ADVANCE PRAISE FOR *CORPORATE CONSPIRACIES*

"America has lost its mind and Belzer and Wayne have found it. Here are hardcore stories of America selling its soul and democracy that have you saying 'Holy shit!' every time you turn to a new page. Worth the price just for the tragic story of Robin Williams's Big Pharma-induced suicide. Burns into you like a fucking tattoo."
> —Greg Palast, journalist, *New York Times* bestselling author,
> *The Best Democracy Money Can Buy*

"Get your hands on *Corporate Conspiracies*, read its succinct and extremely well-sourced and highly corroborated evidence, and finish with a substantial basis for your views, one that may knock you off your feet. This book is the real deal, and there isn't a wasted word in it. Its timing is frightening, its messages urgent. Run, don't walk, to get your hands on a copy."
> —William J. Martin, lawyer, former Chicago assistant state's attorney,
> and author, *The Crime of the Century*

"*Corporate Conspiracies* is a very timely and disturbing look at how controlled American society has become, with the average citizen completely unaware of the extent to which corporations have taken over our democracy. Big Brother is not only watching you—he is making decisions for you! You will never look at Wall Street, the corporate matrix, or 'your' government the same way again after reading this book."
> —Vince Palamara, author of *Survivor's Guilt, JFK,*
> and *The Not-So-Secret Service*

"Insightful, poignant, and timely, *Corporate Conspiracies* is a must read for all who are concerned about the future of democracy and economic justice in our nation at a time of corporate greed and political chicanery."
> —Arthur Blaustein, author, *Make a Difference . . .,*
> former chair of the National Advisory Council on Economic Opportunity

"Reading *Corporate Conspiracies* made me angry. It made me think. It also told me how we can all regain control over our fate as a nation. Richard Belzer and David Wayne show us that corporate conspiracy is real and hidden in plain sight."
> —William Matson Law, author of *In the Eye of History:*
> *Disclosures in the JFK Assassination Medical Evidence*

"*Corporate Conspiracies* reveals what happens when conspiracy *theory* becomes conspiracy *fact*. Authors Belzer and Wayne tell us what we the people can do to get our democracy back. The need for this remarkable, meticulously researched volume has never been greater or more urgent. Start reading it now."

—Alan Axelrod, author, *Full Faith and Credit: The National Debt, Taxes, Spending, and the Bankrupting of America* (Abbeville Press, 2016)

"In *Corporate Conspiracies* Belzer and Wayne document the demise of our representative form of government. Ever since we legalized bribery of our public officials and the equating of money to free speech, we have become captive to what I believe is a form of economic slavery."

—Len Colodny, *New York Times* bestselling coauthor, *Silent Coup* and *Forty Years War*

"Belzer and Wayne authoritatively cite how corporations drive us to war, corrupt the election process, despoil the environment and our bodies and, tragically, more. This is an essential guide for restoring democracy in the US."

—Brad Schreiber, author, *Revolution's End: The Patty Hearst Kidnapping, Mind Control and the Secret History of Donald DeFreeze and the SLA*

"Belzer and Wayne provide a tough, candid view of the powers-that-be in the United States and the harsh impact of their manipulative actions on our lives. This no-holds-barred analysis tells us how things are rather than how we would prefer them to be."

—J. Malcolm Garcia, author, *What Wars Leave Behind: The Faceless and the Forgotten*

"Richard Belzer and David Wayne have raised some very provocative questions about the influence of corporate money on government—from banks to the media and on to energy companies and everything in between. Though you may not agree with the answers, it never hurts to have your preconceptions challenged, and the authors have done just that."

—Mike Farris, attorney, author of *A Death in the Islands: The Unwritten Law and the Last Trial of Clarence Darrow*

"It is obvious that throughout Richard Belzer's acting and comedy career, he remained a voracious reader and close observer of the corruption and decline of American democracy. *Corporate Conspiracies* is a useful and timely guidebook for those engaged in the battle to reclaim our government from the clutches of runaway corporate power."

—Alexander Zaitchik, author, *The Gilded Rage*

CORPORATE CONSPIRACIES

HOW WALL STREET
TOOK OVER WASHINGTON

BY **RICHARD BELZER**
AND **DAVID WAYNE**

Skyhorse Publishing

Skyhorse Publishing books may be purchased in bulk at special discounts for sales promotion, corporate gifts, fund-raising, or educational purposes. Special editions can also be created to specifications. For details, contact the Special Sales Department, Skyhorse Publishing, 307 West 36th Street, 11th Floor, New York, NY 10018 or info@ skyhorsepublishing.com.

Skyhorse® and Skyhorse Publishing® are registered trademarks of Skyhorse Publishing, Inc.®, a Delaware corporation.

Visit our website at www.skyhorsepublishing.com.

10 9 8 7 6 5 4 3 2 1

Library of Congress Cataloging-in-Publication Data is available on file.

Cover design by Brian Peterson

Print ISBN: 978–1–5107-1126-6
Ebook ISBN: 978–1–5107-1127-3

Printed in the United States of America

This book is dedicated to Robin Williams, and the other many thousands of victims of corporate greed.

May your sacrifices not have been in vain . . .

CONTENTS

After the Constitutional Convention, Benjamin Franklin was asked, "Well, Doctor, what have we got—a Republic or a Monarchy?" Franklin's response:

"A Republic—if you can keep it."[1]

1 Jay Cost, *A Republic No More: Big Government and the Rise of American Political Corruption* (New York: Encounter Books, 2015).

INTRODUCTION

Of all the books we researched for this work, the title we loved the most was this one:

Regime Change Begins at Home: Freeing America from Corporate Rule[1]

We love it because it presents—as a hard fact—something that very few people completely understand:

> Since 1980, America has been run by a corporate regime that has co-opted both political parties and shifted sovereignty from "we the people" to transnational corporations.[2]

Since this book covers some corporate conspiracies, we will, no doubt, take a lot of heat for that and be deridingly referred to as conspiracy theorists. So we would just like to remind people that the phrase "conspiracy theorist" was actually invented by the Central Intelligence Agency, to be used as a weaponized term with which to discourage people from seeking the truth. We kid you not. CIA Document 1035–960 was dated April 1, 1967, regarding the Agency's concern about the "reputation of the American government." That document also suggested various tactics for countering "conspiratorial" arguments which confronted the gaping holes critics observed in the findings of the Warren Commission which "investigated" (they did no such thing, in reality) the assassination of President Kennedy. "The agency also directed its members '[t]o employ propaganda assets to [negate] and refute the attacks of the critics."[3] So, as you can see, and as the Freedom of Information Act release of that CIA document clearly reveals, the use of the term "conspiracy theorist" is actually a conspiracy itself. But if you believe (rightly) that Julius Caesar and hundreds of other leaders were the victims of conspirators (as they were), then you're an evil "conspiracy theorist," right? Well, if anybody actually believes that, then you'd better read up on your history, boys 'n girls. Because conspiracies are an ongoing and very common occurrence in human conduct.

Now—Let's get down to the nitty gritty…

Are you aware that many friends of Robin Williams believe that his suicide was the direct result of the prescription drugs he was taking? And that over 23,000 suicides are attributed to psychiatric drugs each year in the United States?[4]

Did you know that turning prisons into a big business has resulted in the United States having the highest incarceration rate in the history of the world—and that most are just drug crimes?[5]

Are you aware that the historic event of the toppling of the statue of Saddam Hussein in Iraq was actually a US military PSYOP (Psychological Operations warfare)—a completely orchestrated event, with the knowledge and assistance of US media—and not a spontaneous event as it was portrayed by the media?[6]

Did you know that the Pentagon is sending $1.5 trillion of our tax dollars to their corporate buddies for a new fighter jet that is already superfluous?

Are you aware that continuing to rely on oil instead of investing in low-carbon energy solutions will cost us $44 trillion due to climate change?[7]

Did you know that companies like General Motors at times know that their products will kill people, but they do nothing, because it is actually cheaper to compensate the victims than it is to correct the problem?[8]

Then read and learn, friends.

American corporations have been getting away with murder—*literally*—for many, many years. Just take a good look at their history. The above example of GM is a proven point:

Consumer advocate Clarence Ditlow, executive director of the nonprofit Center for Automotive Safety, bitterly criticized the settlement. "GM killed over a 100 people by knowingly putting a defective ignition switch into over 1 million vehicles," Ditlow said. "Today, thanks to its lobbyists, GM officials walk off scot-free while its customers are 6 feet under."[9]

Tobacco companies *knowingly lied* about the harmful effects of cigarettes, for *decades*, even though there was plenty of known medical proof of their damage; they even knowingly *hid* that proof from the public. Oil, gas, and chemical companies have been knowingly polluting our planet with cancer-causing products, *also* for decades—and they know that they're doing it. Pharmaceutical companies have lied and attempted to minimize news coverage regarding the deaths that they <u>know</u> their drugs will cause. That's murder, plain and simple. Maybe you can paint a public relations damage control over that landscape if you happen to have all their tons of money and paid political influence. But it's *still murder!* Look the parents of one of their victims straight in the eyes and try to tell them it's *not* murder. Do you *honestly* think they will listen to you?

This book is an effort to reveal the insanity of corporate greed, once and for all.

At this point, most people probably care more about their local football team than they do about the workings of our democratic republic. And while we understand their frustration, *and* their reasons, that's not good enough, folks. We have to all get involved to stop these bastards from getting away with what they have *been* getting away with for far too long. They are robbing us blind, poisoning our planet, hijacking our democracy, and ruining the futures of our children and our grandchildren. *They must be stopped!*

As an agent of the US government employed to implement policies to benefit American corporations, John Perkins noted in his classic work, *Confessions of an Economic Hit Man*, that Corporate America has extended its rule beyond our borders: "What we had previously considered US corporations were now truly international, even from a legal standpoint. Many of them were incorporated in a multitude of countries; they could pick and choose from an assortment of rules and regulations under which to conduct their activities, and a multitude of globalizing trade agreements and organizations made this even easier. . . . Corporatocracy had become a fact, and it increasingly exerted itself as the single major in-fluence on world economics and politics."[10]

It is sad to make this observation, but we have become a government *Of* the corporations, *By* the corporations, and *For* the corporations. You won't see it on the corporate-controlled mainstream media, but "the United States has deposed or helped to depose more than a dozen foreign governments, often for the benefit of US commercial interests operating in those countries."[11] And no one seems to be policing the biggest corpo-rate offenders, even when their frauds are blatantly obvious. Just look at the financial meltdown of 2008—the CEOs of those companies made out like bandits! They walked away with billions of dollars of public tax money, and we mean that literally:

> So what is going on? After all, we're a nation that takes fighting crime so seriously we use SWAT teams and submachine guns to pursue marijuana possessors and dealers . . . But not a single architect of the financial crisis that brought America to its knees has yet been charged. And of all the crimes against "the People," the financial crisis ranks as one of the all-time worst.[12]

We have become a corporatized state, and *they* are whom our government now actually represents—*not* the people. We are now being held hos-tage by a government that has given control of the hen house over to the wolves. Like pigs at the trough, they have all fed on our economic system, at the *expense of the public.*

As Robert F. Kennedy Jr. recently observed, "corporations should not be running our government because they don't want the same thing for America as Americans want. They don't want democracy. They want profits. They want no competition. They are corrupting our democracy. They are stealing everything that we care about in this country."[13]

Recent rulings of the Supreme Court have redefined the very struc-ture of our republic, because corporations were declared to have the same rights as individuals. That differentiation has led to ramifications that threaten the very existence of America as we knew it.[14] Kennedy elo-quently explained why:

The so-called "Citizens United" decision is the "most sweeping expansion of corporate power this century. In an acrimonious split decision, the five 'conservative' justices declared that, in the eyes of the Constitution, corporations were people and money is speech," continued Kennedy.

Corporate campaign donations, in other words, are protected by the First Amendment, making most restrictions on corporate donations to political candidates unconstitutional. "That case effectively overruled a century of corporate campaign finance restrictions that limited a corporation's ability to purchase political candidates."[15]

Kennedy continued with some earth-shaking information:

"And today it's hard to argue that we still have a democracy in this country when you have the Koch brothers, the two richest people in America, who have pledged already to put nearly $900 million into this presidential election, which is comparable to the amount spent by either political party," said Kennedy. "This year's presidential election is going to cost $10 billion with half of that coming from 100 wealthy families. Nearly $1 billion is coming from two brothers."[16]

Corporations still lobby for and receive many billions of dollars in government subsidies that actually work *contrary* to the best interests of the consumer. For example, just in the US sugar program, the government pays corporations $3 billion per year; and the *effects* of that corporate largesse? It <u>doubles the price of sugar</u> for the consumer.[17] Huge corporations have taken over the massive American agribusiness, and it is usually these gigantic farming operations that are being subsidized to the tune of many billions of taxpayer dollars. Why? Because they have driven the smaller farmers out of business. Yet, due to tax loopholes that corporations lobby hard for in Washington, they still qualify for farm subsidies. And if they *can* take it from the American taxpayer, we all know damn well that they *will* take it. And take it, they do.

Many corporations even renounce America, in a formal legal manner, by moving their official headquarters overseas to a tax-friendly location, allowing them to earn profits tax-free in the United States.[18] Another huge loophole for the wealthiest Americans—conveniently left available by their political friends in Washington—is called "deferred compensation," which is a complicated method of pushing assets forward and paying taxes on them far in the future, if at all. According to one tax expert familiar with the issue, the use of deferrals annually "surely amounts to hundreds of billions of dollars" in lost revenues, which we end up paying for.[19]

And don't expect to hear much about that issue from mainstream media either. Because most of them have already been "bought off" too. "You will hear no criticism from the press, the supposed guardians of our democracy. And that's because most of that money will go to media advertising—the 4th estate has been bought off."[20]

And as a result, what we're left with, unfortunately, is a very nasty political predicament, according to Kennedy:

> So democracy is for sale and the Congress that we have today is the best one that money can buy, which by definition, is oligarchy not democracy. Predictably, the rich are now buying themselves politicians and then deploying to reduce taxes on their class and to rid themselves of pesky regulations that protect public health. Our politicians are no longer public servants. They are indentured servants of the Koch brothers and their ilk. They are no longer engaged in public service, but in the mercenary enterprise of ransacking on behalf of Big Oil.[21]

The ramifications of recent court rulings are absolutely astounding: "Tobacco and asbestos companies asserted that they had Fifth Amendment rights to keep secret what they knew about the dangers of their products."[22] Can you *imagine* crap like that in our supposedly free republic? Shouldn't they have to *tell* you that the chemicals you are working with can cause cancer? Well, guess what, folks? *They don't!*

A revolving door between corporate leadership and government positions has also created an untenable ethics situation of glaringly obvious conflicts of interest as they shuffle back and forth during their careers between the boards of directors of major corporations and positions in government entrusted with the oversight of those *very same* corporations. The first chapter will reveal to you who some of the folks are that keep going back and forth through that revolving door.

And the revolving door isn't just between Wall Street and Washington either—it is also mainstream media with all their pals in "public service" (and we use the term loosely). Mainstream journalists and politicians—we repeat ourselves—have been in bed together for ages; and what goes on under the sheets is not a pretty thing to see, either. Isn't it openly preposterous that a guy like George Stephanopoulos goes from being a top White House adviser to the President of the United States, to being the chief anchorman at ABC News? Isn't there something inherently incestuous about that? As in, *wrong*!

The press used to be known as the "Fourth Estate" because they were seen as the watchdog over the various branches of government. They were, supposedly, the ones who presented the unbiased, untainted viewpoint of our government—the one view that we could all trust. That is a *very* important role in a free republic, the importance of which, historically, has been very clearly demonstrated.[23] But now, they just shuffle back and forth freely from working directly with the nation's leadership (and again, we use the term very loosely), to supposedly reporting without prejudice about the very same people they were working with before, and will likely go back to working with again. So why do they behave as though we can trust them to report the news without prejudice when their very actions reveal obvious prejudice?

That string of conservative court rulings we referred to has resulted in a tsunami of game-changers that are currently devastating our republic of a would-be democracy: a flood of billions of dollars in corporate cash contributions they can now use to legally bribe politicians. It "helped create super PACs, which can accept unlimited contributions from corporate and union treasuries, as well as from individuals, and it triggered a boom in political activity by tax-exempt 'dark money' organizations that don't have to disclose their donors."[24] And it eliminated environmental restrictions that now threaten to poison our lands, waterways, and the very air that we breathe.

Here is how one expert, Dr. David Rosner of Columbia University's Center for the History and Ethics of Public Health, summarizes the situation:

It is very troubling to see so many issues, that you would think we should learn from, basically being ignored. Certainly asbestos, tobacco, lead, vinyl chloride (PVC)—you could go through a few classic examples of real mistakes, of major mistakes, in which we allowed these industries to get away with murder.[25]

In 1999, only 1 in every 500 kids had autism. Today, that number is 1 in every 88.[26] Many people believe that the preponderance of chemicals in our daily lives is responsible for that increase, as well as the rise in many types of cancers and other health problems.[27] There are literally no regulations for most of the chemicals in use in our country! Isn't that difficult to fathom in this day and age? A review by the California State Senate in 2010 revealed that out of approximately 83,000 chemicals legally put inside products in the United States, *only about 200 of them* have actually been tested by the EPA (Environmental Protection Agency).[28] The companies *do not* have to prove that they are safe![29]

"Industry in America does not have to prove a chemical is safe before it gets onto the market. Instead, like a defendant in an American court room, a chemical is innocent until proven guilty."[30]

In fact, the chemical industry in America is an excellent example of the horrible games these people play with our families' health. Through their lobbying vehicle, the *American Chemistry Council*, they have spent millions of dollars fighting against the regulations in Congress and state legislatures that would force the companies they represent to register and regulate their toxic chemicals. And you won't believe the absolutely insidious manner in which they defeat the efforts of parents and groups trying to protect us from their poisoning of our bodies. Care for an example? Well, here you go.

It has been established that strong chemicals, known as brominated flame retardants, which are present in almost all American homes in furniture and mattresses, produce toxic compounds that build up in our bodies. It has never been proven that they reduce fire deaths in homes.[31] So, some very responsible parents, groups, health advocates, and some legislators, have worked hard to have these toxic substances eradicated, to stop putting them in our homes. The *American Chemistry Council*, on behalf of the corporations making millions of dollars from these chemicals, spent millions lobbying against those efforts.[32] With no substantive evidence that chemical retardants actually reduced the rate of home fires—but *plenty* of evidence that they could be harming our children via their known toxicity—the chemical industry embarked upon an intentionally deceptive campaign to halt the proposed protective legislation.[33] They did a multimillion-dollar media campaign that blanketed California with very deceptive information about how people would be endangered by fire without the toxic retardants. They even had the audacity to call their campaign *Citizens for Fire Safety.*[34] How's that for deception, folks? Instead of using their own name—which people might realize was done by corporations—they named their campaign like it was a group of concerned citizens working for public safety! *Citizens for Fire Safety, my ass!* It was corporations protecting profits at any cost! They even brought 10-year-old children to come and testify before government committees! They had these little kids televised, reading from scripts that basically said "Please don't let me die in a fire."[35] Do you see how despicable and insidious these companies are? It's like they will not stop at *anything* to continue making obscene amounts of money, even if it means *poisoning* our children. *That's* why we wrote this book! We had to.

Ultimately, it's we—The People—who need to force change against the many transgressions of Corporate America. Europeans don't put up with it and neither should we—in Europe the people have forced manufacturers to get toxic chemicals out of the economic equation, and demanded that *all* GMO foods be labeled as such.[36] And we can easily do that.

The head guy over at a company called Eden Foods sums it all up pretty well, if you ask us:

> If there are no morals and ethics—if nobody cares—there is absolutely no incentive for any business to do anything right. The only incentive remaining, once you remove the morals and ethics, is profit. And if that's the only remaining judgment criteria employed, you get what we have in America today.[37]

That needs to change. Because our tolerance of it is the *only* thing that allows it to continue. Let's *stop* corporations and help our fellow Americans.

This quote is from 2004 and we actually ended up spending a *lot* more in Iraq than $87 billion—but just listen to what we *could have* done with that money instead:

> The United States spends over $87 billion conducting a war in Iraq while the United Nations estimates that for less than half that amount we could provide clean water, adequate diets, sanitations services, and basic education to every person on the planet.[38]

So the point of it all, the *why* of how it all matters, is this: with just a fraction of the waste and greed that we continuously put up with from corporations and politicians, we could really work wonders in this world of ours.

As they say in *The Human Experiment*, a great documentary that is about many of the things that we have mentioned above, "If you aren't outraged, you aren't paying attention to what the hell is going on."[39]

CHAPTER ONE

BOUGHT & PAID FOR:
THE BEST POLITICIANS THAT
MONEY CAN BUY

America has the best politicians money can buy.[1]

—Will Rogers

This is about a group that we call our *political prostitutes*—and it had to be the first chapter of the book because it is what actually allows all the other corruption in our country to exist and thrive. As US Senator Mark Hanna said, way back in 1895: "There are two things that are important in politics. The first is money—and I can't remember what the second one is."[2] Much more recently, a top Senate Democrat came right out and said that the bankers now "own" the US Congress; and, as journalist Glenn Greenwald noted, that Senator's "confession ought to be major news, yet it won't be. Why not?"[3]

It has certainly now reached a new threat level to our republic:

> Former Texas Agriculture Commissioner Jim Hightower told me, "They've eliminated the middleman. The corporations don't have to lobby the government anymore. They *are* the government." Hightower used to complain about Monsanto's lobbying the Secretary of Agriculture. Today, Monsanto executive Ann Veneman *is* the Secretary of Agriculture.[4]

One would think—in a *true democracy*—that the ability to control events would be more in the hands of the masses in the voting booths, than in the hands of a few big power brokers. Unfortunately, events in recent years have brought us dramatically farther in the *wrong* direction.

The situation is clearly out of hand. As President Obama himself noted, in the home of a billionaire supporter:

> "You now have the potential of two hundred people deciding who ends up being elected president, every single time."
>
> "There are five or six people in this room *tonight* that could simply make a decision 'This will be the next president' and probably at least get a nomination. . . . And that's not the way things are supposed to work."[5]

Did you know that "the 100 largest corporations in the world produce $7 trillion in sales and have $10 trillion in assets"?[6] "With this money, they control governments through lobbying and donations, fund academic research so that the 'scientific' view of the world adheres to their perspective—for example, 'There is no climate change'—and, most importantly, dominate consciousness by graffitiing our shared spaces and media with their peculiar philosophies."[7]

President Obama was right. That is clearly *not* the way that the democratic process is supposed to work. But it *is*.

Seven billion dollars was spent on the 2012 presidential election.[8] But, "in 2016, those data points would seem quaint by comparison."[9]

Our political process—once the pride of our democracy—has been virtually put up for sale to the highest bidders. It is no longer a case of the richest 1 percent of Americans controlling the course of the country. That task is now accomplished by a very small group of people. And it is a situation that is now at a point where it is totally disproportionate to the best interests of our republic. If you are not concerned about that, then just get a load of this: *private groups* now spend more on our elections than the Democratic and Republican parties *combined*.[10]

What's new, you might ask? Corrupt politicians have been around for centuries, you say? Crooked leaders are as common as salt. True. Well, how about this? This time the secret pie that the fat cats are feasting on is ridiculously huge. For example, the Wall Street bailout was over one *trillion* taxpayer dollars.[11] And nobody broke up the party! These days they have been perfecting their "skill sets" to a point where it is poisoning whatever we currently have left of a free republic: "Crony capitalism is good for those on the inside. And it is lousy for everyone else. But it does provide a hybrid-powered vehicle to sustain a large base of rich campaign contributors with taxpayer money."[12]

After the financial collapse of 2008, when it came time to pass out the goodies—over a trillion dollars of taxpayer money in the so-called bailout—it was Wall Street insiders and companies who had given large donations to Washington politicians who ended up getting the sweetest deals.[13]

> Access to TARP (Troubled Asset Relief Program) money was not guaranteed. And the terms of the loans were unclear. There was no transparency and no openness to the process. As the economist Robert Kuttner put it, the TARP proceedings were "being done largely behind closed doors and the design is by, for, and in the interest of large banks, hedge funds, and private equity companies. Because there are no explicit criteria, it's very hard to know" if anyone got special treatment. The entire process, he said, reeks of favoritism and special treatment.[14]

The same thing happened with the "American Recovery and Reinvestment Act" of the Obama administration. Billions of dollars' worth of loans, grants, and loan guarantees were passed around—but it was largely wealthy campaign contributors who reaped the most direct benefits![15] These programs should be renamed with a more honest title, such as "No Billionaire Left Behind":

> The game of funneling taxpayer money to friends has exploded to astonishing levels in recent years. Now that annual federal outlays exceed $3 trillion, there are extraordinary opportunities to get a piece of the action. Government checks routinely find their way to very wealthy Americans. Convincing the public that billionaires need the money can, needless to say, be tricky. But if a government check somehow serves the "public interest," it can become part of a larger program and might escape scrutiny.[16]

Billions of taxpayer dollars funneled to the corporate interests of very wealthy campaign contributors: payback. "As a jobs program—the stated purpose—these billions in grants and loans were a failure. But as a method for transferring billions in taxpayer funds to friends, cronies, and supporters, they worked perfectly."[17] It's basically a "can't miss" situation—if you happen to be a billionaire. And it amounts to a legalized system of theft:

> Imagine for a minute that you are a corporate executive and you start using your company's assets to "invest" in projects that in turn benefit you directly. What would happen? You would be risking possible criminal charges for the misuse of those assets. But if it's taxpayer money? Suddenly it becomes legal. Even acceptable. And for the billionaire who is looking to get a big return on his investment, there are few returns that can be higher than those resulting from campaign contributions. After all, how else can you turn half a million dollars from yourself and your friends into hundreds of millions of dollars after a single election?[18]

That mention of half a million dollars, above, is in reference to a venture capitalist, Steve Westly, who brought in contributions to the Obama campaign in the amount of approximately half a million dollars.[19] Westly sat on the board of directors for Tesla Motors and his venture capital firm had a big stake in Tesla. Now, we happen to like electric cars—but get a load of this. This is an example of how the political process actually works. After Obama came into office, many of his major campaign contributors were on the boards of companies and had major financial interests in corporations that were on the receiving end of huge grants and loans, under very beneficial terms. One of those was Tesla, which received $465 million in government loans.[20] That money—taxpayer money—made the IPO (Initial Public Offering of stock in the company) of Tesla possible.[21] Their IPO was very successful, and made their big investors infinitely richer. Mr. Westly's firm had 2.5 million Tesla shares and he personally has an undisclosed amount of the company's shares on top of that. (Also, you would think that he would have to disclose the number of those shares, but since he is not technically a federal employee, he is apparently exempt from disclosure laws.)[22] He and other big investors made millions, as a result.[23] Then, the Obama administration announced its plan to offer a rebate to boost electric car sales, and Tesla shares shot up an additional 6 percent.[24] The potential conflict of interest has been widely noted; at the same time that his companies have benefited directly, Mr. Westly has had the close attention of and special access to the Energy Secretary who, obviously, is a key decision-maker in the process of giving out those funds.[25] "Companies in The Westly Group portfolio have benefited from more than half a billion dollars in loans, grants or stimulus money from the Energy Department. . . . Relatively few companies succeed in winning such benefits."[26]

As we wrote this book, Tesla Motors has risen to a stock market value of over *thirty billion* dollars. And yes, we know—you could make the argument that it all created a great company, in a great business. But *how* were they created and *who* benefited the most? They were made great with the help of taxpayer dollars. So you could also argue—successfully, we believe—that the American taxpayers, who *provided* that relief, were not the beneficiaries of the positive results. The average American has not benefited from Tesla's success, nor does the average American have $100,000 to go out and buy a new Tesla. Their millionaire shareholder investors were clearly the big beneficiaries of that taxpayer assistance. Fat cat investors made fortunes from taxpayer-provided relief. And that's just plain wrong.

But the Energy Department was small potatoes compared to what was going on over at the Treasury Department. Over at Treasury, the revolving door between Wall Street and Washington was reaping rewards beyond the wildest dreams of most business people.

> Goldman Sachs had a direct line to Treasury Secretary Hank Paulsen, its *former managing partner*, as well as incoming officials in the Obama administration.[27]

As you will see below, as well as in the following chapter on Wall Street, banking firms like Goldman Sachs now play far too large a role in our election and governing processes. As Glenn Greenwald observed:

> Nobody even tries to hide this any longer. The only way they could make it more blatant is if they hung a huge Goldman Sachs logo on the Capitol dome and then branded it onto the foreheads of leading members of Congress and executive branch officials. Of course, ownership of the government is not confined to Goldman or even to

bankers generally; legislation in virtually every area is written by the lobbyists dispatched by the corporations that demand it, and its passage then ensured by "representatives" whose pockets are stuffed with money from those same corporations.[28]

As people have said before, these damn politicians should be forced to wear patches of their corporate sponsors on their jackets just like NAS-CAR drivers do. Then we'd know who the bastards are actually working for. Because it sure as hell isn't us. They have sold out to their corporate masters long, long ago. The only question now is which companies are they working for? Care for examples? There are literally *thousands of them*.

Remember US House of Representatives Minority Leader, Richard Gephardt? Gephardt's congressional district was centered around St. Louis, Missouri, the home of the huge defense contractor, McDonnell-Douglas. Back in 1996, Gephardt lobbied hard for McDonnell-Douglas, which was hoping to get awarded the hugely lucrative Pentagon contract for its new Joint Strike Fighter plane. Gephardt used his influence, vehemently explaining to the Defense Department that this was a program our country truly needed, that the new Joint Strike Fighter was an "affordable solution to our future strike warfighting needs."[29] But instead of McDonnell-Douglas, the Pentagon awarded the contract to Boeing and Lockheed corporations. How did Gephardt react? *The very next day* Gephardt withdrew his support for the entire program.[30] Because, apparently, his dramatic concern about our need for the plane was actually based on the desires of his biggest corporate sponsor. *That's* how it all works, in reality.

And here's another little gem for you.

This example is another one of our favorites: the B-1 bomber. Would you like to know how Boeing Corporation made sure that they had a way to threaten *every single member* of the US House of Representatives? They came up with a very devious method. It was brilliant. Actually, *diabolical* would be a more appropriate word. What they did was ensure that the B-1 program was practically invulnerable to attack because it had some of its many parts made in every single one of the country's 435 congressional districts.[31] So it didn't really matter that the B-1 bomber was a ridiculously expensive and unnecessary addition to our forces. What *mat-*

tered, at the nuts-and-bolts level of the American political system, was that if the program didn't continue, jobs would be lost. They could argue that cancellation of the B-1 program would devastate American labor all over the place. Or, they could bully a congressional representative by even suggesting that they were planning to take those jobs out of his or her district and move them somewhere else.[32] That's the way that the ugly game of corporate politics is played.

These groups have all been in bed with each other for so long that they don't even seem to realize that it's an incestuous relationship. "As the *New York Times* reported in February 2011, senior Pentagon officials began meeting in secret with investment advisers in New York to give them information regarding defense-related companies."[33] Isn't that outrageous? What the *hell* do they think they're doing? That's obscene! Further, on the same meetings: "The message was direct: even with defense cutbacks on the horizon, 'the Pentagon is going to make sure the military industry remains profitable.'"[34]

It's reached the point where these people really don't seem to even *care* anymore about the obvious appearances of conflict of interest. In October 2010, the Deputy Defense Secretary, William J. Lynn, met with a large group of Wall Street stock analysts. According to the *New York Times*, he laid out the Pentagon's plans "in astonishing detail."[35] And guess what happened as a result? "The Big Five defense contractors—Lockheed Martin, General Dynamics, Raytheon, Northrup Grumman, and Boeing—all saw their stocks rise shortly after that October meeting."[36] So tell us, plain and simple, because we have a very direct question: Who exactly is working for whom here?

Corporations have always used the political system to gain advantages, but recently companies have been using politicians to pave their corporate interests to the extreme. And the concept of *fairness* has got *nothin'* to do with it, folks. If the bastards think that they can get away with it, they will try. That has been proven to us time and again. "The political success of the income tax always rested upon a broad sense that it was fair, but . . . major companies like Boeing, Dow, and General Electric were not only paying no taxes, but actually receiving net benefits through the tax code."[37] There is a well-documented recent history of top Congressional leaders receiving bundles of cash contributions from big oil and gas corporations and then suddenly deciding to "push bills for fossil fuel industry" projects.[38]

Many Americans still tend to believe that Big Business is generally "Republican" as far as their politics goes. Nothing could be further from the truth. They'll buy *anybody*! They can and do and, in fact, they already have.

> Corporate America's effort to mold both political parties to do its bidding was increasingly successful as politicians needed ever more contributions to buy the television ads that got them reelected. Politicians insisted that no one bought their vote with their donation and that was true.[39]

But it was only true on a *technical* level. It just gave them plausible deniability that they hadn't sold their vote to the corporations. Realistically, everybody in Washington knew what it meant. "But what donations did buy, every politician acknowledged, was access. That access meant that every senator and representative was listening primarily to the concerns and ideas of the super rich, of the political donor class."[40]

If you don't think that the American political process has been totally corrupted by the wealthiest Americans, then just pay close attention to the following sentence. Two individuals—the extremely conservative, multibillionaire Koch Brothers, who are the damn poster boys for the richest 1% who *own* this country now—spend as much on a presidential election as the entire Democratic Party or Republican Party (which, historically, have been the two major forces in every election); and that comparison, by the way, also includes "the party's two congressional campaign committees."[41] The Koch Brothers budget for the 2016 presidential election is actually *far greater* than either political party spent on all their elections of 2012.[42]

Environmental attorney and activist Robert F. Kennedy Jr. had some very cogent observations on that topic:

> "What do you think accounts for the Koch Brothers' generosity to our political system?" He answers his question with a battery of new questions. "Do you think that Charles and David Koch are putting

nearly $900 million into the election because of some patriotic impulse? Do you think they are putting nearly $900 million into this election because they love America? Do you think that they are putting nearly $900 million into the election because they love humanity? Our environment? Or our purple mountain's majesty? Our democracy? Or free market capitalism?"[43]

Kennedy pulled no punches, and that's putting it mildly!

Koch Industries is not a benign corporation. It's a suicide pact for creation. It's the archetype of "disaster capitalism." It's the command center of an organized scheme to undermine democracy and impose a corporate kleptocracy that will allow these greedy men to cash in on mass extinction and the end of civilization.[44]

And Kennedy blasted them with both barrels, also noting the lethal effects and thinly disguised roles of their so-called foundations and "institutes":

The real purpose of their 'think tanks' they created and fund—like the Heritage Foundation and the CATO Institute—is not to promote free market capitalism, but to gin up the philosophical underpinnings for a scheme of uncontrolled corporate profit taking. And the press, consolidated as it is into private monopolies and relieved of social obligation, are on the carbon and pharma payroll and in full cahoots with the scheme. [45]

Unfortunately, our so-called Congressional "leadership" (and *damn*, we wish there was a better word for it than that because it is *so* inaccurate), has made it all too clear that they will gladly sell their political influence to fatten their pockets. There is practically no end to the specific and numerous examples of our political prostitutes, officially known as the elected representatives of our electoral process. So that is not a theory or an allegation—that is a fact.[46]

When we think about how corporate money pollutes democracy, we generally infer that the election process makes political posts go to the highest bidder and that votes can effectively be bought with advertising.

But it's actually a much more malignant disease. It may not seem of paramount importance in our everyday life, but in the following chapters we will show you how this "purchased influence" is directly responsible for everything from legalized slavery to the mass marketing of drugs that their manufacturers know full well, in *advance*, are going *to kill* people. Put simply, this is the evil that allows all the other evils to happen. If our Democratic process is virtually "for sale to the highest bidder," then it opens the door to blatantly corrupt misuses.

And, if you don't think that corporations and their co-conspirator politicians have successfully engineered the hijacking of our economy and the transfer of wealth from the disappearing middle class to the wealthiest—just take a good look at the following chart. It shows how America measures up to other developed countries; or, actually, how we *fail* to measure up.

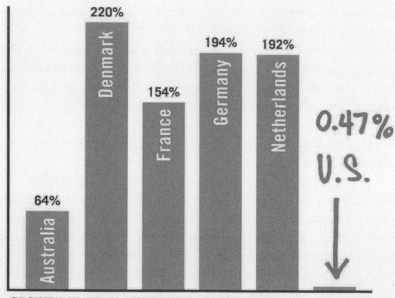

Graph courtesy of George R. Tyler, *What Went Wrong: How The 1% Hijacked the American Middle Class . . . And What Other Countries Got Right,* (Dallas: BenBella Books, 2013).

"In 2007, the year of the crash, the top 1 percent of American house-holds took in almost two-and-a-half times the share of our nation's pre-tax income that they had grabbed in the 40 years following World War II. This was no accident—the rules of the market underwent profound changes that led to the upward redistribution of trillions in income over the past 30 years."[47]

Corporations got so greedy that they even stopped trying to hide their nasty behavior. General Electric, at one time, was the world's largest com-pany.[48] But they took from the poor and gave to the rich. It became widely viewed that management's game was "to squeeze the pay and numbers of the rank and file and then richly reward executives."[49]

You've probably seen articles and news shows on television implying that corporate money "influences" US politicians. But actually, the reality is quite a bit worse than that. They're not just "influenced"—they're even *controlled*. They are often bought and paid for to do a corporation's bid-ding for them. These political prostitutes are often little more than glori-fied corporate employees without the name tag.

Actually, it's even worse than that. There used to be strict legal limits to the amounts that corporations were allowed to donate to politicians. But all that changed with the Supreme Court decision in the case of *Citizens United v. Federal Election Commission* in 2010. That decision by the high court "overturned key provisions of the McCain-Feingold campaign finance law, rules that kept corporations—and their lobbyists and front groups (as well as labor unions)—from spending unlimited amounts of cash on campaign advertising within 60 days of a general election for fed-eral office (or 30 days before a primary)."[50]

Former US Representative Alan Grayson summarized the impact of the *Citizens United* decision in blunt terms: "We're now in a situation where a lobbyist can walk into my office . . . and say, 'I've got five million dollars to spend, and I can spend it for you or against you. Which do you prefer?'"[51]

Corporate interests have "overpowered 'government of the people, by the people, and for the people,'" to quote another memorable Lincoln phrase. "Corporations' power over the government is at the root of a wide array of issues of deep concern . . . including campaign finance reform, the growing gap between rich and poor, environmental degradation, globalization, and whether democracy itself has been reduced to a mere charade or a sideshow in a global bazaar."[52]

Politicians aren't just "influenced" by campaign contributions; they are manipulated, and practically even controlled by these vermin who are politely referred to as "lobbyists." And you almost can't blame corporations for hijacking the political process. For them, it's just a really good investment—it makes excellent business sense. Here's an example. An article in *Time Magazine*, in 2010, pointed out that the political donations of hedge funds and other money managers had made them a fortune. The financial groups had invested about $15 million to weaken the impact of legislation that was attempting to reform Wall Street.[53] The successful "dilution" of the would-be reform act, saved those big money people a fortune; about $10 billion in taxes per year. That's a return of 660 percent on their investment.[54] Not bad, huh?

Russell Brand said it best:

> We've got more in common with the people we're bombing than the people we're bombing them for. That is why it takes some pretty well-drilled, old-fashioned optimism to get down to the polling station on Election Day. The very system in which we are invited to ritualistically but irrelevantly participate is designed, DESIGNED, to prevent significant change occurring.[55]

It was the laws passed by these corrupt political prostitutes that removed the restrictions against huge corporations. And that was what opened the floodgates of multibillion-dollar accounting scandals at gigantic companies like Enron, Tyco, Global Crossing, Adelphia, Waste Management, and many others.[56] In fact, calling them "accounting scandals" is an understatement of the highest degree. In reality, they were planned and coordinated thefts, massive fraud and premeditated criminal activity in the board rooms of some of the country's biggest corporations, as "the collapse of Enron exposed widespread risks and deceitful practices at the world's leading corporations . . . financial scandals at companies ranging from Adelphia to WorldCom, from Anadarko to Xerox."[57]

A long wave of corporate corruption was exposed, as one company after another admitted to "cooking their books," or, in cases like American Express, they confessed to not completely understanding their own investments. "Thus, American Express joined the long list of supposedly sophisticated financial experts that had been unable to assess the risk and value of their own investments in derivatives: Bankers Trust, Salomon Brothers, Askin Capital Management, Barings, Kidder Peabody, Enron, and so on."[58]

One after another, the dominoes started to tumble. WorldCom, a telecommunications giant, announced they had suddenly discovered another $3.3 billion in "accounting mistakes."[59] It was revealed that a highly questionable $1 billion tax shelter set up by Citigroup and Merrill Lynch had been related to the "discovery" of an additional $2.4 billion in liabilities for Williams Companies, and it brought their stock crashing down to earth.[60] Dell Computer revealed that they had put options on their own stock in over-the-counter deals arranged with Goldman Sachs and Morgan Stanley.[61] Five executives of Adelphia Communications were arrested for not disclosing important financial dealings.[62] Xerox Corporation confessed that it had "overstated" (where we grew up, we called that lying!) company revenues by almost $2 billion.[63] AOL Time Warner confessed that their accounting practices were the subject of an SEC investigation.[64] The CEO of Tyco International suddenly resigned after being charged with evading taxes.[65] Qwest Communications disclosed that they were the subject of a criminal investigation.[66] Martha Stewart, the television homemaker icon, was charged with criminal insider-trading.[67] Martha Stewart would go on to become the sacrificial lamb of the whole financial fiasco, leading to the question: Why did she go to jail when the Wall Street shysters who actually caused it, all walked away scot-free?

All told, as the market value of companies plummeted, investors had lost over $7 trillion in stocks.[68] That's what it costs when corporate corruption goes unchecked. And that's why you can always count on large political contributions from American corporations. Because they know what side their bread is buttered on.

And guess what? It's still happening. Even though everybody—especially mainstream media—treats the financial crises (there were several) of the early 2000s as though they are now a thing of the past, gigantic corporations continue in their corrupt financial practices. After their paid-for politicians had removed the historically necessary and prudent restrictions upon the entire financial services industry—by repeal of the Glass-Steagall Act—the boys and girls on Wall Street really had their hands free to invent entirely new ways to financially devastate the economy as they enriched themselves beyond belief. The foxes were finally in control of the hen house and they knew exactly what to do with it, too.

Companies use every trick in the book and—thanks to their hefty campaign contributions that ensure those loopholes are kept open by politicians—there are *literally* thousands of little tricks.

> Corporations are busy moving intellectual property such as patents, trademarks and the title to the company logo to entities organized in tax havens like Bermuda. These corporations then pay royalties *to use their own intellectual property, allowing them to convert taxable profits in the United States into tax-deductible payments* sent to Bermuda and other havens that impose little or no tax.[69]

In other words, they actually get a tax credit as a reward for avoiding the taxes they should have rightfully paid to begin with! And guess who pays for that. You guessed it. We do. "You pay for this through higher taxes, reduced services or your rising share of our growing national debt. You also pay for it through incentives in the tax system for companies to build new factories overseas and to reduce employment in America." Great, huh? They win—we lose. The politicians lower taxes on corporations and the wealthy, and we foot the bill.[70]

Corporations pay attorneys a fortune to navigate through an intentionally complex tax code that provides a world of riches in the form of reduced taxes:

> "One method that multi-national corporations are using to pay lower international taxes is offshore transfer payments," said analyst Jill Gonzalez, a researcher at WalletHub. This is done by creating foreign subsidiaries to make raw materials or parts in countries with low tax rates. The corporations' US operations then buy these parts from the overseas units above cost. Thus, the foreign unit makes a large profit, which avoids the US tax rate.[71]

Offshore tax havens—registering a corporation or its subsidiary in a very financially friendly location, such as Bermuda or the Cayman Islands—is a gigantic loophole that Congress could have closed up a long, long time ago. So why haven't they? Because their "corporate clients" make hundreds of billions of dollars off it, that's why. Many times they do not even have actual employees in the foreign company—it's just an address, a shell game to avoid taxes.[72] And avoid taxes they do—*big time*. The United States Public Interest Research Group Education Fund reported recently that in 2014, a whopping 72% of US Fortune 500 companies used offshore tax havens—and doing that *hid $2.1 trillion in offshore profits that they should have paid $620 billion in US taxes on!*[73] Now do you see why corporations make huge donations to their friendly politicians across the country? It's an *investment*—and one that keeps on reaping billions of dollars in profits and unpaid taxes. They are gifts that just keep on giving.

We should care a lot about that because it's *us* that picks up the tab, when all is said and done.

> When corporations dodge their taxes, the public ends up paying. The American multinationals that take advantage of tax havens use our roads, benefit from our education system and large consumer market, and enjoy the security we have here, but are ultimately taking a free ride at the expense of other taxpayers.[74]

The examples of corporate abuse of the tax system are massive. And companies often fail to even cooperate with the Internal Revenue Service, refusing to provide requested documentation.[75] "ChevronTexaco, the world's fourth-largest oil company, evaded $3.25 billion in federal and state taxes from 1970 to 2000 through a complex petroleum pricing scheme . . ."[76] Sometimes these corporate schemes are so complicated that it takes investigators years to even figure them out. And many of them probably escape detection. One lawmaker said that "for every narrow loophole that is closed, there are dozens if not hundreds more tax shelter schemes that remain available to be exploited by those who choose not to pay their fair share for necessities like national security."[77]

Diabolically ingenious tax experts find intricate ways in which the rich just get richer and richer. One of the best tax lawyers is a guy named Jonathan Blattmachr, and here is an example of his work.

> Once, Blattmachr devised a way that Bill Gates, the richest man in America, could reap $200 million in profits on Microsoft stock without paying the $56 million of capital gains taxes that federal law required at the time. The plan was so lucrative that Gates would not have to pay a single dollar in tax and would even be entitled to an income tax deduction of $6 million or so. And that was just the initial plan. The concept could be applied endlessly, allowing Gates to convert billions of dollars in Microsoft stock gains into cash over the years.[78]

Corporate CEOs use a million tax dodges like tax-free salaries and bonuses and deferred income on stock market capital gains.[79] They also have built-in tax schemes for their luxurious lifestyles, like corporate jets that grace them with a benefit of 30- to 200-times profit on every dollar of tax they put toward their corporate jet.[80] It's criminal and Congress does nothing about it because they are basically paid by these corporations to look the other way.

Deferring millions of dollars in income and capital gains is a trick that has really been perfected by corporations and their fat cat executive officers and board members. "Deferral, the tax lawyers say, is 90 percent of tax planning. Delay a tax for thirty years and its cost in today's money is almost nothing."[81]

Meanwhile, capital gains taxes—the realm of the wealthy and their massive stock market and real estate profits—has been steadily *reduced* and is now about half of what it originally was. Capital gains are "the source of more than half of income for the super rich."[82] But the capital gains tax rate, which was 28 percent in 1987, has been steadily *reduced* by Congress and was lowered again in 2003, to *only 15 percent*.[83] That was made possible by our politicians and through the campaign donations of wealthy corporate and fat cat special interests.[84] But they cap the social security tax for wealthy Americans. After income passes $118,500, they stop deducting Social Security taxes.[85] They get a free ride after that.

The deck is stacked against the working person in a rigged game that favors the rich and corporations, made possible by their co-opting of the political system via massive donations to purchase influence. As columnist Matt Taibbi put it: "Bankers on Wall Street pay lower tax rates than most car mechanics."[86] The tax breaks made possible by all their political cronies have now reached a point where their behavior should be considered criminally fraudulent:

> Goldman Sachs in 2008—this was the same year the bank reported $2.9 billion in profits, and paid out over $10 billion in compensation—paid just $14 million in taxes, a 1 percent tax rate. . . . Bank of America last year paid not a single dollar in taxes—in fact, it received a "tax credit" of $1 billion. There are a slew of troubled companies that will not be paying taxes for years, including Citigroup and CIT.[87]

Like we said . . . And the rich get richer. And that's not just an expression either. It's a fact, and it has never been truer than recently in American history. The middle class is disappearing and most of the income gains are going to the wealthiest Americans. "Across the political spectrum, economists found the same basic trend: the rich really are getting richer and the poor really are getting poorer."[88]

Every single election that comes along, we all hear politicians promising that they are going to close the loopholes that allow corporations and millionaires to avoid paying taxes. Yet, those loopholes seem to mysteriously always survive. At this point, it's almost a joke. The whole thing is just a charade. We should stop believing their vacant promises because they are *employees* of the corporations and the wealthy—they are paid to do their bidding and those loopholes are left open intentionally: "Indeed, experts believe that the structure of the tax code encourages corporations to shuffle money overseas to hide from the US taxman."[89] And that's not to mention billions of dollars in tax credits that they bestow upon them, as well.

They are all nice, fat loopholes, made generously possible to corporations by the politicians who have received many corporate-based campaign contributions, for many years, from the same companies who benefit.

By shifting profits on American sales to tax havens abroad, blue-chip firms such as Apple, Chevron, Cisco Systems, GE, Google, Microsoft, Oracle, and Pfizer perforce end up with sizable portions of their corporate cash resting in havens like the Cayman Islands or Luxembourg. For example, Cisco holds 80 percent of its $40 billion cash balance abroad and Apple holds two-thirds of its even larger hoard abroad. In May 2011, American multinationals held over $1 trillion abroad in such accounts . . . [90]

That process of corporate theft goes by the hyperbole of "offshoring capital." But the offshoring of jobs is an even bigger issue.

Apple is America's largest corporation and is generally esteemed in glowing terms for being our huge success story.[91] But there is another side to that story.

Offshoring virtually everything in the value chain from R&D to production with barely 6 percent of its workforce in America, it is also an unusually disloyal American multinational.[92]

That may surprise some people, but it's true. "Moreover, like most multinationals, much of its profit is channeled through overseas cutouts to be hidden in tax havens, its tax burden shifted onto families and purely domestic US enterprises."[93] Because every time that a corporation evades taxes and offshores jobs, it's the taxpayers—we—who, ultimately, are forced to pick up the tab.

The American technology jewel Apple is a poster child for this category of offshoring. Despite its products being envisaged, conceived, researched, financed, developed, and managed from America, Apple fabricates most of its products—iPhones, for example—in low-wage countries, such as China, for export to the United States.

So Apple apparently isn't the answer to the problems of the American economy—in fact, they're part of the cause of those problems.

The late visionary Steve Jobs was an innovative genius, but . . . his successor, Timothy D. Cook, has proven to be far from an economic patriot. . . . About 43,000 of Apples' 63,000 or so direct employees reside in the United States, but almost none of the 700,000 contract employees work in America.[94]

Apple annually has "earned more than $400,000 in profit per employee, more than Goldman Sachs, Exxon Mobil or Google." But American workers, even at Apple, have not shared very highly in that success.[95] And the fact that American workers have been largely cut out of that success story comes in spite of the fact that Apple sells about 40 percent of its products in the United States.[96]

So instead of being embarrassed by the obvious disparity and apparent unfairness of the matter, they should just repatriate—bring the jobs back home. They *are* embarrassed by it, and rightfully so—they *should be* embarrassed. It's a disgraceful and very unpatriotic act and their actions indicate that they are aware of that point. This was a defensive comment in that regard from an Apple executive in 2012: "We shouldn't be criticized for using Chinese workers. The US has stopped producing people with the skills we need."[97] Well, hold on there, Charlie, because there's just one little problem with that statement. It's not true! American workers are actually *more* productive than most of their foreign counterparts and that's a proven fact.[98] "Not long ago, Apple boasted that its products were made in the US. Today, few are."[99] Bringing those jobs back home would help everybody, Apple included, because it would be inexpensive and labor is actually only a fraction of the cost of manufacturing.[100]

With the big banks, the situation is even worse. Neil Barofsky's title was Special United States Treasury Department Inspector General. Here's what Mr. Barofsky had to say about the tainted relationship between the big banks and the politicians who gave them hundreds of billions of dollars of taxpayer money, in the form of "bailout" money:

> The suspicions that the system is rigged in favor of the largest banks and their elites, so they play by their own set of rules to the disfavor of the taxpayers who funded their bailout, are true. It really happened. These suspicions are valid.[101]

Well *that's* pretty damn clear. Thank you, Mr. Barofsky.

Look at the facts, folks. Jeff Cohen is a media critic who is a real watchdog for the people and he put together a great list which, taken in full, really tells the story of how corporations have taken over the political show. After all his campaign oratory, here's who Obama put in key positions once he was elected:

- "Three successive White House chiefs of staff who'd made fortunes in the financial industry: Rahm Emanuel (amassed $16 million within a couple years of exiting the Clinton White House), William Daley (JPMorgan Chase) and Jacob Lew (Citigroup/Now US Treasury Secretary).
- Wall Streeters to dominate his economic team, including Clintonites like Larry Summers as Chief Economic Advisor and Peter Orszag as Budget Director.
- Monsanto executives and lobbyists for influential food and agriculture posts.
- A corporate health-care executive to preside over health-care 'reform,' while allowing pharmaceutical lobbyists to obstruct cost controls.
- An industry-connected nuclear power and fracking enthusiast as Secretary of Energy.
- Two successive chairs of the Federal Communications Commission who've largely served corporate interests, including former lobbyist Tom Wheeler now undermining Net Neutrality."[102]

And then, these same wealthy vermin go back and forth through a revolving door that should not even exist, between corporate boardrooms, lobbying and public relations firms, and politically-appointed government positions. "The revolving door also incentivizes lawmakers themselves to weaken regulation, because they have their own subsequent careers to consider. The purchase of obliging legislators is a well-established tradition of American pay-to-play politics . . . "[103]

And "play" the game they do, at a rate that is increasingly alarming: "In the 1970s, only about 3 percent of retiring members of Congress went on to become Washington lobbyists. But by 2009, more than 30 percent did, because the financial incentives for lobbying had become so large."[104]

The amount of people who have traveled through this magical revolving door is far too numerous to mention. Literally thousands have passed back and forth through the career-enhancing effects of political appointments and the private sector. And the nasty, obscene acts of these folks are also too numerous to mention. But here are just a few choice examples of the obvious conflicts of interest that we're talking about here.

THE REVOLVING DOOR BETWEEN WALL STREET AND WASHINGTON

- Michael W. Wynne, who had worked for both General Dynamics and Lockheed Martin (two of the largest arms producers), was nominated for Secretary of the Air Force, in spite of the fact that he was one of those blamed by the "Pentagon inspector general for a failed 23.5-billion-dollar deal with Boeing, which many lawmakers call *the most significant case of contract abuse in decades.*"[105]

- Edward C. Aldridge Jr. joined the Board of Directors at Lockheed Martin a month prior to leaving his job at the Pentagon. While at the Pentagon, he approved a $3 billion contract to purchase twenty Lockheed Martin planes "after having long criticized the program as overpriced and having threatened to cancel it."[106] He was then named as Chairman of the President's Commission on Implementation of United States Space Exploration Policy.[107]

- Dick Cheney was a Secretary of Defense with no business experience, but became CEO of a multibillion-dollar conglomerate when he left the Defense Department. As Charles Lewis of the Center for Public Integrity observed: "Why would a defense secretary, former chief of staff to a president and former member of Congress with no business experience become the CEO of a multibillion-dollar oil services company? He was brought in to raise their government contract profile and he did."[108] After Halliburton, he then became Vice President. Vice President Dick Cheney "denied that he had any ties with Halliburton Company after he left his position as CEO of the company in 2000. An investigation by the Congressional Research Service revealed that while VP, Cheney received deferred compensation from Halliburton to the tune of $500,000 to $1,000,000. . . . Questions about 'sweetheart deals' with Halliburton arose as the company was awarded no-bid contracts for reconstruction in Iraq. The contracts were estimated to be worth about $1.5 billion. Probes into Halliburton led to allegations of overcharging the military for importing oil from Kuwait into Iraq, $6 million in kickbacks for the awarding of contracts to a Kuwaiti company and $180 million in bribes to land a natural gas project contract in Nigeria while Cheney was CEO."[109] In total, Halliburton received at least $39.5 billion in contracts related to the Iraq War.[110] The actual amount of "no-bid" contracts, where "companies get to name their price with no competing bid,"[111] to Halliburton in Iraq, was $7 billion.[112]

- Paul O'Neal was CEO (Chief Executive Officer) of Alcoa Corporation, as well as RAND Corporation. He was then appointed Treasury Secretary by President Bush. After leaving the Treasury Department, he became an adviser to The Blackstone Group, a major player in the world of finance.[113]

- Robert E. Rubin began his career at Goldman Sachs, the huge investment bank that is very involved in politics (we will have a lot more to say about the tactics of the infamous Goldman Sachs in the following chapter). Rubin became Vice Chairman, then Co-Chairman of the company. He then became Treasury Secretary under President Clinton. After leaving the Treasury Department, he served as a member of the Board of Directors at Citigroup and was also Senior Advisor to the company.[114] That's the same "Citigroup that was bailed out during the financial crisis, even though the company was more bankrupt than Lehman Brothers."[115] Lehman Brothers was "allowed" to go bankrupt—and the world didn't come to an end. "Rubin decamped from Treasury in 1999, shortly after the passage of Gramm-Leach-Bliley, to join Citigroup, which at the time was the principal benefactor from the law. He has become Exhibit A when progressives talk about the 'revolving door' between banks and Washington . . . [US Senator, Elizabeth] Warren cited Rubin by name, noting that three of the last four Treasury secretaries under Democratic presidents, 'starting with Robert Rubin,' have been affiliated with Citigroup either before or after their service."[116] It's a funny thing with all these big corporate CEOs—they're "too big to fail" but they're not too big to be appointed Treasury Secretary!

- Lawrence Summers became Treasury Secretary after Robert Rubin, while Clinton was President. He was influential in the financial deregulation—including the repeal of the Glass-Steagall Act—which led to the whole financial runaway act until it all imploded in the autumn of 2008. Then Summers became Managing Partner of a big hedge fund. Then he became President Obama's chief economic adviser. After leaving government, Summers made many millions of dollars. When he was nominated as Treasury Secretary, he reported having assets of only $900,000 and debts of $500,000.[117] But after leaving the Treasury, his income ballooned up after government service. When he returned to his post in the Obama administration, "he reported a net worth of between $7 million and $31 million" from working as a "paid consultant" to Citigroup, a NASDAQ group, and a hedge fund.[118]

- Henry Paulson was the CEO of Goldman Sachs. Paulson then became Treasury Secretary under President Bush. As Secretary of the Treasury, he was in charge of "doling out" over $700 billion to the big banks.[119]

- Timothy Geithner was an Under-Secretary at the Treasury Department, who was then named President of the Federal Reserve Bank of New York. Geithner reportedly arranged the rescue and sale of the huge investment firm, Bear Stearns.[120] He was offered the top position at Citigroup, but declined, though "he had extensive interaction with Citigroup."[121] He became Treasury Secretary under President Obama and was responsible for disbursing hundreds of billions of dollars in "bailout" funds. After serving as Treasury Secretary, he became President and Managing Director of Warburg Pincus, a huge investment firm.

- Jack Lew became Treasury Secretary after Geithner. Lew had been an attorney in private practice and went to work in Washington as a Special Assistant to President Clinton. He became Director of OMB (Office of Management and Budget). He then returned to the "private sector" (and the reason that we place that in quotation marks is because, these days, we find almost nothing to distinguish it from the public sector), as the Chief Operating Officer at Citigroup which, at that time, was one of the largest banks.[122] He was then nominated for Treasury Secretary in 2013 and approved by the United States

Senate in February, 2013. Oh, and by the way—while he was COO at Citi, he oversaw a group which invested heavily in a hedge fund "that bet on the housing market to collapse,"[123] and, as we all know, it did. Also during his time as COO at Citi, the number of Citigroup subsidiaries in the Cayman Islands' tax haven increased to 113.[124] "Of the past six secretaries of the Treasury, four have been top executives of major companies and two were from the financial and investment giant Goldman Sachs."[125]

- Michael Taylor was an attorney for Monsanto Corporation. Then, he joined the FDA (the United States Food and Drug Administration that is supposed to *regulate* companies like Monsanto) as the FDA's Deputy Commissioner for Foods. Then he went back to Monsanto as Monsanto's Vice President for Public Policy. Then he went back to the FDA as its Deputy Commissioner for Policy, "in the same cushy position as he was before, rubber-stamping pro-Monsanto legislation."[126]

- Bechtel Corporation is another company which is infamous as a revolving door. Bechtel has a history of pushing US policy toward war and then profiting from it.[127] They made billions from the Iraq War. "Bechtel consistently uses insider connections at the highest levels of government to obtain its contracts."[128] And a US government audit "exposed gross mismanagement by the company."[129] "Bechtel has longstanding ties to the national security establishment. One director is George P. Schultz who was secretary of state under President Ronald Reagan. Before joining the Reagan administration, Mr. Schultz, who also serves as a senior counselor to Bechtel, was the company's president, working alongside Caspar W. Weinberger, who served as an executive at the San Francisco–based company before his appointment as defense secretary."[130] Bechtel's CEO, Riley Bechtel, received a presidential appointment to serve on the President's Export Council.[131]

- President George H.W. Bush: "After leaving the Central Intelligence Agency in 1977, George H.W. Bush was made a director of Eli Lilly. Future Vice President to Bush Dan Quayle's father, James C. Quayle, owned controlling interest in the Lilly company and the the *Indianapolis Star* at that time. Bush actively lobbied both within and without the Reagan administration as Vice President in 1981 to permit drug companies to sell obsolete or especially domestically banned substances to Third World countries. While Vice President, Bush continued to act on behalf of pharmaceutical companies by personally going to the Internal Revenue Service for special tax breaks for certain drug companies, including Lilly, who were manufacturing in Puerto Rico. In 1982, Bush intervened with the US Department of Treasury in connection with proposed rules that would have forced pharmaceutical companies to pay significantly more taxes. Bush was personally ordered to stop lobbying the IRS on behalf of the drug companies by the US Supreme Court."[132]

- "Alex Azar, was deputy secretary of Health and Human Services under George W. Bush, serving as chief operating officer for two years. In that role, he oversaw such agencies as the Food and Drug Administration, the National Institutes of Health, the Centers for Disease Control and Prevention, and the Centers for Medicare and Medicaid Services. In May 2007 Azar became Senior Vice President of Corporate Affairs and Communications for Eli Lilly, reporting directly to Chief Executive Sidney Taurel."[133]

- Attorney General Eric Holder was formerly an attorney at the law firm Covington & Burling, which ranked the megabanks among their top clients: the "Four Horsemen" of the banking industry— JPMorgan Chase, Citigroup, Bank of America, and Wells Fargo.[134] Holder brought many of his law firm colleagues with him when he left Covington to head up the Justice Department.[135] As is well known, Holder's Justice Department failed to prosecute the banks vigorously, even though many felt they were guilty of criminal activity.[136] As Attorney General, "he let the big banks skate by with nothing more than a slap . . . " and deprioritized investigations of mortgage fraud.[137] The title of Matt Taibbi's *Rolling Stone* article says it all: "Eric Holder, Wall Street Double Agent, Comes in From the Cold: Barack Obama's former top cop cashes in after six years of letting banks run wild."[138] "He even, at one point, said that big banks are too big to prosecute."[139] Then, Mr. Holder returned through the revolving door, back to the prestigious Covington & Burling where his office had even been kept there waiting for him—literally.[140] But, needless to say, there was no conflict of interest there, folks. Of course not! How dare you! How could one even suspect such a thing? Actually, articles have pointed out that if we truly had a responsible mainstream media, it should have been a widely covered spectacle (and it wasn't) that Holder returned to the law firm from which he came after giving Wall Street a free pass—and that it was "an unquestionable conflict of interest."[141]

"Deferred prosecution" is another way that politicians get remunerated—some people would call it *bribed*—for their political service to corporations. Deferred *compensation* would probably be a more accurate term for it. The scumbags are creative, you've got to give them credit for that. Need an example? Well, here you go. This is how the system works:

> John Ashcroft, a former Senator, Presidential Candidate, and US Attorney General, earned little during a career of public service before retiring in 2005. His net worth was dramatically enhanced, however, when his former Justice Department subordinate (and currently New Jersey Governor) Chris Christie appointed Ashcroft as "monitor" of a remedial agreement involving illegal kickbacks to physicians.[142]

And here's *how* it is enhanced. This is a perfect example of the slick games going on between corporations and politicians. "Zimmer Orthopedics avoided prosecution by agreeing to a Justice Department bargain including paying Ashcroft at least $29 million for 18 months of work as monitor. Worse, the firm wasn't required to pay fines to the federal government, apparently because the monitor fees were considered sufficient punishment—even though they enriched Ashcroft's law firm rather than reimburse victimized patients or taxpayers."[143] Nice, huh? Like the old expression goes: good work if you can find it.

Unfortunately, there are far too many examples of corporations effectively bribing politicians through a thinly disguised form of corrupting the system: Bristol-Myers Squibb, the huge pharmaceutical firm, cut a deal to avoid prosecution and one of the conditions was to endow a chair at a Bush appointee's old university, Seton Hall law school—in "Business Ethics," of all things![144] As a former investigator for the Internal Revenue Service appropriately observed: "It looks too much like the boys are taking care of buddies, because these are lucrative contracts."[145] That whole gambit of "enterprise monitors" was actually a system that lavishly reimbursed 30 politically connected hotshots.[146]

Corporations get tax benefits via loopholes generously provided them by their bought-and-paid-for politicians. It's simple. A huge corporation like Medtronic just moves its headquarters out of the United States and then, thanks to the Congressionally protected sweet little loophole, instead of being subject to the 35% US corporate tax rate on profits earned overseas, it only pays 5%.[147] *That is why jobs continue to leave the United States. Not* because of US workers. But because of corporations taking advantage of the loopholes made possible by Congress, *to whom corporations make generous campaign contributions.* It all stinks to high heaven.

It not only makes no sense—it's blatantly *wrong*: "We give tax breaks to immensely profitable corporations that don't need the money and boondoggles that wouldn't exist without government favoritism."[148]

We would submit that even a president of the United States is beholden to his or her masters and, in the case of twenty-first century America, those masters are Wall Street. They are the same Wall Street contributors who anointed Barak Obama with their financial blessing that made him president, led by Goldman Sachs, the folks who invented the revolving door between Wall Street and Washington political posts.

You may have heard Governor Martin O'Malley's statement: "Recently the CEO of Goldman Sachs let his employees know that he'd be just fine with either Bush or Clinton. I bet he would."[149]

> "The key for Goldman is to have its bets hedged both in its businesses and in politics," said William Cohan, a journalist and former banker who wrote a history of Goldman. "And you can't get any better for them than Jeb and Hillary, it's a dream come true, they would win either way."[150]

But *think* about that for a minute. Shouldn't it scare the *hell* out of us if the Wall Street hotshots don't care whether a Jeb Bush or a Hillary Clinton gets elected President of the United States? Because they know the simple fact—that they win either way! Isn't it pretty clear at this point that the bankers and the corporations are running the show, not the Republicans or the Democrats?

> The United States acts like an army that enforces the business interests of the corporations it is allied to . . . the American government subsidizes the development of weapons. They literally give massive companies grants to make missiles and whatnot, as well as creating ridiculously favorable tax conditions for them to prosper in. That's state-funded industry—America does believe in communism but just communism for the rich.[151]

We have to change the game of political prostitution because it is only working for the corporations, not for the people. "Unless we get money out of politics—campaign finance, lobbying, and the revolving door between governments and the most powerful global corporations—we are not going to create change within those old obsolete and decaying governmental systems."[152]

To us, calling our current political system obsolete and decaying is being pretty generous with the terminology, folks. It's a *poisoned* system, *not the democratic republic* we grew up thinking it was. And that has been *proved* true; in fact, they have proved it themselves:

> Princeton University recently did a study revealing what those of us paying attention already know all too well: The United States is, *in scientifically proven fact, not a democracy*. They concluded that the United States is controlled by economic elites.[153]

And those economic elites need a *real* wake-up call from the 99%. What do you say we *give 'em one*!

And get this clear, because *this* is the overriding point of it all:

<u>It is corporations that are to blame for the hijacking of our precious democratic republic!</u>

In the following one paragraph, the reason for the above is clearly demonstrated. We urge you to read it carefully, and then read it again, to correctly understand what has happened to the American political system:

> The structural reason that voting is redundant is that through the funding of political parties, lobbying, and cronyism, corporations are able to ensure that their interests are prioritized above the needs of the electorate and that ideas that contravene their agenda don't even make it into the sphere of public debate. Whoever you vote for, you'll be voting for a party that represents a big-business agenda, not the will of the people.[154]

Amen, brother!

FURTHER RESEARCH:

Derber, Charlie. *Regime Change Begins at Home: Freeing America from Corporate Rule*. Oakland, CA: Berrett-Koehler Publishers, 2004.

Brand, Russell. *Revolution*. New York: Ballantine Books, 2014.

Lewis, Charles. *935 Lies*. New York: Perseus Books, 2014.

Schultz, Jim. *The Democracy Owner's Manual: A Practical Guide to Changing the World*. New Brunswick, NJ: Rutgers University Press, 2002.

Cost, Jay. *A Republic No More: Big Government and the Rise of American Political Corruption*. New York: Encounter Books, 2015.

Perkins, John. *Confessions of an Economic Hit Man*, Oakland, CA: Berrett-Koehler, 2004.

Johnston, David Cay. *Perfectly Legal: The Covert Campaign to Rig Our Tax System to Benefit the Super Rich—and Cheat Everybody Else*. New York: Portfolio, 2003.

Palast, Greg. *The Best Democracy Money Can Buy*. Greg Palast. New York: Plume, 2004.

Partnoy, Frank. *Infectious Greed: How Deceit and Risk Corrupted the Financial Markets*. New York: Times Books, 2014.

Vogel, Kenneth P. *Big Money: 2.5 Billion Dollars, One Suspicious Vehicle, And A Pimp—On the Trail of the Ultra-Rich Hijacking American Politics.* New York: Public Affairs, 2014.

Schweizer, Peter. *Throw Them All Out: How Politicians and Their Friends Get Rich Off Insider Stock Tips, Land Deals, and Cronyism That Would Send the Rest of Us to Prison.* Boston: Houghton Mifflin Harcourt, 2011.

Tyler, George R. *What Went Wrong: How The 1% Hijacked the American Middle Class…And What Other Countries Got Right.* Dallas: Benbella Books, 2013.

Reich, Robert. *Aftershock: The Next Economy and America's Future.* New York: Vintage Books/Random House, 2010.

Achbar, Mark, and Jennifer Abbott, directors. *The Corporation.* New York: Zeitgeist Films, 2005. DVD. https://www.youtube.com/watch?v=Z4ou9rOssPg.

Kornbluth, Jacob, director. *Inequality for All.* Los Angeles: Radius TWC, 2014. DVD.

Hardy, Don Jr. and Dana Nachman, directors. *The Human Experiment.* Santa Clara, CA: KTF Films, 2013. DVD.

Holland, Joshua. "The Fascinating History of How Corporations Became 'People'—Thanks to Corrupt Courts Working for the 1%." *AlterNet* (November 23, 2001). http://www.alternet.org/story/153201/the_fascinating_history_of_how_corporations_became_%22people%22_—_thanks_to_corrupt_courts_working_for_the_1.

Greenwald, Glenn. "Top Senate Democrat: Bankers 'own' the US Congress." *Salon* (April 29, 2009). http://www.salon.com/2009/04/30/ownership/.

Taibbi, Matt. "Wall Street Isn't Winning—It's Cheating." *Rolling Stone* (October 25, 2011). http://www.rollingstone.com/politics/news/owss-beef-wall-street-isnt-winning-its-cheating-20111025.

Cohen, Jeff. "Hillary's Candid Motto for Democratic Party: 'Represent Banks.'" *Huffington Post* (July 14, 2014). http://www.huffingtonpost.com/jeff-cohen/hillary-clinton-banks_b_5584870.html?utm_hp_ref=tw.

Morgenson, Gretchen. "Into the Bailout Buzzsaw." *New York Times* (July 22, 2012). http://www.realclearpolitics.com/2012/07/22/into_the_bailout_buzz-saw_285380.html.

Taibbi, Matt. "Eric Holder, Wall Street Double Agent, Comes in From the Cold: Barack Obama's former top cop cashes in after six years of letting banks run wild." *Rolling Stone* (July 8, 2015). http://www.rollingstone.com/politics/news/eric-holder-wall-street-double-agent-comes-in-from-the-cold-20150708.

CHAPTER TWO

NO BANKER LEFT BEHIND: TOO BIG TO FAIL, *OR* JAIL
- OR-
WHERE $30 TRILLION WENT (AND IT SURE AS HELL WASN'T TO YOU!)

Give a man a gun and he can rob a bank. Give a man a bank and he can rob the world.

—Anonymous

Now we get to the nitty gritty of the largest theft in the entire history of humanity—in a daring robbery that was pulled off in broad daylight too. It's an epic tale that might have easily been called "How the Wolves of Wall Street Mauled the Men and Women of Main Street."

But first off, to give you an idea of what charm and integrity this particular group of business people hold, here's what Andrew Jackson, seventh President of the United States of America, had to say about the large banks:

You are a den of vipers and thieves.[1]

It is to be regretted that the rich and powerful too often bend the acts of government to their selfish purposes.[2]

If one of us goes into a casino and we place a bet and we lose—then that's it. We lost. Right?

But—if one of the big banks or any major player in the financial industry places a big bet and loses—they get bailed out by the government. We ask you, is that fair? Imagine if you could keep placing bets in a casino and you're allowed to keep whatever you win, but you also get reimbursed for whatever you lose. You'd have to be crazy not to keep playing with that setup, would you not? Of course, you'd have to be crazy to give somebody that kind of a deal, wouldn't you? *So why do we?* Why do we put up with that crap? Why do we let the government come to the rescue and bail out these ruthless bastards, so that they can foreclose on the homes of hard-working Americans who, just like them, hit some bad luck? How come the billionaires always get bailed out and it is hard-working American families that always get screwed, having their homes foreclosed by the same folks that got bailed out with taxpayer dollars? How the *hell* can anybody say that is fair? It's Robin Hood *in reverse*!

> With the dramatic events surrounding the 2008 financial crisis, beginning in 2009 the United States embarked on the greatest reverse–Robin Hood transfer of wealth in its history. Tax money was taken from all, rich and poor, and given to billionaires. Under the guise of an economic stimulus plan to create jobs and to develop alternative energy, Washington has handed out billions of dollars in cash and federal loan guarantees.[3]

We'd say that spells it out pretty clearly, don't you think? Robin Hood in reverse. The rich getting richer, and as a direct result of financially supporting the right politicians.

And next thing, folks, for once and for all, let's <u>stop blaming the victims</u>. Millions of families had their homes foreclosed by the same ruthless banks that caused the whole problem to begin with. Thirty million people lost their jobs.[4] *Those* are the folks who should have been financially assisted. And instead we gave a fortune to the big banks and other gigantic corporations.

Calling it the "sub-prime mortgage crisis" or the "credit crunch" is *incredibly* inaccurate and inappropriate. It makes it sound like it was simply borrowers failing to pay their bills that caused the whole financial collapse, and that was not *at all* the actual case. It was the actions of reckless corporations that caused the meltdown.

So let's get that straight, right from the start. It, categorically, *was not* the American public that caused the financial collapse of 2008. It was the wolves of Wall Street and the Big Banks that leave no billionaire behind. As Jesse Ventura stated, "Don't let them fool you into thinking it was reckless borrowers and subprime loans that built the house of cards."[5] Ventura said it like it was: "We've had a revolving door between Wall Street and Washington, which led to a Wild West mentality on 'the Street.'"[6] They invented horribly speculative financial instruments with confusing names like credit default swaps, and they finally got so drunk with speculation that they drowned in a pool of their own making and they couldn't get out of it. So they came crying to the government for help, and together with their pals in Washington, they managed to put together a false scenario where it's supposedly the public's fault for increasing their feeding frenzy. Why? Because working people were trying to buy a home for their family, which *used* to be called the American Dream. Therefore, according to the logic of an insane financial system, instead of rescuing the people who were losing their homes, *millions* of them, as a result of these tyrants, they instead shelled out trillions of dollars of taxpayer money to the *very* people who caused the problem to begin with! And that's right—we said trillions—because that's what it actually was when you add it all up. Although the usual TARP (Troubled Asset Relief Program) figure bandied around in mainstream media is "only" $700 billion, the true figure, as we are about to show you, is actually in the *trillions* of dollars. So keep reading.

But this habit of blaming the victims is even present in some of the mainstream media analysis that points its institutional fingers at the public as though too much consumer greed—like trying to buy a nice home for our families—was responsible for the whole financial fiasco. But even conservative analyses prove the point that it was not the public who was to blame for that huge mess. Here's how one very mainstream author put it at the time: "Tax money was taken from all, rich and poor, and given to billionaires."[7] We "bailed out" the wrong people! Billionaires did not need bailing out—American consumers did.

Millions of those American consumer borrowers, who tend to officially take the blame for much of that crisis, actually *lost their homes* as a result of it. That's the reality of the situation. And meanwhile, crooked CEOs like Angelo Mozilo, who was the CEO of Countrywide Financial, one of the biggest lenders to those home buyers, walked away with a cool $148 million that year: an annual salary of $48 million, plus another $100 million that he made from dumping his stock in Countrywide right before the whole house of cards came crashing down on the American public.[8] And did Mozilo ever go to jail? *Hell* no, he didn't! He was never even charged! He cut a deal. The proclaimed "king of predatory lending" just walked away.[9] And, as a former federal prosecutor put it:

> Mozilo was the boss of bosses of predatory lending. . . . If prosecutors are not going to go after low-hanging fruit like Mozilo, the rest of the bankster bosses can sleep well, assured that their fortunes are secure.[10]

It has been observed that "if big banks operate under different legal rules than the rest of us, it makes a mockery of democracy."[11] Well then, boys and girls, you better get used to it. Because that's the way our system of "justice" now operates. The big banks really put the "mock" in democracy. And make no mistake about it. Corporations and their cronies in the government were the primary components of the corrupt actions that brought down our economy in 2008:

> Anybody in a position to harm (mortgage maker) Fannie Mae's interests was either bought off or intimidated into backing down, even as the GSE (Government-Sponsored Enterprises, such as Fannie Mae) was perfecting the sort of accounting shenanigans that brought down Enron and WorldCom, and later on as it was loading up its balance sheet with the subprime mortgages that eviscerated the economy in 2008.[12]

The roots of The Wall Street Fiasco—and that's what it *should* be called—were in the unscrupulous financial practices of corrupt corporate greed, facilitated by the richly rewarded politicians who removed the obstacles that had been in place to control that corporate greed, such as The Glass-Steagall Act that, for decades, had controlled the excesses of the banking industry. Anti-trust issues have almost disappeared from America's business landscape. "Bigger is Better" is the new corporate battle cry. The repeal of the Glass-Steagall Act—engineered by Wall Street and passed by their "employees" in Congress—blew up the dam that was effectively the only thing holding back the big banks from a reign of financial terror. And *sure enough*—they took advantage of it with a feeding frenzy that didn't abate until the broad financial crisis of 2007–2008.

> Deregulation was also endorsed by the Clinton administration, including the Commodity Futures Modernization Act of 2000, which minimized regulation of credit derivatives, removing them from bucket shop prohibitions. Underwriters such as AIG were not required to back derivative issues with a reasonable amount of reserves, causing the derivative market to grow enormously.[13]

That deregulation spawned the problem. Because "AIG, with Lehman Brothers and Bear Stearns not far behind, issued $3 trillion (not *billion—trillion*, which is 1,000 billion!) of credit derivatives with little reserve backing."[14] They invented a new way to play the game. New rules that were designed expressly for their best economic interests. "These changes enabled the debt of the American private financial sector to quadruple, growing from an amount comparable to 26 percent of GDP (gross domestic product) in 1985 to 108 percent in 2009."[15] So *there's your bubble*, boys and girls. That's how they started to blow it up.

> We now know that banks and mortgage companies were indulging in all sorts of fraudulent practices to pump up their mortgage business. . . . It was no accident that the most complex mortgages were sold to the least sophisticated buyers, especially in poor and minority neighborhoods.[16]

Although the usual figure stated for the TARP program is $700 billion, the United States government has actually spent $2.5 trillion "propping up" these thankless bastards, and "the government has made commitments of about $12.2 trillion."[17] That's how the *New York Times* tallies up the tab, at least. But the most comprehensive study actually places the bailout figure at $29 trillion.[18] That's one helluva *lot* of money—and for what? They didn't just "rescue the banks," as the news usually parrots. They rescued the banks, the mutual funds, Fannie Mae, Ginnie Mae, Freddie Mac, the insurance giant, AIG, General Motors, General Electric, Chrysler, Bear Stearns, and many others.[19] You might wonder what GM is doing on that list. But, actually, all of the Big Three automakers—GM, Ford and Chrysler—jumped onto the bandwagon, showing their financial wounds and pointing out that *they* should be "too big to fail" as well.[20] And it worked. They, too, received billions of dollars of taxpayer money:

> The bailout of the Big Three automakers sends the message that although mismanagement at an average-size firm will be punished with losses, gross mismanagement on a gigantic scale will be rewarded with credit and funds purloined from innocent third parties. People who are good stewards of wealth are thereby forced to subsidize people who are disastrously poor stewards of wealth.[21]

That's what they did to save their pals' asses at their big banks and corporations when they hit hard times. Trillions of dollars, representing the greatest theft from the public—and make no mistake about it, that means *us*—in our entire history:

> During the bailout of Wall Street, $30 trillion in support and subsidies went to the most powerful players on Wall Street. That was the greatest theft of wealth in history. Throughout the entire world, the Federal Reserve, IMF (International Monetary Fund), World Bank, ECB (European Central Bank), and BIS (Bank for International Settlements) carry out genocidal economic policies. Just because that sounds hyperbolic and incredibly harsh doesn't mean it's not true.[22]

Another in-depth study, in fact, the most in-depth study of the issue known, confirmed that high number, by the way, and placed the true figure for the bailout at $29,000,000,000,000.[23] Twenty-nine trillion dollars. And that's not $29 trillion in lost economic production, or inclusive of broader factors of that type; that's $29 trillion in "funding provided by the Federal Reserve to bail out the financial system."[24]

As journalist Matt Taibbi learned, Citigroup's input was even very present in the "search" for the next Treasury Secretary:

> Geithner, in other words, is hired to head the US Treasury by an executive from Citigroup—Michael Froman—before the ink is even dry on a

massive government giveaway to Citigroup that Geithner himself was instrumental in delivering. In the annals of brazen political swindles, this one has to go in the all-time Fuck-the-Optics Hall of Fame.[25]

They've been sleeping together so long that they don't even notice it anymore. As one Congressman put it, as a question to Treasury Secretary Paulson: "Is it possible that there's so much conflict of interest here that all you folks don't even realize that you're helping people that you're associated with?"[26]

We are told that the bailout actually worked—that it rescued our economic system and everything is fine now. Well guess what? That could not be farther from the truth. Matt Taibbi had a great article in *Rolling Stone* called "Secrets and Lies of the Bailout":

> It was all a lie—one of the biggest and most elaborate falsehoods ever sold to the American people. We were told that the taxpayer was stepping in—only temporarily, mind you—to prop up the economy and save the world from financial catastrophe. What we actually ended up doing was the exact opposite: committing American taxpayers to permanent, blind support of an ungovernable, unregulatable, hyperconcentrated new financial system that exacerbates the greed and inequality that caused the crash, and forces Wall Street banks like Goldman Sachs and Citigroup to increase risk rather than reduce it.[27]

As columnist William Safire aptly noted, *before* the fact on this one:

> "No private enterprise should be allowed to think of itself as 'too big to fail,'" wrote Safire in a foreshadowing of exactly what would ensue. Having the support of the FDIC (Federal Deposit Insurance Corporation)—the federal government guaranteeing your accounts—had to come with restrictions, or it would be exploited, he argued . . . "If a huge group runs into trouble, it should take the bank down with it; no taxpayer bailouts should allow executives or stockholders to relax."[28]

We say amen to that. However, we don't tell our elected officials what to do—Wall Street does that! And, as we all now know, they bailed the rich bastards out anyway, and told us that they had to, because they were "too big to fail."

Make no mistake about it, folks—this was a rigged, closed-end game of financial musical chairs that was *designed* to fail, right from the start (and if you guessed that it was the taxpaying citizen who was the one who was left without the chair when the music stopped, then you guessed right). When you learn the facts, you are going to hate these bums as much as we do! Pay attention to the following, please—we beg that of you; it's *so* illuminating as to what was *really* going on, while they tried to blame it on consumers for actually attempting to own their own home!

Now, let's take a good look at *how* they caused the collapse, re-engineering our entire financial system, as they blew up a bubble that was pre-destined to bust:

> Goldman Sachs originally packaged those derivatives with an expectation of their failure and, indeed, placed counter bets that ensured even higher profit on the downturn that left tens of millions throughout the world destitute when the housing bubble collapsed. As the *New York Times* editorialized on December 28, 2009: "During the bubble, Goldman Sachs and other financial firms created complicated mortgage-related investments, sold them to clients and then placed bets that those investments would decline in value." The practice, detailed in the *Times* by Gretchen Morgenson and Louise Story, allowed Wall Street to profit handsomely as its clients tanked.[29]

Goldman Sachs is a story in itself. There is a pervasive "screw-the-client culture that permeated Goldman" and "ultimately costs consumers billions of dollars."[30] Investigators "concluded that Goldman had misled clients and Congress about its investments in securities related to the housing market."[31]

> Goldman was a key participant in that "shadow banking system" that precipitated the housing market collapse and the consequent financial debacle that slammed America's middle class.[32]

And get this: "A congressionally created panel set up to investigate the economic meltdown, approvingly cited a financial expert who concluded that Goldman practices had 'multiplied the effects of the collapse in [the] subprime' mortgage market that set off the wider financial implosion that nearly threw the nation into a depression."[33]

Which is why *we* say they should not only have been "allowed" to fail, we should have been dancing on the ashes of those heartless, greedy companies' multiple bankruptcies! They are the *scourge* of democracy and *no one* better deserved failure than they did. They truly *earned* their bankruptcies—and we should have given them to 'em.

But the point is, it's not the average home-buying American who was to blame for the financial crisis. What *really* happened is that all the Wall Street fat cats started going way too far with their "exotic" (read "insane") investment products. They created new financial products out of thin air. And thin air is the appropriate expression because thin air is about how much their newly packaged products were worth; and also because the air must get pretty thin in the uppermost altitudes of the financial world where these uncompassionate, fat pigs live and play. Here's what they did:

> Wall Street re-engineered residential mortgage portfolios into structured bonds called collateralized mortgage obligations (CMOs). A portfolio of mortgages would be dedicated to support the issuance of a family of bonds. The bonds would be tiered in horizontal slices, or tranches . . . The bottom tranches absorbed all initial defaults but paid high yields.[34]

In other words, they created a bunch of invisible *crap* that literally did not exist before. Then they packaged it up and sold it off to their financial cronies around the world and created a whole new investment market in their gift-wrapped crap! Then, all they had to do was follow their own predatory instincts, feed off their insatiable greed, and expand the new market: "Wall Street inevitably pushed the tranching technology to an extreme . . . and every almost unimaginable concept of debt was collected, packaged, and then re-sold"[35]:

> The floodgates were opened. So long as you did the gritty, credit-by-credit documentation work with the rating agencies, you could securitize

anything . . . Then it got more complicated. About the same time as the securitized, or structured, finance industry was evolving at a breakneck pace, some brilliant financial engineer introduced new families of credit derivatives, the most important of which is the credit default swap.[36]

Credit default swaps were basically a way for banks to package the risk of their billions of dollars in mortgages and sell it to other investors. It became a new financial market that grew very rapidly. The size of credit default swaps portfolios grew at an astronomical rate, from $1 trillion in 2001, to $45 trillion by the middle of 2007, before the bubble finally burst.[37]

The creation of this new credit default swaps market actually *encouraged* subprime higher risk loans, because those loans carried higher interest rates and were generally more attractive packages for the banks' big clients who were investing in the credit default swaps.[38] Thus, the financial house of cards—destined to collapse—was built up and fed upon itself until it *did* indeed ultimately collapse.

Then, of course, they did what greedy bastards like them have always done since the beginning of time immemorial: they pushed the envelope to squeeze every last drop of profit out of the bubble until the laws of gravity finally came into play and the damn thing popped.

Keep in mind that it's the "little guy" that got screwed—as usual! It's the middle class hard-working couples trying to buy their family a home—The American Dream—who truly suffered as a result of the financial meltdown. What happened to the fat cats, one might ask? Well— they made out like the bandits they truly are! They made fortunes, left and right. There was money to be made and they took it! As usual in this country, the rich get richer, and the richest get most of the new riches too. Look at the numbers:

> Overall, the top tenth of 1 percent more than tripled their share of cash income to about 9 percent, while the top one-hundredth of 1 percent, or fewer than 15,000 taxpayers, quadrupled their share to 3.6 percent of all taxable income.[39]

Angelo Mozillo, that fat cat CEO of Countrywide with a $48-million-a-year salary who made *another* $100 million by *dumping his stock right before his company went under with the rest of the financial meltdown,*[40] was but one of many scores of CEOs who reaped gigantic bonuses as a reward for driving our economy into the ground, for which they should have been stoned in the public square (or showered with rotten tomatoes, at the very least!).

Let's also take a look at some of the crooks in government who engineered this whole financial fiasco. How did they do financially? That's a fair question, isn't it? They did fantastic, actually. Let's take a look at a few of them. Lawrence Summers was a Wall Street fat cat (a hedge fund managing partner and frequent speaker at the "Holy Grail" of Wall Street, meaning Goldman Sachs, JPMorgan, Citigroup, and Merrill Lynch), who went through the "revolving door" and became Treasury Secretary under Clinton, then back to Wall Street, and then a key economic advisor to President Obama. In between, he was also kicked out of Harvard University, as a standing President of that university, after receiving a no-confidence vote by the Harvard faculty (unfortunately, we did not get to vote on our confidence about having him in key governmental positions!):

> Among the winners was Lawrence Summers, who remains convinced that he deserved every penny of the nearly $8 million that Wall Street firms paid him in 2008, when he was an Obama campaign adviser. And why shouldn't he be cut in on the loot from the loopholes in the derivatives market—money now toxic—that he pushed into law when he was Bill Clinton's Treasury secretary? No one has been more persistently effective in paving the way for the financial scams that enriched the titans of finance while impoverishing the rest of the world than the man who became the top economic adviser to President Obama.[41]

You see what we mean? Are you starting to see why there should be a special section in hell for these bastards?

Wall Street's greed was what was *really* responsible for the whole crisis:

> To read the newspaper reports, the credit crunch is a sub-prime crisis. It's much broader than that . . . Taken together, the deafness of the (Bush) administration and congressional leadership to alternative plans

. . . all suggest that directing large new flows to Wall Street was at least as important an objective . . . [42]

The first huge scandal involved the multibillion-dollar energy-trading company, Enron. It became apparent that their financial numbers were being dramatically misstated. A huge accounting scandal emerged and it just kept getting bigger and bigger.

> From the moment Enron admitted to having misstated its books, Wall Street and also a considerable stretch of Corporate America were never the same . . . The main components of the scandal—the unvarnished greed, the conspiratorial neglect by gatekeepers, the hysterical attention to share price—were simply too common to think that Enron was unique.[43]

And it suddenly started to become apparent that the audacity of these corrupt thieves was unmatched by anything we had ever seen. For example, prior to Enron going down like a sinking ship, the executives of Enron granted themselves—and *cashed out*—stock options worth <u>over a billion dollars</u>.[44] But they *prevented* their loyal employees from even selling their own stock![45]

> Its seamier revelations turned the public's stomach. The news that Enron had locked down its 401(k) program to prevent rank-and-file employees from selling stock—even as executives whose own pensions were protected were bailing out—presented a revoltingly greedy picture of the corporate suite.[46]

In other words, they gave themselves fat rewards for driving the company into the ground, while at the same time *preventing* their employees from even being able to sell their stock in the company before the stock price eventually crashed and became worthless! These people are corporate criminals!

We, the public, gradually realized that the Enron/Arthur Andersen scandal was just the tip of the iceberg. What these bastards had been doing ran *all* the way through our financial system, and it stank to high heaven.

It showed us just how low the vermin who run theses corporate empires can go and <u>proved</u> that they really don't give a rat's ass about their own employees: "The revelation that Enron had paid $55 million in retention bonuses in the month before the bankruptcy seemed too shocking to believe."[47] But cheer up—it got worse.

What did their huge corporate accounting firm, Arthur Andersen, do about all of Enron's dirty lies on their accounting books? Well, by law, they're obligated to report them, so that's what they did, right? Wrong, boys and girls. Not in the crooked world of cooked corporate books. Arthur Andersen jumped into action all right. They shredded trunk loads of documents! It all went *straight* into the big document shredders![48] And why would they do a thing like that, one might ask? For the obvious reason—to shield their client from disclosing its ugly truths.

> The appearance of criminality at Andersen, formerly the gold seal of trust, heightened the public's impression that Enron was the result of a systemic, as distinct from a singular, breakdown. The bull market had already cracked, and after Enron/Andersen it seemed not just over but invalidated—as though it had been based on shoddy premises all along.[49]

The corruption of Corporate America seemed pervasive. "The top energy and telecommunications firms did the most notorious transactions, including questionable round-trip swaps (a complicated layered financial scheme) with each other, many of which were arranged by Wall Street's top banks and blessed by Big Five accounting firms."[50] The top US accounting firms, known as the Big Five, were Arthur Andersen (which surrendered its license after being found guilty of criminal charges in the Enron scandal), PricewaterhouseCoopers, Ernst & Young, Deloitte Touche Tohmatsu and KPMG (Klynveld, Peat, Marwick Goerdeler). "Some of these swaps merely inflated the companies' revenues, without affecting the bottom line; others puffed up profits."[51]

And it just gets worse and worse and worse, too, folks. The inequities of our financial system keep *expanding*, even in an era of unprecedented global expansion:

Distribution and profits are at an all-time high. Instead of this dramatic increase in wealth creation delivering a healthier standard of living to everyone, it has been consolidated within a mere fraction of the global population. In the United States, *95 percent of income gains since the recession began have gone to the top .01 percent.*[52]

The level of inequity in a country that presumes itself a democracy has reached the level of financial insanity. Consider that "in the United States, the 400 richest people have as much as 185 million people, over 60 percent of the population."[53]

And while the economy still mostly sucks overall, there's never been a better time to be a Too-Big-to-Fail bank. Wells Fargo reported a third-quarter profit of nearly $5 billion last year, while JPMorgan Chase pocketed $5.3 billion—roughly double what both banks earned in the third quarter of 2006, at the height of the mortgage bubble.[54]

So we ask you: Why do we, as a people, continue to put up with crap like that? None of that wealth, in the form of a "bailout," or anything else for that matter, went to hard-working Americans. In fact, quite to the contrary. Now: How much do you think they spent to save people's homes that were going into foreclosure, when *they* hit hard times, as a direct *result* of those sinister banks and corporations? You guessed it. Zero. Nada. Zip. There was virtually no relief offered by the government to the homeowners who suffered the frigging *results* of the actions by these Wall Street bastards and banks. Do you know how many people lost their homes? "13.1 million American people had their homes foreclosed."[55] Other sources put the number at slightly under 5 million foreclosures, but those are foreclosures that are legally completed and that number does not include homes locked in default or homes that people just dropped off the keys and walked away from.[56] But any way you look at it, *those* were the people who *should* have been bailed out. And they weren't. Why? We'll *tell* you why. "Because their debt, it turns out, was real; it was only the debt within the financial sector that was imaginary. It was only the people who generated the crisis who got three magical wishes from an economic genie. There was no abracadabra for ordinary people; they just got abraca-fucked."[57]

In other words, when the fat cats get into trouble financially, there is a bottomless pit of money to throw at them. But when plain old hardworking Americans get into trouble, they're on their own! The same damn banks that were "bailed out" with public funds—with *our* money—foreclose and take away people's homes when they get a little behind on *their* mortgage payments! Does that sound like a fair system to you? It's criminal. Which leads us to another point. Were any of those bastards held to account for their criminal actions? Did they go to jail or even face charges? No, instead they were *rewarded*, with fat bonuses ranging in millions of dollars. *Now* do you understand why we say our entire financial system is rigged in favor of the rich?

United States household wealth fell by $16.4 trillion with the 2008 collapse.[58] The average American household lost *a third of its net wealth*.[59] And those households have recovered less than half of that lost wealth.[60]

It's almost like we woke up in the Dark Ages or something. What the hell happened?

> A stunning 76 percent of the US population is living paycheck to paycheck. While US millionaires have $50 trillion in wealth, an all-time record number of people are toiling in poverty, hunger, prison, and severe debt. When you fully grasp the situation, you realize that this is the greatest crime against humanity in the history of civilization . . . almost everyone is getting fucked.[61]

These people have been in bed together for so long that they forget to even wash the sheets! "Neel Kashkari went from Goldman to running the bailout under the government Office of Financial Stability. So it's no surprise that Goldman, along with AIG, were the biggest beneficiaries of the bailout!"[62]

As Governor Ventura said: "This crisis wasn't about the little guy. It was a bailout of these financial giants unprecedented in our history, because they were 'too big to fail.' Nomi Prims was a managing director at Goldman Sachs who "jumped ship" and wrote a book called *It Takes a Pillage*. Here's a bombshell that she had on the greatest theft in the history of humankind: 'For the money spent on subsidizing the industry, the government could have bought every single outstanding mortgage in the country. Plus, every student loan and everyone's health insurance. And on top of that, still have trillions of dollars left over.'"[63]

And make no mistake about it, even while driving their companies into the ground with reckless speculation, the Wall Street fat cats made out like bandits. "While driving their firms bankrupt with risky behavior, Bear Stearns CEO James E. Cayne, Lehman CEO Fuld, and their top four lieutenants cashed out over $2.4 billion from 2000 to 2008, according to the Program on Corporate Governance at Harvard Law School."[64]

This is criminal, folks! *Listen* to this: "Almost 70 execs who participated in running our economy into the ground have received more than a million bucks apiece in bonuses. Goldman Sachs had a spectacularly profitable first half of 2009 (the year *after* the bailout) . . . Goldman's 30,000 employees will each earn an average of $700,000."[65]

And guess who President Obama's largest contributor was? You guessed it: Goldman Sachs. How do these people sleep at night? Obama's chief economic adviser, Lawrence Summers, came from a hedge fund. In 2008, he earned $2.7 million in speaking fees from firms like Goldman Sachs and Citigroup.[66] Get it through your head! They are all in bed together. Timothy Geithner became Obama's Treasury Secretary. Before that he was head of the New York Federal Reserve, an important position. His five-year reign there has been summarized as a total disaster of risk-taking that led to the financial collapse.[67] And who were the people who wined and dined with Geithner? You guessed it! Goldman Sachs, Citigroup, and JPMorgan were some of his highest-occurring contacts after he came to Washington and headed up the Treasury Department.[68] It's very clear. We have left the wolves in charge of the hen house and it's not a pretty story.

These are some of the very same people who "led the way in blocking any regulatory efforts of the derivatives market whatsoever on the ground that the financial industry and its lobbyists were objecting."[69] That's what *caused* the whole financial crisis to begin with!

These are *pigs* feeding at the trough of our taxpaying dollars.

> We all think of General Electric in terms of light bulbs and home appliances, but its finance wing is GE Capital . . . They'd be the seventh largest bank in the United States, if they were classified that way. But

since GE Capital is an arm of an industrial corporation, they can put forth handsome finance arrangements for those who purchase their products. And when the bailout happened, they ended up qualifying for a government-guaranteed program allowing them to raise almost $75 billion by the close of the first quarter in '09.[70]

The fat cat bankers also borrowed a page from the Mafia and found a way to skim a fortune in profits right off the top of public municipal bond auctions. And the fact that it was illegal didn't slow them down a bit either:

> Along with virtually every major bank and finance company on Wall Street—not just GE, but JPMorgan Chase, Bank of America, UBS, Lehman Brothers, Bear Stearns, Wachovia and more – these three Wall Street wise guys spent the past decade taking part in a breathtakingly broad scheme to skim billions of dollars from the coffers of cities and small towns across America. The banks achieved this gigantic rip-off by secretly colluding to rig the public bids on municipal bonds, a business worth $3.7 trillion.[71]

But they don't go to jail for a thing like that. They don't even get in trouble. They get *rewarded* with bailout funds! Take a good look at what they did:

> By conspiring to lower the interest rates that towns earn on these investments, the banks systematically stole from schools, hospitals, libraries, and nursing homes—from "virtually every state, district and territory in the United States," according to one settlement. And they did it so cleverly that the victims never even knew they were being cheated. No thumbs were broken, and nobody ended up in a landfill in New Jersey, but money disappeared, lots and lots of it, and its manner of disappearance had a familiar name: *organized crime.*[72]

These are the ways our crooked so-called pillars of industry steal from us, folks. They rob us blind and they laugh in our faces while doing it:

> In the bankruptcy of Jefferson County, Alabama, we learned that Goldman Sachs accepted a $3 million bribe from JPMorgan Chase to

permit Chase to serve as the sole provider of toxic swap deals to the rubes running metropolitan Birmingham—"an open-and-shut case of anti-competitive behavior," as one former regulator described it.[73]

It's nothing new. They do it all the time:

> Banks and hedge funds routinely withhold derogatory information about the instruments they sell, they routinely trade on insider information or ahead of their own clients' orders, and corrupt accounting is so rampant now that industry analysts have begun to figure in estimated levels of fraud in their examinations of the public disclosures of major financial companies.[74]

Audits of major banks, like Washington Mutual (WaMu), showed huge disparities in their accounting procedures. "As early as 2005, internal audits by WaMu revealed stunning lapses in underwriting standards. An audit of two large Southern California origination offices had confirmed fraud rates of 58 and 83 percent."[75] And what was done about that, you rightfully inquire? Absolutely nothing! "The extensive—and perhaps systemic—fraud uncovered by these audits was never disclosed, and yet WaMu officials chose to continue with business as usual."[76]

And let's not forget who Corporate America and their slyly purchased politicians made pay for the financial crisis that they caused—*us*! Let's never forget that. It was not just a matter of blaming the victims, people who had lost their homes as a direct result of Wall Street's rampage over any sensible investment policies. *Now* the victims of the crisis were to be punished as well. Everywhere you looked, people were losing their benefits and losing their jobs as companies "downsized"; aka throwing their loyal workers out onto the street because it helped the "bottom lines" of their business model. Millions of Americans lost their jobs.

> Millions who kept their jobs had their benefits cut. Instead of a pension, which came on top of their salary, they would have to save for their old age in a 401(k) plan with money that came out of their salary. . . . It was also a huge savings for the employer. . . . Medical and dental plans were also cut, with growing numbers of workers being shunted health

maintenance organizations (HMOs), which many people found were skilled at erecting obstacles to seeing a doctor or getting needed care.[77]

And they gave us a big sob story about how all these cutbacks were vitally necessary. Why? Why were they necessary? Well, if you really want to know, they were necessary to maximize profits for Corporate America, plain and simple.

> Companies making these cuts all said they just could not afford to provide the same benefits as before. The question that was not pressed hard at the time was just why this was so, especially at companies that continued to report solid profits.[78]

And time and again, for decades now, corporations have been employing an old trick to cut the retirement pensions and health-care benefits of their workers—by labeling them "entitlements."

> *Entitlements* was the watchword for management at Frontier and many other companies working to reduce compensation of those down in the bowels of the company, even as dollars flowed ever more generously to management, especially those at the top.[79]

It should be noted that the example of Frontier was only one of many who used that dirty little trick to rob from their workers and enrich upper management. "Every Frontier manager, down to the lowliest foreman, was given a booklet that labeled the pension and health-care benefits negotiated between the company and the union as 'entitlements.'"[80] Also note that in this example, as in many others, what they were attacking was the agreed result of negotiated arrangements on behalf of the workers of the company. "The union members, Frontier managers were told, were like the lazy bums who collect welfare checks because they are entitled to them, the only difference being the unionists show up for work."[81] It is hard to believe that corporations actually get away with the crap they pull against their own employees. It is an outrage.

And meanwhile, the average compensation of America's best-paid corporate chief executives has risen from $1.7 million in 1973 to <u>$10.5 mil-</u>

lion in 2014, with many of them in the $50 million range—while they were "downsizing" jobs and slashing their workers' health care and pensions for them and their families.[82] By any standard of fairness: *That sucks!* And it is *still* going on, too. Just last October the huge conglomerate 3M Corporation—a company with a market value hovering around $100 billion—announced that they had higher-than-expected, record-breaking profits, surprising even the forecasters on Wall Street. So what's the first thing that 3M did? They immediately announced that they were eliminating 1,500 jobs "to lower expenses."[83] Corporations have made it brutally clear that what they care about is their financial bottom line and their stock price—their employees, who are what actually make the company successful, are now a *very* low priority.

Standard & Poor's, the corporate ratings agency, has been called the "Watchdog That Didn't Bark" because their ratings *should have* warned us about an impending financial crisis long before it happened.[84] So what happened to them, one might rightfully ask? They *settled*. They agreed to pay a fine. Part of the settlement was that, technically—and get a load of *this* bullshit—they made no admission of guilt.[85] So just *think* about that for a minute. If you are one of the big corporate government fat cats, even if you are guilty as sin, if you agree to pay a fine, you can claim—with a straight face even—that you did nothing wrong. You are blameless. Plus, if you fail, you get bailed out by the taxpayers. And you can do it again, because the politicians are in your pocket and corporations can't be jailed. *And* you even have a clean record because you were never even forced to admit any wrongdoing at all!

The big banks and the entire financial services industry continues to get richer via practices that keep the poor in a downward cycle of predatory lending practices. "Lenders are squeezing US consumers for as much as $4.2 billion annually in the steep fees charged on payday loans. . . . To pay back a $325 loan, the average payday-loan borrower pays a total of $793. The average annual interest rate on such loans runs about 400%, according to the study."[86] They borrowed another page from the Mafia on these payday-type loans; because they are just like some unforgiving loan shark: "Borrowers often find themselves taking out new payday loans to cover old payday loans and ultimately end up owing thousands of dollars on what started out as a few hundred dollars of debt."[87]

As if we didn't already know it, "The average investor is being systematically taken advantage of by the financial services industry."[88] And worse yet, those financial "services" prey specifically on the military and the poor.[89] Just over 42 percent of Americans carry credit card debt, and with an average balance of about $11,000; and 75.7 percent of those are paying an interest rate higher than 15%, according to a study done in 2014.[90] American consumers are now indebted—a more accurate word would be enslaved—to financial institutions to the tune of about 12 trillion dollars.[91]

To make matters worse, Goldman Sachs has also entered the online loan market.[92] And there is every reason to believe that they will continue to build on their well-deserved reputation for being irresponsible in the financial products they offer to consumers.[93]

And now, as a *real* sign of trouble, Goldman has *also* entered into a potentially very lucrative new field: the privatization of America's infrastructure.[94] Just as our politicians have been "outsourcing" our nation's prisons, which we discuss in a following chapter, and turning them into corporate profit machines instead of what they were designed to be—they are also privatizing the infrastructure of our country. We kid you not—bridges, highways, you name it—all for sale to the highest bidder. Everything from power plants to parking meters, public health and food programs, *airports*, toll roads, everything from entire shipping ports to libraries—it's all potential "monetization" for folks like Goldman Sachs, and they are in it, big-time.[95] Disturbing, isn't it? And it's bipartisan, because selling out to corporations is *one* thing that Democrats and Republicans can always agree on. Just when you thought it couldn't get any worse, they are selling the infrastructure of this country right out from under us.

And if you think that the *past* history of the big banks is scary, then we've got a big news flash for you, folks: the future is a lot scarier. Just get a load of who JPMorgan Chase recently hired as their security consultant.

> Proving yet again the ubiquitous ties between government and private interests, four-star General Ray Odierno—who retired as the US Army's Chief of Staff on August 14—made a rather abrupt leap in career choice to senior adviser for JPMorgan Chase less than a week later.[96]

General Odierno's "notorious reputation during the Iraq 'War' included a penchant for indiscriminate, mass detention and extrajudicial killings of civilians."[97] This guy's unit in Iraq was so notorious that *even a member of its PsyOps team* found it necessary to file a formal complaint about that brigade's treatment of civilians.[98] And now he goes to work for the big banks. Great, huh? If you put this stuff in a movie, nobody would even believe it. And it's true! Pretty damn scary, if you ask us. Because it makes you wonder what the ruthless bastards might be up to next.

So, folks, when we say that this is not the America that we grew up in, these are the types of examples that we are talking about. In the America we grew up in, loyal employees were *rewarded* for their work. But in the America that corporations have co-opted away from us, loyal employees have no place—they are just supposed to follow orders, be blindly grateful that they even have a job, and know that they can have their benefits stripped away or be tossed onto the street any old time that it happens to be in the best interests of the corporation.

Because, sadly, corporations now *are* America.

One positive note is that the Obama administration did at least effectively kill a deal that the drug giant Pfizer was seeking—a merger with a huge Irish company, Allergan, for the sole purpose of avoiding paying its share of US taxes.[99] The tax rules that affected their specific merger were changed in a way that negated the tax dodge that the deal was designed for, in a surprise move by rule changes at the Treasury Department that observers suspected were designed toward derailing that specific merger.[100] When they found out they wouldn't receive the tax shelter that the merger was specifically designed to give them, Pfizer immediately backed out of the deal, even though it meant having to pay a $150 million "break-up fee" to cancel the deal.[101] That shows us how loyal these bastards really are. Their only loyalty is to increasing their obscene profits by evading taxes.

It's a loophole that these atrocious corporations still have open through their paid servants in Congress, but at least in that one case, Obama scored a point for the people:

> When a large corporate entity keeps relying on US roads, patents, research funding, and workers while ensuring they don't kick as much

money back into public coffers as they are supposed to, they are effectively changing their corporate passports in order to loot American society.[102]

But the big loophole game is still played and we taxpayers are always the loser. Even though President Kennedy tried to close it way back in 1963, progressives in Congress have never had enough clout to shut one of the biggest corporate loopholes in history, known as the inherited capital gains clause. It's known as the "Angel of Death" tax loophole, and for a very good reason too.[103] It allows the wealthiest Americans to pass along their stock assets and other capital gains to their heirs without <u>ever</u> being taxed. Get a load of this little gem:

> The inherited capital gains loophole has major effects on the budget, on the economy, and on tax fairness. It results in about <u>half of all capital gains going permanently untaxed</u>. It costs the US Treasury an estimated $50 billion per year (perhaps more). It encourages people to hold onto assets even when they would otherwise want to sell them. And since capital gains are highly concentrated at the top end of the income scale, it undermines progressivity.[104]

What can you say? There's progress—and then there are rich bastards . . .

Still . . . Exposing these bastards for what they are gives us a deep, abiding joy.

FURTHER RESEARCH:

Henkels, Stan V. *Andrew Jackson and the Bank of the United States: An interesting bit of history concerning "Old Hickory."* Philadelphia: Privately Printed for Stan V. Henkels, Junior (Gollifox Press), 1928. http://kenhirsch.net/money/Andrew-JacksonAndTheBankHenkels.pdf.

Ventura, Jesse and Dick Russell. *American Conspiracies: Lies, Lies, and More Dirty Lies that the Government Tells Us.* New York: Skyhorse, 2010.

Graeber, David. *DEBT: The First 5,000 Years.* New York: Melville House, 2014.

Schweizer, Peter. *Throw Them All Out: How Politicians and Their Friends Get Rich Off Insider Stock Tips, Land Deals, and Cronyism That Would Send the Rest of Us to Prison.* Boston: Houghton Mifflin Harcourt, 2011.

Felkerson, James. "$29,000,000,000,000: A Detailed Look at the Fed's Bailout by Funding Facility and Recipient." Working Paper no. 698. Annandale-on-Hudson: Levy Economics Institute of Bard College, December 2011. http://www.levyinstitute.org/pubs/wp_698.pdf.

McKenna, Terence, director. *Meltdown.* Ottawa: Canadian Broadcasting Corporation, 2010. https://www.youtube.com/watch?v=k5q6z_FpxIY.

Morris, Charles R. *The Trillion Dollar Meltdown: Easy Money, High Rollers, and the Great Credit Crash.* New York: Public Affairs, 2008.

Woods, Thomas E. Jr. *Meltdown: A Free-Market Look at Why the Stock Market Collapsed, the Economy Tanked, and Government Bailouts Will Make Things Worse.* Washington, DC: Regnery Publishing, 2009.

Scheer, Robert. *The Great American Stickup: How Reagan Republicans and Clinton Democrats Enriched Wall Street While Mugging Main Street.* New York: Nation Books, 2010.

Lowenstein, Roger. *Origins of the Crash: The Great Bubble and Its Undoing.* New York: Penguin Press, 2004.

Taibbi, Matt. "Obama's Big Sellout: The President has Packed His Economic Team with Wall Street Insiders." *Rolling Stone* (December 13, 2009). http://www.commondreams.org/news/2009/12/13/obamas-big-sellout-president-has-packed-his-economic-team-wall-street-insiders.

Field, Abigail. "Justice Denied: Why Countrywide Chief Fraudster Isn't Going to Prison." *DailyFinance.com* (February 23, 2011). http://www.dailyfinance.com/2011/02/23/countrywide-mozilo-fraud-no-prison-trial-sec-mortgage-meltdown-deal-crisis/.

Taibbi, Matt. "Obama and Geithner: Government, Enron-Style." *Rolling Stone* (December 20, 2011). http://www.rollingstone.com/politics/news/obama-and-geithner-government-enron-style-20111220#ixzz3p4t9gJVh.

Taibbi, Matt. "The Scam Wall Street Learned from the Mafia: How America's biggest banks took part in a nationwide bid-rigging conspiracy—until they were caught on tape." *Rolling Stone* (June 21, 2012). http://www.rollingstone.com/politics/news/the-scam-wall-street-learned-from-the-mafia-20120620#ixzz3raJzhTC9.

Taibbi, Matt. "Secrets and Lies of the Bailout: The federal rescue of Wall Street didn't fix the economy—it created a permanent bailout state based on a Ponzi-like confidence scheme. And the worst may be yet to come.*" Rolling Stone* (January 4, 2013). http://www.rollingstone.com/politics/news/secret-and-lies-of-the-bailout-20130104#ixzz3raJ6uDZu.

Delgass, Michael N., JD, Nicole R. Hart, JD, and Eric Dostal, JD. "Why the 'Angel of Death' Tax Loophole Will Remain Alive and Well," *CPAPracticeAdvisor.com* (February 27, 2015). http://www.cpapracticeadvisor.com/news/12049501/why-the-angel-of-death-tax-loophole-will-remain-alive-and-well.

CHAPTER THREE

MAINSTREAM MEDIA CONSOLIDATION FOR CONTROL (OF *YOU*!)

If you're not careful, the newspapers will have you hating the people who are being oppressed, and loving the people who are doing the oppressing.[1]

—Malcolm X

In this chapter we're going to get into some very interesting revelations about 9/11, the Iraq War, Edward Snowden, and our government spying on us with the willing assistance of telecom and social media companies. But first we want to cover some general trends that, unfortunately, are very disturbing in their nature.

Maybe we should tell mainstream media that <u>the airwaves actually belong to the people</u>. Corporations <u>lease the airwaves from us</u>! Did you know that? That's a function of the Federal Communications Commission (FCC). Most Americans don't even know that. And they don't *want* you to know that either. But they do. The airwaves are in the public domain.

> Ever since the first broadcast radio stations were authorized more than 75 years ago the United States has maintained that the airwaves belong to the public and are to be operated by broadcasting companies as a public trust. As radio and later TV and cable properties have grown to become big business, the corporations that control them have chafed at or ignored the public trust responsibilities.[2]

In fact, the Federal Communications Commission even acknowledges in its own manual that it operates "as the trustees of the public's airwaves."[3] The airwaves do not belong to the mega-media corporations. They actually belong to the public. They are licensed to corporations to broadcast, *on behalf of* the public.

Furthermore, since the FCC provides broadcasters with "a valuable license to operate a broadcast station using the public airwaves, each radio and television licensee is required by law to operate its station in the 'public interest, convenience and necessity.' This means that it must air programming that is responsive to the needs and problems of its local community of license."[4]

Well, well, well. You can bet it would come as a big shock to the boards of directors of all the big media corporations to actually read the above regulations regarding their actual <u>responsibilities for licensing of the **public's** airwaves</u>.

> Because the airwaves belong to the public, broadcasters are in theory required to serve the public interest—by keeping us informed and giving us a voice.[5]

But they don't, if you think about it. Not really. They don't really "give us a voice"—they do *all* the talking. And it's a very debatable point on whether or not they actually "keep us informed."

> A democracy cannot thrive without an informed public, which is why the press is called The Fourth Estate—the citizens' facility for oversight of their government. The founders of the United States of America understood this, and so enshrined a free press in our Constitution's Bill of Rights.[6]

But bigger media companies have been taking over smaller ones for decades. There are now very few major players. "Today, roughly ninety percent of the media is owned by "The Big Six." The Big Six includes General Electric, Walt Disney, News Corp, Time Warner, Viacom, and CBS."[7] Comcast should be added to that, especially after their purchase of NBC Universal from GE.[8] That deal made Comcast a 150-plus-billion-dollar megamedia company—now the largest media company on the planet, with revenues of $68 billion annually.[9]

In terms of maintaining a free-thinking, well-informed democratic republic, that consolidation has resulted in a problem of gargantuan proportions:

> Massive corporations dominate the US media landscape. Through a history of mergers and acquisitions, these companies have concentrated their control over what we see, hear, and read. In many cases, these companies control everything from initial production to final distribution.[10]

Studies have clearly established that "Though people may believe that by watching Fox, CNN, NBC, or ABC that they are receiving a different perspective, it is very likely that they really aren't."[11] The press used to seriously be considered that Fourth Estate, our system of government's extra branch that stood as watchdog against misuse. Instead, they have turned mass media into a corporate money machine with very narrow parameters when it comes to actually informing the public.

That's *not* the way it is supposed to work. Remember—the airwaves supposedly belong to the public. Media outlets used to have a formal mandate to serve the public interest. But now, they control what we see and hear as they rack up the profits:

> Broadcasters make billions in profits while using the public airwaves for free. In return, they are supposed to provide programming that fulfills community needs. Instead, lobbyists have successfully fought to make it easier for broadcast companies to gobble up even more free airspace while doing less to serve the public.[12]

It was termed the "Fourth Estate," because it meant that the function of the press is "as a fourth branch of government and one that is important to a functioning democracy."[13]

> The First Amendment to the Constitution "frees" the press but carries with it a responsibility to be the people's watchdog.[14]

But, as many have observed, mainstream media, in our recent history, has failed in its watchdog role, and failed miserably.[15] The press has now become more of a lapdog than watchdog.[16] Glenn Greenwald made the astute observation that "our mainstream media willingly acts as 'stenographers' to the high and mighty," following wherever they are led, parroting whatever they are told.[17] And, as noted in an article which was very appropriately entitled "The Failure of Our 'Free' Press":

> That last statement is the kicker. The media's stenographer-types market the "poison" of the elites, whether governmental or corporate, and they often do so under the cover of source anonymity.[18]

Glenn Greenwald, who was the journalist who broke the story about the NSA's massive surveillance program, PRISM, explains how that breakdown is threatening our form of governance:

> The theory of a "Fourth Estate" is to ensure government transparency and provide a check on overreach, of which the secret surveillance of entire populations is surely among the most radical examples.[19]

However, when that "check" on balance is corrupted by maligned interests in the mainstream media, the system then fails:

> But that check is only effective if journalists act adversarially to those who wield political power. Instead, the US media has frequently abdicated this role, being subservient to the government's interests, even amplifying, rather than scrutinizing, its messages and carrying out its dirty work.[20]

Russell Brand, the British celebrity and social activist, summarized the matter very succinctly: "Six corporations own 90 percent of all media in the United States. If you want the truth, you're not going to get it there."[21] And Brand makes an excellent point in the observation that the amount of wealth that has been generated in the Information Age has been squandered away in wars by the military and in massive thefts by corporate bankers:

Due to the mainstream media, the average person has no understanding of this unprecedented increase in wealth. Imagine if the average American understood that US millionaires now have $50 trillion in wealth. $1 trillion is 1,000 billion. For an estimated $30 billion you can end world hunger. You can wipe out the entire national debt of the United States with just 25 percent of that wealth."[22]

But, in a process where one hand washes the other, mainstream media has become bedfellows with the very people they were supposed to be warning us about:

The leading members of the media work for the very corporations that benefit most from this process. Establishment journalists are integral and well-rewarded members of the same system and thus cannot and will not see it as inherently corrupt (instead, as *Newsweek*'s Evan Thomas said, their role, as "members of the ruling class," is to "prop up the existing order," "protect traditional institutions," and "safeguard the status quo").[23]

If you've ever wondered about the commingling of politics with mainstream media, one need look no further than George Stephanopoulos, who went from a role as Senior Advisor to President Clinton, and "*de facto* press secretary" in which he was basically telling us what to think—to a job as Chief Anchor at ABC News, co-anchor of *Good Morning America*, and host of ABC's Sunday morning show *This Week*, with a $105-million contract, where he is—basically *telling us what to think*.[24] Pretty cozy, huh?

Robert F. Kennedy Jr. has also noticed that "deafening silence" coming from mainstream media on all the current major issues:

"This year's presidential election is going to cost $10 billion with half of that coming from 100 wealthy families. Nearly $1 billion is coming from two brothers." And, said Kennedy, "You will hear no criticism from the press, the supposed guardians of our democracy. And that's because most of that money will go to media advertising—the 4th estate has been bought off."[25]

As Kennedy further observed, the same is true of big media concerning the uncontrolled profits of corporate giants: "And the press, consolidated as it is into private monopolies and relieved of social obligation, are on the carbon and pharma payroll and in full cahoots with the scheme."[26] So it has now reached a level of complicity that the "Fourth Estate" is clearly failing us.

> Given the job done by the mainstream media, is it any wonder that our national dialogue is in such a woeful state? So many cable channels constantly beam out something that looks vaguely like "news," but nothing that ever resembles analysis—constantly replaying the same footage, working on the principle that every viewer is "just tuning in." Issues deemed to not have sufficiently wide appeal are neglected. What little analysis is provided is usually thin, scaremongering, or sensational. Coverage of the most critical issues, like the Syrian refugee crisis, is dominated by those with hateful and intolerant views.[27]

Their crime against our democratic form of government is that they malign our thinking, with nationalistic slogans like "Freedom isn't free" that deter us away from the actual logic and what *should* be intelligent debate on the important topic of whether or not our nation should go to war. Instead, they lull us into oblivion with those mindless slogans.

Freedom has *never* been free, but that doesn't have a place in deciding whether or not we go fight another war.

But now, those empty explanations are an acceptable tactic, a notion that is supported in high-budget Hollywood movies, financed by American megamedia corporations.

Because the new role of the media is *also* to support America's appetite for foreign wars.

> From reckless corporate consolidation of the media industry, the Presidential persecution of whistleblowers to the targeting of independent wartime journalists by the military, our system has completely failed us . . . The war drums beat to the tune of our racing hearts—which rage with fury over manipulated messages driven by those in power.[28]

We should take a close look at the role of mainstream media companies in shaping and conforming public opinion to the wishes of the military-corporate system. It is a *major* role that they play and one that is also glaringly obvious. Just take a good look at some of the big war movies of the past few years.

Even though a movie like *American Sniper* was very popular and many apparently thought it very "patriotic," we are *very* happy to report that not everyone agrees with that. Some people think it's actually a truckload of crap designed to justify our barbaric and ongoing war-like mentality as a nation.

Many also saw troubling historical similarities to disturbing trends in government propaganda and have reviewed it in terms such as "warmongering trash, the popularity of which exposes a sickness in the American psyche."[29] As journalist Chris Hedges points out, *American Sniper* resembles "the big-budget feature films pumped out in Germany during the Nazi era to exalt deformed values of militarism, racial self-glorification and state violence."[30]

Movies like *American Sniper* are basically just a very effective method of propagating US propaganda, for public consumption. Critics have mentioned that, in thinking terms, the film doesn't even really make sense. They point out glaring inconsistencies in the supposed logic that forms the base of the misled patriotism: "Kyle's father tells him that there are three kinds of people: sheep; wolves, who prey on the sheep; and sheepdogs, who protect the sheep from the wolves. The father wants Chris to be a sheepdog . . . The irony is that soldiers like Chris Kyle, who conform to and never question their culture's pro-war values, could be described as sheep."[31]

Lone Survivor is another film that has been accused by critics of being morally corrupt government propaganda.[32] Check out the very blunt points made in some of these reviews:

- "A pro-war propaganda surprise hit—Mark Wahlberg kills Taliban by the dozens in Hollywood's first 2014 smash hit, a shameless war-porn spectacle" (*Salon.com*)[33]
- "Crude propaganda" (*Vulture*)[34]
- "It's about a politically-charged situation but has almost no political point of view" (*Los Angeles Times*)[35]

- "*Lone Survivor*'s Takeaway: Every War Movie is a Pro-War Movie" (*The Atlantic*)[36]
- *Salon* reviewer Andrew O'Hehir labeled it a "pornographic work of war propaganda" and added "that people want to see a competent action picture in the depths of winter isn't all that depressing, but the fact that they're swallowing the disgusting symbolism of this one definitely is."[37] (And "swallow" it up they did—it was a very successful movie.)
- Calum Marsh of *The Atlantic* termed it "a film-length recruitment ad" for the US military and added that "movies like *Lone Survivor* do begin to resemble multimillion-dollar recruitment videos—tools of military indoctrination geared toward the young and the impressionable."[38]

Zero Dark Thirty, according to some critics, was an even worse case of government propaganda finding its way into movie theaters—and our homes and our families' minds.[39] As one scholar noted about the films *Zero Dark Thirty* and Brad Pitt's recent movie, *FURY*, "the message is that in war, we must do terrible things, like killing kids, and the sooner we accept this truth, the better. This is not truth, of course, it's repulsive pro-war propaganda."[40]

And the most disturbing fact of all is that the CIA took an active role in making sure that *Zero Dark Thirty* played right along with the CIA position that "enhanced interrogation techniques"—a *sick* hyperbole for **torture**—are justifiable in war because they produce results.[41] What the *hell* is the CIA doing even being *involved* in movie-making for the entertainment industry? That really gives you an idea of the disturbing extent to which our so-called democracy has been corrupted by these warped individuals.

The entire basis of *Zero Dark Thirty* was false, according to a well-researched article by veteran journalist, Seymour Hersh.[42] Hersh's article in the *London Review of Books* was entitled "The Killing of Osama bin Laden" and it exposes what his research revealed are many lies:

> Hersh asserts that the accounts given by President Barack Obama and members of his administration "might have been written by Lewis Carroll," author of *Alice in Wonderland*. Among the claims exposed as fabrications are that the CIA torture program contributed to the

discovery of bin Laden's hideout; that the raid was carried out without the knowledge of the Pakistani government; that the Special Operations team intended to take bin Laden alive, and only killed him after he resisted; and that bin Laden was given an Islamic burial at sea from the carrier USS *Carl Vinson*.[43]

And, possibly of even greater importance, the article also establishes the current role of mainstream media as merely a mouthpiece of a broader agenda:

> The wealth of details laid out in Hersh's article calls attention to the reality that nothing that any government official says on the record can be taken as the truth, and that the mainstream media operates as an echo chamber for official lies.[44]

The good news is this: "If the urge to wage war were embedded deep in our genes, Americans wouldn't need propaganda like American Sniper to persuade them that their wars are just."[45]

Those are what could be termed "general" maladies and influences. But let's look at specifics. Let's look at a huge and extremely obvious example—the Iraq War. It has become clear that "our most prominent journalists served as little more than cheerleaders for an administration that lied repeatedly as it steered America into a misguided debacle."[46]

> It's no secret that the period of time between 9/11 and the invasion of Iraq represents one of the greatest collapses in the history of the American media. Every branch of the media failed, from daily newspapers, magazines, and Web sites to television networks, cable channels, and radio.[47]

Now—here is a very disturbing fact about the actual *results* of media manipulation. *More than half of Americans actually believed that there were WMDs (weapons of mass destruction) in Iraq.*[48] That came despite the facts—facts which overwhelmingly confirmed that there were *no* WMDs.[49] And—*get this*—millions of Americans *still believe* that falsehood![50] Why? Because it was a falsehood that was used to help us accept the rationale to go to war, so it was perpetuated in mainstream media. The Bush administration paraded that falsehood in front of the cameras continually and—as Charles Lewis of the Center for Public Integrity vividly documented—"President George W. Bush and seven of his administration's top officials made at least 935 false statements about the national security threat posed by Iraq."[51]

The Bush administration really went all-out to parade that lie around, you have to say that for them. You probably remember General Colin Powell's famous testimony where he asserted there was a deadly chemical threat, even though there was not—General Powell didn't let the facts get in the way of a good story.[52] But do you know some of their other shenanigans to lead us falsely into war? Do you know, for example, that "the Pentagon had quietly recruited and coached seventy-five retired military officers to be 'independent' paid consultants and radio and television analysts whose true role was to make the case for war in Iraq."[53] Isn't that infuriating and disgusting? Bet when you watched all those generals and admirals being interviewed that you had no idea they were actually acting as paid consultants for the Bush Administration's media campaign to send us into war with a blatantly false rationale. That's the kind of thing that makes the media as blasphemous as the politicians these days. It is absolutely despicable.

The media was complicit in the Iraq War from start to finish. We are all familiar with the classic film footage of Saddam Hussein's statue being toppled and brought to the ground, dramatically symbolic of America's victory over his regime in Iraq. In fact, CNN constantly uses that footage as an example of the victory and perseverance of America in the world today. The toppling of the Saddam statue, for all of us, marked the iconic moment of the victorious Iraqi citizens taking back their country from a dictator. Right? They use it as an example, displaying it over and over, as a type of "visual reward" for our sacrifices of war.

What they don't tell you, though, is that it was a staged event. The whole thing was a fraud! The toppling of that statue was a stage-managed media event—with the press playing right along with the military.[54] It was what is referred to in Military Intelligence parlance as a "PsyOp"— a psychological operation designed to enhance your prospects and lessen your enemy's stature.[55] Of course, you will never see that story picked up in mainstream media. But if you google "Saddam statue PsyOp" you will quickly find dozens of credible accounts, mostly in alternative media sources, which document the true facts surrounding the toppling of that statue.

In reality—*appearances in mainstream media aside*—there were very few people in that square that day and most of the ones who *were* there were US media and US military, along with a few disinterested Iraqi observers.[56] But mainstream media people, apparently working with US military people, used their "magic" to make it *appear* that a large crowd was present at an event of great interest to them. Get a load of this little gem—the truth can be enlightening, folks:

> **Media Vastly Exaggerated Attendance:** Though we're all familiar with the photos of a crowded-seeming square, ProPublica reproduces photos showing that the square was actually mostly empty, but that media portrayals used tight-focus shots of a small cluster of people to suggest it was packed. Maass adds, "very few Iraqis were there. If you were at the square, or if you watch the footage, you can see, on the rare occasions long shots were used, that the square was mostly empty. You can also see, from photographs as well as video, that much of the crowd was made up of journalists and Marines." Of even the small number of Iraqis there, Maass says most were subdued, standing with their arms crossed. "Close-ups filled the screen with the frenzied core of the small crowd and created an illusion of wall-to-wall enthusiasm throughout Baghdad. It was an illusion that reflected only the media's yearning for exciting visuals." But that just isn't accurate.[57]

There are wider angle photos accessible online that reveal the fraud of the whole thing. Take a look for yourself. Search online for "global research saddam statue" or go to: http://www.globalresearch.ca/articles/ NYI304A.html.

Isn't it disgusting how they intentionally distort the news like that? When you watch that clip of the statue on the news it gives you the sense that a huge crowd of Iraqi civilians, delighted at their liberation, are pulling down that Saddam statue in a state of euphoria. And that *simply was not true.*

Much the same level—and *method*—of public ignorance as a result of mainstream media's rubber-stamping of government propaganda in the Iraq War, was also achieved regarding the events of 9/11. A poll in 2006 found that an astounding 40 percent of the American public was completely unaware that a third skyscraper—World Trade Center Building 7—also collapsed on September 11, 2001.[58] Those are *facts*. But they are facts that you will find in an article entitled "Building What?" And that article is in a book called *Censored: The News That Didn't Make the News*— because they are facts which you will *not hear discussed* in mainstream media.[59]

Building 7 is the thing that mainstream media refuses to discuss, because it is clearly the Achilles' heel of 9/11. The Twin Towers collapsed prior to 10:30 am. The South Tower came down at 9:59 am and the North Tower collapsed at 10:28 am.[60] But what many people are *still* unaware of is that another World Trade Center skyscraper, the 47-story skyscraper known as World Trade Center Building 7, also collapsed, coming down rapidly at 5:20 pm that same day, almost seven hours *after* the Twin Towers.[61]

There was absolutely no indication whatsoever that Building 7 was structurally weakened; there were small fires visible on three or four floors. So—make sure you *get* this—it was a 47-story steel-reinforced skyscraper, with minimal fires—that _no plane_ had crashed into. Nevertheless, at 5:20 p.m. on 9/11—about *seven* hours after the Twin Towers came down— Building 7 suddenly imploded neatly into its own footprint at near free-fall speed, in *precisely* the method and appearance of planned demolition. In fact, the film of its collapse was shown to an independent expert who confirmed that it *indeed was* an act of demolition.[62]

The strangest thing of all about the matter, were the *premature* media reports. *Incredibly*—several minutes before Building 7 collapsed—there were televised news reports on both CNN and the BBC that Building 7 already *had* collapsed. On the long BBC report, you can clearly see Building 7 standing in the background of the shot as the news reporter *incorrectly* reports that Building 7, also known as the Salomon Brothers Building, has also collapsed. You can't miss it! It's a 47-story steel-reinforced skyscraper.

You *have to watch* this video clip. Search the Internet for "BBC Building 7" or watch this link: https://www.youtube.com/watch?v=ltP2t9nq9fI.

Building 7 did not collapse until 5:20 p.m. It is a matter of public record. Yet, quite a bit *prior* to its collapse, at about 5:00 p.m., those televised news reports began discussing how Building 7 had collapsed in exactly the same manner as had the Twin Towers. The problem was—and *still is*—obvious. Building 7 had *not* collapsed at that time—it can be clearly seen in the film—standing and structurally intact. "Yet, somehow, news networks and many others knew it was going to happen."[63] CNN's Aaron Brown announced on the air, over an hour before it happened: "We are getting information now that one of the other buildings, Building 7 in the World Trade Center complex, is on fire, and has either collapsed, or *is* collapsing."[64] Really? *So*—apparently a very good question would have been: Where exactly *were you getting that information*, Mr. Brown?

We're not making this up, folks! You can listen to it online. That's exactly what he said, live, on CNN, and you can check it out online by searching for "Original ReThink911 video" or going to:

https://www.youtube.com/watch?v=rNR6Kbg5jJ8

This is documented evidence. So, apparently, our buddies from "across the pond"—who just happened to be our biggest partners in the Iraq War—were somehow in on the whole thing too. And somebody, somewhere, must have messed up, big-time. There is proof that is well documented:

> Several videos have surfaced on the Internet showing BBC journalists reporting that Building 7 had collapsed well before it had actually done so. Not only was the broadcast time-stamped at 21:54 (4:54 PM EST), a full twenty-six minutes before the event had actually occurred, but the building in question was still standing clearly in the background.[65]

Are you following this? Nobody could even make this up! "After the commotion over the BBC clips, Google removed the footage from Google Video."[66]

As an archivist at CNN concluded:

"No one is saying the BBC is 'part of the conspiracy,' we're saying that someone gave that reporter the information ahead of time."[67]

Well, that's a pretty serious conclusion, folks! If they gave "that reporter the information ahead of time,"[68] then it means that they were planning to bring down Building 7 as a staged event, such as a controlled demolition of that building, just as over 2,000 architects and engineers have been alleging for many years![69]

So what the hell was going on there? Think about that for a minute. Mainstream media reports stated that Building 7 had collapsed just like the Twin Towers—only it *hadn't*. Mainstream media reports stated that the collapse of Building 7 looked just like one of those planned demolitions. That statement came from anchorman Dan Rather, no less—and then quickly disappeared from the hallowed halls of major media.[70] But you can watch and hear that for yourself. Search online for "WTC 7 collapse with Dan Rather commentary" or go to: https://www.youtube.com/watch?v=XL3kL0nXZvk

In Washington, the same day, a live, mainstream media report stated that there was no plane wreckage at the destroyed section of the Pentagon. A reporter *at the scene* basically said—*on the air*—that he was right there and that there was no plane! That was on CNN. The transcript of that live reporting follows:

"9/11 CNN Pentagon Report - NO PLANE - Only Aired Once" (videoclip online):
https://www.youtube.com/watch?v=7BNqgNvUhRQ

CNN Anchor Judy Woodruff and CNN Military Affairs Correspondent Jaimie McIntyre

JUDY WOODRUFF: Outside the Pentagon, CNN's military affairs correspondent Jamie McIntyre. And, Jamie, you got very close to where that plane went down.

JAMIE MCINTYRE: That's right, Judy. A short—a while ago I walked right up next to the building, firefighters were still trying to put out the blaze . . .

JUDY WOODRUFF: . . . Jamie, Aaron was talking earlier—or one of our correspondents was talking earlier—I think—actually, it was Bob Franken—with an eyewitness who said it appeared that that

Boeing 757, the American jet, American Airlines jet, landed short of the Pentagon. Can you give us any better idea of how much of the plane actually impacted the building?

JAMIE MCINTYRE: You know, it might have appeared that way, but from my close-up inspection, there's *no evidence of a plane having crashed anywhere near the Pentagon.* The only site is the actual site of the building that's crashed in, and as I said, the only pieces left that you can see are small enough that you can pick up in your hand. There are no large tail sections, wing sections, fuselage, nothing like that anywhere around, which would indicate that the entire plane crashed into the side of the Pentagon and then caused the side to collapse. Now, even though if you look at the pictures of the Pentagon you see that the floors have all collapsed; that didn't happen immediately. It wasn't until almost about 45 minutes later that the structure was weakened enough that all of the floors collapsed.[71]

Well, gee whiz! That's <u>not the official story at all</u>! *No wonder* that only aired once and then was never heard again!

Major General Albert Stubblebine III, a 32-year veteran who "served with distinction," was Commanding General of US Army Intelligence and, in 1990, was inducted into the Military Intelligence Hall of Fame.[72] He was "responsible for all of the Army's strategic intelligence forces around the world."[73] Among his responsibilities were the photographic surveillance and analysis of US military intelligence, including imagery interpretation. He analyzed the damage at the Pentagon. The General is a very sane and logical man. You can watch him online, in various video clips. What he says will astound you. He knew it was not a jet that crashed into the Pentagon. He didn't "think" that—he *knew*:

"Conclusion: Airplane did not make that hole."[74]

"I was very careful to not say what it was, because I couldn't prove it. I *was* careful to say that it was *not* the airplane that did that, because I *can prove* that it was not the airplane."

"I am the highest-ranking officer, I believe, that has ever gone public."

"The official story was not true."

Search "Major General Albert Stubblebine's views on 9/11" or see him at this link: http://discerningkate.com/2012/12/10/high-ranking-us-major-general-exposes-september-11/.

There was also an incredibly small debris field at the supposed crash site of the other plane, in Pennsylvania. Many witnesses at the crash site at Shanksville, Pennsylvania related "how little it resembled what they expected the scene of a plane crash to look like."[75] You can also hear TV reporters, who eyewitnessed the site, describing how surprisingly small it was.[76] Here is a good news feed regarding observations that the crash site was extremely small (if that link disappears, then do an Internet search: "9/11 Pennsylvania crash site too small"): https://www.youtube.com/watch?v=_0eC3uns3pA

Dr. Steven E. Jones is a respected physicist who scientifically examined the evidence surrounding 9/11. He concluded that "the official explanation for the collapse of the World Trade Center buildings is implausible according to laws of physics."[77] That's very straight-forward, and so is Dr. Jones, a "show-me-the-science" no-nonsense guy who was a university professor for decades. And listen to what he concludes: "In fact, the evidence shows very strongly that there were explosives used, in the way the buildings came down, that is, the completeness of the destruction, the rapid acceleration, the symmetry. All of these things argue for controlled demolition using explosives."[78]

If you watch the video of Building 7 coming down, you can vividly see what he is talking about. In fact, to Dr. Jones, as well as many others, it is very obvious: "It doesn't take a rocket scientist to see that there is something very strange, especially when you compare with controlled demolition."[79] As Dr. Jones determined, *scientifically*, the official government version would be in violation of an accepted and fundamental law of physics, mechanics, and structural engineering—*Newton's Third Law*—that for every action, there is an equal and opposite reaction. Dr. Jones loves America and states that he has no political agenda:

> You have to go with science, I figure, and science says that buildings don't just collapse onto their footprint at freefall speed unless you get the material out of the way. . . . Society is mesmerized by this myth,

this official story of 9/11 being due to the Muslims. Everyone knows it—you can't challenge this myth. If you do, you're a conspiracy kook. Well, I'm sorry, good science *cuts* through all that nonsense, it *doesn't* care.[80]

But have you seen Dr. Jones on mainstream media recently? Nope. And you probably won't, either. But, scientifically, there is simply no other explanation possible except controlled demolition. As one Civil/Structural Engineer puts it, rather sarcastically:

"This is high school physics."[81]

And, by the way—you can watch that collapse on *YouTube*. Just see it for yourself. It only takes 30 seconds of your time to see *exactly* to what Dr. Jones and others are referring. If you just computer search "Building 7 collapse," there are many film clips. Here is a good one:

https://www.youtube.com/watch?v=Mamvq7LWqRU

We urge you to think with an open mind, just as groups like Firefighters For 9/11 Truth are urging people to view the simple science of an important historical event:

"If we live in a free country, why are we afraid to just talk about an event that was the most traumatic event in our history?"[82]

That's from their video and, in just two minutes, you will see what they mean:

https://www.youtube.com/watch?v=2Sft5b2qr14&feature=youtu.be

And here is another link with a scientific discussion of the facts, or, just do a search of "Official ReThink911 Video": https://www.youtube.com/watch?v=rNR6Kbg5jJ8.

Oddly enough, another perfect example of the problem of media consolidation is the Edward Snowden case. Ed Snowden was a whistleblower, by the very definition of the word. He alerted the American people that they were being spied upon by their own government—*without* their knowledge, and *without* their consent. Mainstream media sure in hell wasn't going to tell us. That heads-up from Mr. Snowden was a public service, and since it was one where he knew that he would be vilified by our government for revealing the truth to us, it was a public service that required a great deal of courage, in our opinion and the opinions of many all around the world.

Consider the actual facts of the matter, especially from a personal standpoint. Edward Snowden risked his life to warn us—to divulge extremely important information that every American citizen had the right to know:

That we are being spied upon by our own government!

That is *not* an act of treason. That is not an act of cowardice. That is an act of patriotism. That is an act of bravery.

So, what did mainstream media do? Instead of congratulating him for revealing information crucial to the public and an informed citizenry—information that was being intentionally hidden from the public at large—the media immediately branded Snowden a "traitor" to his country. Bullshit! As informed world citizens, we have a news flash for you too—he is only branded a traitor in the US media, and by the US corporate-military complex. The rest of the world considers Ed Snowden a hero!

And by any fair standard of true American justice, Ed Snowden *is* a hero. His actions were *very* heroic—exposing the totalitarian lies of the corporate-military power structure that is in control of this country. That power structure uses the American flag as a shield to brandish in their own totalitarian interests instead of the best interests of "the Republic for which it stands."[83] And by that measure, Ed Snowden embodies exactly the type of actions on behalf of our freedom that the founders of our Republic were proponents of.

So let's get something straight, right here, and right now. The forbears of our Republic would be *damn* proud of Edward Snowden. Because he personifies what the founders of our democracy truly believed and fought for:

That the freedom of the individual outweighs the interests of the State!

That is the principle of democracy that millions of Americans have fought and died for. It goes all the way back to the Bill of Rights. What we have been fighting for is *not* to protect the best interests of the corporate-military complex. What we have been fighting for is to protect the rights of the citizens that were established to *protect us from* entities like the corporate-military complex.

Allow us to speak very plainly here. Mainstream media is now a freaking puppet of the people who actually run this country. They all line up in mainstream media and march to the tune of that corporate-military complex that now rules this country in its perpetual state of war, whether we citizens like it or not.

Edward Snowden is a whistleblower. He should have been *protected* by the very people who mercilessly persecuted him instead. He alerted the American people that they are being illegally spied upon. He did that at great risk to himself. He gave up a $200,000 a year job in Hawai'i to go live at the airport in Moscow—the only place at which he was safe—for quite some time.[84] To do what he thought was right, so that we could be informed citizens. As Ed Snowden himself put it:

"I'm willing to sacrifice all of that because I can't in good conscience allow the US government to destroy privacy, Internet freedom and basic liberties for people around the world with this massive surveillance machine they're secretly building."[85]

That's a hero. Not a traitor. And we don't care how mainstream media twists it all around. They do that because they are bought and paid for. It's just like the quote at the start of this chapter. It's so important that you should read it again:

"If you're not careful, the newspapers will have you hating the people who are being oppressed, and loving the people who are doing the oppressing."[86]

Malcolm X (the author of that quote) knew a lot about media manipulation. He also said:

"The media's the most powerful entity on earth. They have the power to make the innocent guilty and to make the guilty innocent, and that's power. Because they control the minds of the masses."[87]

And it now appears that US mainstream media is merely a puppet of the interests of the corporate-military complex. As Noam Chomsky observed, in a brief sentence that should scare the *hell* out of us if we have any brains:

Any dictator would admire the uniformity and obedience of the US media.[88]

It is also disturbing how much *cooperation* the NSA and other spying agencies receive from Corporate America. For example, AT&T exhibited an "extreme willingness" to give the NSA access to billions of private emails—"it bent over backwards to help the National Security Agency (NSA) spy on Americans' Internet usage, according to *The New York Times*, which based its report on classified documents released by Edward Snowden."[89] And even though gigantic corporations like AT&T have shown that they are "eager" to help the government spy on American citizens who have committed no crime, the record shows that domestic surveillance has "no discernible impact on preventing acts of terrorism . . . "[90]

And guess what. They are *still spying on us*:

> Federal law makes it a crime to reveal the existence of classified programs but no law makes it a crime to lie to the public about the existence or nonexistence of such programs.
>
> The Obama Administration recently argued in a court case that public discussion of telecom surveillance would make any such programs ineffective and pose a threat to national security.[91]

It would be extremely naive to think that companies like Facebook, LinkedIn, Google and many others operate their services for us out of kindness. They do not. They are not your friends. They are corporations. They operate for profit. And they make that profit by selling your personal information—to anyone interested in buying it.

You probably think that's not that big a deal, because you are probably careful about what you put out on the Internet, and delete anything that might be misconstrued. But guess what? When you press "Delete" and it removes an item from your Google or YouTube or Facebook, it only removes it from *your* view, it doesn't really delete it from existence.[92] You are only hiding it from yourself—the social media company still has it and, therefore, <u>so does the government</u>![93]

California Senate Majority leader, Ellen Corbett, tried to get a bill passed that would put limits on the sharing of our personal information and offer private citizens some level of protection from gigantic social media corporations. Google and Facebook were against the bill and it seems their influence was successful in killing that bill.[94] Senator Corbett learned a lot from that struggle and, when asked if we should be worried about these developments, she looked straight into the camera and responded: "We should be worried."[95] That, and a lot of other great things, are in a documentary that everyone should watch, called *Terms and Conditions May Apply.*

And then there are other companies who "mine" and store *all* your personal and professional information. They take *all* that data on you, *combine* it, and then sell it to anyone who can benefit from it. So, a word of warning—you may *think* that your professional information at LinkedIn is separate from your personal photos at Instagram. But you're wrong—they are no longer separate, in reality. When you apply for a job, if your prospective employer goes to the right company, they can see your *entire* social profile—Instagram, Snapchat, Facebook, Google history, Twitter, YouTube, you name it. Your entire story is there. In fact, much of your *whole life* is there. A child born in the past few years will have their *entire life history* online and totally accessible to anyone willing to pay for that information—or any government that decides to look at it.

Those companies—and we include Google and Facebook—*sell your personal information* to advertisers who then target your interests. They also *share your personal information with the government.* They know a *lot* about you, and they spread it around—and really well, too. Companies like Google even map your location—they know where you are and where you go.[96]

It's even worse than that, boys and girls. A *lot* worse. What would you say if we told you that the United States government actually had access to every phone call you have ever made, access to every email you have ever sent or received, access to everything you have ever done online? An NSA whistleblower came forward and stated *precisely* that, as a set of facts. Here is a transcript of what that former NSA analyst, Russel Tice, had to say about the level of government spying upon American citizens. And, just for the record, when he is asked a "light" question below, his response to that question was not light at all—his response to it was with the utmost seriousness:

NSA ANALYST: The National Security Agency had access to *all* Americans' communications: faxes, phone calls, and their computer communications.

REPORTER: Is there a recording somewhere of every conversation I had with my little nephew in upstate New York? Is it like that?

NSA ANALYST: It would be everything. Yes. It would be everything.[97] It didn't matter whether you were in Kansas, in the middle of the country, and you never made foreign communications at all. They monitored *all* communications.[98]

So the next time that you hear some blurb on the business news about how much money Facebook and Google are making—maybe you should ask yourself exactly how they are making all that money . . .

All Americans should be concerned about programs and policies that threaten our privacy—like the Pentagon's Total Information Awareness program. The American Civil Liberties Union called it "the closest thing to a true 'Big Brother' program that has ever been seriously contemplated in the United States."[99] The very wide scope of the program is what was so disturbing. As ABC News reported: "The Pentagon is clearly moving to create the largest electronic eye ever, to look at any and all Americans" with every type of data collection conceivable.[100] Did they receive assistance from US companies in the collection of their data on American citizens? *You betcha* they did. And although the project was technically cancelled due to public outcry—over its very name, among other things—you can bet that they just rolled it over into another departmental project within their black ops off-the-books budget and with some title that will be less shocking if anyone ever even finds the damn thing. Because there was no law made against it—it was simply a disbanded project.[101] Here is NSA expert Shane Harris, from his excellent book, *The Watchers: The Rise of America's Surveillance State*:

So behind closed doors, the people who were in charge of TIA (Total Information Awareness) and others in the intelligence committees in

Congress struck a deal that TIA would be as they say defunded from the Defense budget but that all the money for it would be moved over to the classified side of the budget, the black budget as it's often called. And it was disbanded in name, and all of the various components of the research program were separated, were given new cover names, and almost all of them were then shifted over to the management and control of the National Security Agency, which unbeknownst to everyone in America—most people in America at the time—had been running its own Total Information Awareness program.[102]

So the program was shut down—technically. But it wasn't shut down in reality. It was secretly rolled over into the NSA's PRISM program—which we would not even know about today, were it not for Ed Snowden.[103] If you think the NSA has a history of admitting that they spy upon American citizens who have not committed a crime, then you need to learn more about the NSA. They admit nothing unless it is in their *own* best interests—such as when Snowden's revelations started to expose their massive domestic surveillance program, PRISM, and they went "public" trying to put the spin on that its actual purpose is benign and that "the database is only used for counter-terrorism and foreign intelligence efforts."[104] Yeah, *right*. Like anybody actually *believes* that crap! That was a "damage control" publicity push. But we know different now, thanks to what Ed Snowden revealed.

So TIA is shut down publicly, and privacy advocates really declared a great victory for this, but unbeknownst to them, the work just continued in secret at the NSA and became part of this larger, vast surveillance apparatus that we're learning more about now.[105]

Then there is yet another very disturbing development called "pervasive monitoring" with "retrospective surveillance." With the help of your personal information—notice we did not say "private" information, because it no longer is, folks—but with your personal data supplied to the government by public corporations like AT&T, Facebook, Google and many others, they can basically "reverse engineer" you! They can wait until someone becomes a "person of interest" and *then* they can go back through all of their recorded and preserved computer data banks and *reconstruct* what that person did in the period leading up to their commission of a crime, or to becoming a "person of interest." We kid you not. Get a load of this—it comes from the research of the think tank, the Brookings Institution, and it is one of the scariest things you will ever read:

> Pervasive monitoring will provide what amounts to a time machine allowing authoritarian governments to perform retrospective surveillance. For example, if an anti-regime demonstrator previously unknown to security services is arrested, it will be possible to go back in time to scrutinize the demonstrator's phone conversations, automobile travels, and the people he or she met in the months and even years leading up to the arrest.[106]

Of course, in the above example, it would not necessarily have to be a criminal's actions that are reconstructed. It could be an average citizen's life they track down every trace of—which seems to be the authoritarian direction in which we are headed, *unless* we take action to stop it.

The future is *here*, boy and girls. Now, it is simply a question of how we will grapple with it. To give you an idea of the outrageous arrogance of these pompous fascists in their suits and ties, this is what Eric Schmidt, the CEO of Google, had to say about protecting your privacy:

> If you have something that you don't want anyone to know, maybe you shouldn't be doing it in the first place. If you really need that kind of privacy, the reality is that search engines—including Google—do retain this information for some time and it's important, for example, that we are all subject in the United States to the Patriot Act and it is possible that all that information could be made available to the authorities.[107]

Sometimes you hear something and you have to ask yourself an important question: Does it stand up to actual logic? Think about what that Google CEO actually said: "If you have something that you don't want anyone to know, maybe you shouldn't be doing it in the first place."[108]

Isn't that disgusting? What kind of a sick mind can actually think in such a way? That's like saying "If you didn't want me to *slap* you across the face then you shouldn't have been standing there with your face unprotected."

But hey—get a load of this. The *same* guy—the same CEO of Google, Eric Schmidt—got all pushed out of shape when a picture of his house was published.[109] We're not kidding! Is that two-faced, or what? "Eric Schmidt's Google blackballed CNet's reporters after CNet published personal information about Schmidt's private life."[110]

So apparently it's not so harmless when *you're* the one who is losing their privacy, huh Eric? As one reporter responded to the issue, echoing the would-be logic of Mr. Schmidt's comments:

> Hey, Eric: if you don't want us to know how much money you make, where you live, and what you do with your spare time, maybe you shouldn't have a house, earn a salary, or have any hobbies, right?[111]

These maniacs have to be stopped. We have to take back our right to privacy. It's not for sale, and we never knowingly put it *up* for sale. But the *fascists* of Corporate America took it away from us anyway. And now we must take it back.

Here, below, is a very solid update on where we currently are in this dramatic scenario surrounding our privacy—or the *lack* of it:

> You are under surveillance right now.
>
> Your cell phone provider tracks your location and knows who's with you. Your online and in-store purchasing patterns are recorded, and reveal if you're unemployed, sick, or pregnant. Your emails and texts expose your intimate and casual friends. Google knows what you're thinking because it saves your private searches. Facebook can determine your sexual orientation without you ever mentioning it.
>
> The powers that surveil us do more than simply store this information. Corporations use surveillance to manipulate not only the news articles and advertisements we each see, but also the prices we're offered. Governments use surveillance to discriminate, censor, chill free speech, and put people in danger worldwide.[112]

Alex Jones at *InfoWars* was right. There is a war going on—and it's the war for your mind! And *believe* us—when it comes to Corporate America, your rights and your privacy are the *last* things on their minds.

FURTHER RESEARCH:

Greenwald, Glenn. *No Place to Hide: Edward Snowden, the NSA and the U.S. Surveillance State*. New York: Metropolitan Books, 2014.

Haas, Elizabeth, Terry Chistensen, and Peter J. Haas. *Projecting Politics: Political Messages in American Films*. London: Routledge, 2015.

Harris, Shane. *The Watchers: The Rise of America's Surveillance State*. New York: Penguin Press, 2010.

Schneier, Bruce. *Data and Goliath: The Hidden Battles to Collect Your Data and Control Your World*. New York: W.W. Norton & Company, 2015.

Lewis, Charles. *935 Lies: The Future of Truth and the Decline of America's Moral Integrity*. New York: PublicAffairs, 2014.

Whitten-Woodring, Jennifer and Patrick James. "Fourth Estate or Mouthpiece? A Formal Model of Media, Protest and Government Repression." *Political Communication* 29 no. 2(April 26, 2012):113–136. https://www.uml.edu/docs/Fourth%20Estate%20or%20Mouthpiece%20whitten%20woodring%20jennifer_tcm18–146237.pdf.

Horgan, John. "What War Propaganda Like American Sniper Reveals about Us." *Scientific American* (February 2, 2015). http://blogs.scientificamerican.com/cross-check/what-war-propaganda-like-8220-american-sniper-8221-reveals-about-us/.

Hersh, Seymour M. "The Killing of Osama bin Laden." *London Review of Books* 37 no. 10(May 21, 2015). http://www.lrb.co.uk/v37/n10/seymour-m-hersh/the-killing-of-osama-bin-laden.

Schwarz, Jonathan. "Lie After Lie After Lie: What Colin Powell Knew Ten Years Ago Today and What He Said." *Huffington Post* (April 7, 2013).

http://www.huffingtonpost.com/jonathan-schwarz/colin-powell-wmd-iraq-war_b_2624620.html.

Kamiya, Gary. "Iraq: Why the media failed: Afraid to challenge America's leaders or conventional wisdom about the Middle East, a toothless press collapsed." *Salon* (April 10, 2007). http://www.salon.com/2007/04/10/media_failure/.

Martin, Rachel, host. "Reminder: Saddam Statue Was Toppled by Psy-Ops." National Public Radio (April 9, 2008). http://www.npr.org/templates/story/story.php?storyId=89489923.

"The pulling down of the Statue was a staged media event," New York Indymedia, *Centre for Research on Globalisation* (April 11, 2003). http://www.globalresearch.ca/articles/NYI304A.html.

Griffin, David Ray. "Building What? How State Crimes Against Democracy Can Be Hidden in Plain Sight." In Huff, Mickey, Peter Phillips, and Project Censored, eds. *Censored: The News That Didn't Make the News-The Year's Top 25 Censored Stories—2011*. New York: Seven Stories Press: 2010.

"Physicist Challenges Official 9/11 Story." In Phillips, Peter, Andrew Roth, and Project Censored, eds. *Censored 2008: The Top 25 Censored Stories of 2006–07*. New York: Seven Stories Press, 2007.

Johnston, Kate. "High Ranking US Major General Exposes September 11." *DiscerningKate.com* (December 10, 2012). http://discerningkate.com/2012/12/10/high-ranking-us-major-general-exposes-september-11/.

The Official ReThink911 Video. https://www.youtube.com/watch?v=rNR6Kbg5jJ8.

Smith, Brett, director. *Hypothesis*. Logic Gate Productions (2010). DVD. https://www.youtube.com/watch?v=wkaX5n3pfZE.

"BBC Reports Collapse of WTC Building 7 Early – Twice." *MVR (BBC Motion Gallery)* (February 28, 2007). https://www.youtube.com/watch?v=6mxFRigYD3s.

Dykes, Aaron and Alex Jones. "*CNN, BBC 24* Reports Conclusively Prove Media Prior Knowledge and False-Start Scripting of Building 7 Controlled

Demolition." *Jones* Report (February 27, 2007). http://www.jonesreport.com/articles/270207_bbc_lost_response.html

"Science of 9/11: Who We Are." Architects & Engineers for 9/11 Truth. http://www.ae911truth.org/about.html.

Firefighters For 9/11 Truth & Unity. "Firefighters, Architects & Engineers Expose 9/11 Myths." September 2, 2015. https://www.youtube.com/watch?v=2Sft5b2qr14&feature=youtu.be.

Flux, Elizabeth. "Google Maps Has Been Tracking Your Every Move, And There's a Website to Prove It."*Junkee* (August 15, 2014). http://junkee.com/google-maps-has-been-tracking-your-every-move-and-theres-a-website-to-prove-it/39639

"Q&A on the Pentagon's 'Total Information Awareness' Program." American Civil Liberties Union (2015). https://www.aclu.org/qa-pentagons-total-information-awareness-program.

Hoback, Cullen, director. *Terms and Conditions May Apply.* Toronto: Phase 4 Films (2013). DVD. https://www.youtube.com/watch?v=Yn0mglH7XLk.

Edwards, David and Muriel Kane. "Whistleblower: NSA spied on *everyone, targeted journalists.*" *Raw Story* (January 21, 2009). http://rawstory.com/news/2008/Whistleblower_Bushs_NSA_targeted_reporters_0121.html.

Hayes, Chris. "Before PRISM there was Total Information Awareness." *MSNBC.com* (September 12, 2013). http://www.msnbc.com/all-in/prism-there-was-total-information-awar.

Villasenor, John. "Recording Everything: Digital Storage as an Enabler of Authoritarian Governments." *Center for Technology Innovation at Brookings* (December 14, 2011). http://www.brookings.edu/~/media/research/files/papers/2011/12/14-digital-storage-villasenor/1214_digital_storage_villasenor.pdf.

CHAPTER FOUR

AMERICA'S BIGGEST EXPORT: PERPETUAL WAR

Peace makes a lot of sense. It just doesn't make a lot of dollars.
—Jesse Ventura

War is a racket . . . A few profit—and the many pay. But there is a way to stop it. You can't end it by disarmament conferences. You can't eliminate it by peace parleys at Geneva. Well-meaning but impractical groups can't wipe it out by resolutions. It can be smashed effectively only by taking the profit out of war.[1]
—US Marine Corps Major General Smedley D. Butler,
two-time Medal of Honor recipient

Those wise words of General Butler, above, have unfortunately gone completely unheeded. If we can't pay attention to teachers and philosophers then you would think that we would at least be interested in what the generals who have seen the blood-soaked battlefields have to say about the uselessness of the endeavor.

A very disturbing event has taken place. The American geopolitical landscape has been manipulated to a point where a state of perpetual war is now acceptable to large factions of our two main political parties.[2] "The Federation of American Scientists has cataloged nearly 200 military incursions since 1945 in which the United States has been the aggressor."[3] Gore Vidal wrote those words in 2002—you can now add many more "conflicts" to the list. We act as though we are the self-appointed policeman of the world (no one gave us that authority; we simply took it, without consent). We have now reached a point where, as Normon Solomon recently observed: "The 'war on terror' now looks so endless that no one speculates anymore about when it might conclude."[4]

As we explained in detail in chapter 1, the gigantic arms corporations keep politicians in every state handcuffed by linking their production programs to a labor-intensive industry that creates jobs in every Congressional district.[5] Threatening the removal and transfer of those jobs is a poison spear that can always be pointed at them—and that is just one of the ways in which corporations buy the willing cooperation of politicians.[6] But it is the *cost* of that corrupt process that is so incredibly disturbing. Just to give you an idea of how much money we're talking about with the weapons business, please think long and hard about one specific example. The US military will spend $1.5 trillion on a new fighter jet that is already superfluous. We will get to the specifics of that later in this chapter.

General Dwight D. Eisenhower was Supreme Commander of Allied Forces in Europe during World War II then, as a war hero, was elected 34th President of the United States. Here's what he took away from all of that experience and they are words that deserve our attention:

> Every gun that is made, every warship launched, every rocket fired signifies, in the final sense, a theft from those who hunger and are not fed, those who are cold and are not clothed. This world in arms is not spending money alone. It is spending the sweat of its laborers, the genius of its scientists, the hopes of its children. The cost of one modern heavy bomber is this: a modern brick school in more than 30 cities. It is two electric power plants, each serving a town of 60,000 population. It is two fine, fully equipped hospitals. It is some fifty miles of concrete pavement. We pay for a single fighter with a half-million bushels of wheat. We pay for a single destroyer with new homes that could have housed more than 8,000 people. . . . This is not a way of life at all, in any true sense. Under the cloud of threatening war, it is humanity hanging from a cross of iron."[7]

When Eisenhower wrote those words, the cost of that "one modern heavy bomber" was only a few *million* dollars. Think about that for a minute. Then think about 1.5 *trillion* dollars. How do you think Dwight would feel about that? That's a crime against humanity. That is unacceptable.

One and a half trillion is the cost of just *one Air Force program*, and a highly-flawed program, at that.

Remember the good old days when it was "only" millions of dollars that would mysteriously disappear? Well, folks, technology isn't the only thing that's improved! So has thievery, fraud, and corruption. A recent report revealed that *8.5 trillion dollars is missing from the Pentagon budget.*[8] That's trillion with a "T"—which is a million-million! Eight and a half trillion dollars.

> In an interview, Linda Woodford, an employee at the Defense Finance and Accounting Service—the Pentagon's main accounting agency—reveals to Reuters that she spent the last 15 years of her career simply "plugging in" false numbers every month to balance the books;
> **"A lot of times there were issues of numbers being inaccurate. We didn't have the detail . . . for a lot of it."**
> In the REAL WORLD, that would be called MASSIVE FRAUD.[9]

The day before the 9/11 attacks, Secretary of Defense Donald Rumsfeld made an astounding announcement: "According to some estimates, we cannot track $2.3 trillion in transactions."[10] Ooops! Can you imagine if you ran a business that way? Oddly enough, nobody seemed to think that matter was worth looking into.

> That was Sept. 10, 2001. The next day, al Qaeda hijacked commercial airliners and flew them into the World Trade Center and the Pentagon. It would be nearly a decade before Pentagon accounting drew the attention of Congress.[11]

After the 9/11 attacks, then Congress approved the stringently authoritarian Patriot Act without even reading it and went back to sleep for a few more years.[12] Apparently they didn't think it was worth looking for the missing $2.3 trillion. But, over a decade later, a reporter at the news organization *Reuters* continued looking into the matter and the results of *that* investigation showed that the missing monies that the Pentagon had been disbursing to the defense contractors had magically risen to $8.5 trillion by 2013—that's eight trillion, five hundred billion dollars.

So, while we were taking a nap (or busy at work, more likely), the "defense" industry has apparently managed to take over Washington, D.C. And we placed the word defense in quotation marks for a very good reason: it's not! We're no longer "defending" our country. We're locked in a state of perpetual war against an "enemy" that doesn't technically even exist. If the "War on Terror" sounds like a reasonable idea, then perhaps we should consider the fact that the United States of America declared war on an abstract noun. Even national security experts have observed that it "is a politically expedient slogan without real substance, serving to distort rather than define."[13] As author Gore Vidal once pointed out, you can't have a "War on Terror" because "terror" is an abstract concept, not an actual enemy.[14] The "War on Terror" is simply a metaphor; it's symbolic, not literally applicable.[15] You can only have a war against a country or a specific and identified group of individuals. Otherwise, you're fighting an abstract which is not even a winnable war. But that's what they want: perpetual war. Because that keeps on sending the endless billions of dollars into the pipeline of their never-ending war machine. Get it?

A little bit of history puts all this into perspective. In the post–World War II era, two nations, the United States and the Soviet Union, vied for power. Their military strength far exceeded other nations of the world and they became known as the Superpowers—the two gargantuan competitors of the planet.

The United States defeated the Soviet Union in that Battle of the Superpowers—largely based on a policy of outspending them. The United States spent so much on military advances that, although they tried, the Soviets could not keep up with that level of spending and, as a result, the Soviet economy thus collapsed. It was a war based on spending rather than actual fighting, and America won it.

After the collapse of the Soviet Empire in the late 1980s, most progressive Americans reasoned that there would then be huge amounts of money available for major domestic issues: for health care, for jobs programs, for education. They reasoned that since the United States was now the world's only superpower, the massive amounts of military spending were no longer necessary and would be reduced. It seemed quite a logical argument.

But *they were wrong*. The insanely high levels of military spending simply continued as though nothing had changed. The defense contractors kept sending massive weapons development programs to the Pentagon. The Pentagon kept approving them and sending them to Congress. Congress did little to challenge the system. It had become an ingrained part of the American economy and they just kept playing the game, oblivious to the point that there was no longer a solid rationale to support it.

As author and defense analyst Chalmers Johnson observed, that irrational system was maintained via a very calculating process employed by defense contractors that had become highly successful and is strongly evident in today's American economic landscape as well. It's accomplished by employing a two-part method that has become foolproof in maintaining absurdly high levels of military spending on projects that are often of little use to the actual "defense" of America.

The "two crucial Pentagon gambits" designed to keep us deadlocked in this horrible system of endlessly expensive military expenditures are known as "front-loading" and "political engineering."[16] Front-loading is appropriating funding for new weapons systems without actual proof of their necessity—just based on the vague assurance from corporate and military people about what a particular plane or other weapons program can achieve. The project is dramatically "lowballed," touted at a bargain price that eventually turns out to be absurdly and inaccurately low. That's why weapons systems generally go way over budget and can increase to an actual cost that is ten times that of the original proposal.[17] Political engineering is even simpler—it is the deviously intentional strategy of awarding defense contracts in as many different congressional districts as possible—thereby ensuring that both voters and congressional incumbents are dependent upon military money and then, when the *true* costs of the falsely front-loaded programs begin to appear, they can be pressured to keep rubber-stamping their support of the expensive project.[18] Front-loading and political engineering are the way the game is played:

> They both involve criminal intent to turn on the spigot of taxpayer money and then to jam it so that it cannot be turned off. They are de rigueur (required) practices of our military–industrial complex.[19]

This absurd system has resulted in a situation that is incredibly maligned, yet earth-shatteringly important—because it *defines* what the real problem is:

**Congress has been corrupted by the military–industrial complex
into believing that by voting for more defense spending, they are
supplying "jobs" for the economy.**[20]

It's _not true_. Do _not_ believe it. "In fact, they are only diverting scarce
resources from the desperately needed rebuilding of the American infrastructure and other crucial spending necessities into wasteful muni-
tions."[21] Sustaining absurdly high levels of military spending is not in our
economic interest. The argument that it creates jobs is flawed reasoning; it
is "the determination to maintain a permanent war economy and to treat
military output as an ordinary economic product, even though it makes
no contribution to either production or consumption."[22]

Some high-profile security experts have tried to stop the endless
spending spiral—but none have ever succeeded. Immediately prior to his
death, William Colby, the former CIA director, was publicly advocating
an immediate 50% unilateral reduction in US defense spending. If that's
true, then Colby's demise was actually in the best interests of the military–
industrial American power structure. Mr. Colby's death was also under
highly suspicious circumstances. Some researchers even suspect that he
was murdered as a result.[23]

Security experts have been warning Americans for many years about
the dangerously excessive levels of military spending by the United
States. But, as one would suspect these days, in the corporate oligarchy
that America has become, those ridiculously high levels of spending are
strongly _supported_ by the corporate defense industry which builds and
sells those weapons. They make massive campaign contributions to congressional representatives and, lo and behold, those high spending levels
keep getting passed in Congress. If that surprises you, then you better
keep reading, folks. Because it has reached a point that the whole thing is
insane.

Add to that, America's extremely overzealous forward-basing system of
literally hundreds of major military installations scattered around the entire globe, in its self-appointed role of "world policeman." The cost of these
bases is astronomical and, many experts believe, completely unnecessary.

As Chalmers Johnson has also detailed, the United States spends more
on military expenditures than the _rest of the world's countries combined_.[24]

And meanwhile, they tell us that there simply isn't enough money to fund social security, health care, jobs programs, infrastructure, and other basic needs for our citizens. The US military is in 147 different countries, which is 75% of this planet.[25] We have somehow developed into what is basically a military empire and that empire consists of 865 military facilities scattered all around this planet.[26] If that doesn't sound excessive to you, then you better have your pulse checked.

> US and NATO military operations have grown exponentially over the years, as the Western nations have taken it upon themselves to police the world and use that position to their benefit at every possible opportunity. The fact that military agents have been deployed to this many different areas in just a year reveals that the US empire is involved in an even deeper war than most American citizens can imagine.[27]

The fact is that an astonishing *54 percent of the of US discretionary budget goes to Military* spending; only 6 percent of it goes to Education.[28] Docs that convey to you the true wishes of the would-be and so-called leaders of this country? They benefit from war, they want war, and they will continue to get us into wars!

> Our annual spending on "national security"—meaning the defense budget plus all military expenditures hidden in the budgets for the departments of Energy, State, Treasury, Veterans Affairs, the CIA, and numerous other places in the executive branch—already exceeds a trillion dollars, an amount larger than that of all other national defense budgets combined.[29]

Some of the examples of that excessive military spending are mind-boggling, both in their high cost and their notably poor performance.

Take the V-22 Osprey helicopter, for example, which as the *New York Times* noted, "has become a case study of how hard it is to kill billion-dollar Pentagon programs."[30] One analyst refers to it bluntly as "a piece of junk"—is that frank enough for you?[31] At about $100 million per unit, it's a very expensive piece of junk too.[32] It's also a monumental problem that the Marine Corps is now stuck with because the Pentagon remained committed to the project.[33] *Dozens* of good pilots and their passengers have been killed during its development—yet the Pentagon would not reconsider.[34] With a wingspan over 84 feet (making it a big target for the enemy), the V-22 is a massive, double-rotor monstrosity.[35] Its list of short-falls are almost too numerous to count: "Able to do only a few missions with any level of competence" is just one of the short summaries of the ridiculously expensive and dangerous Osprey craft.[36] In fact:

Sailors have a joke: "The Osprey can wave at you while you drown."[37]

One member of Congress, US Representative Lynn Woolsey of California, referred to it as the "poster child for the excesses and inefficiencies of the military–industrial complex."[38] But they ordered more of them anyway![39] Because waste is what they do best in Washington. The Pentagon remains committed (and they *should be committed*, actually—to a mental institution!).

So the V-22 Osprey is basically a good way to waste $50 billion—that's the cost of just that one program. But wait, it gets even better—*much*. Because that's mere child's play compared to some of their other projects.

Then there is the new and most expensive warship in the history of the United States Navy: America's new $13 billion aircraft carrier—and yes, your fears are correct—that's $13 billion *each*.[40] And you can bet that it'll end up costing a lot more than that. It always does. The point is this: If we're really a peace-seeking nation—as we officially purport to be—then why do we possess such an insatiable desire to bomb the shit out of other countries? And many question whether it even makes any sense to build them at all, because countries like China continue to develop missiles that can blow them right out of the water. Frankly, that sounds like a pretty good reason to question building them at all!

But for all the advances within the Ford-class carrier group, some have questioned the wisdom of continuing an astronomically expensive carrier-heavy naval strategy in a time when interstate warfare is rare and nations like China continue to develop potentially carrier-killing long-range antiship cruise missiles.[41]

A former Captain in the US Navy makes an argument that has a lot of logic, stating that the new carrier is an "easy target" that is "simply not suited to the future of naval warfare" because it is staking too much on something that could be entirely taken out by one strike.[42] China has invested heavily in those anti-ship cruise missiles, as well as in submarines that are capable of launching those missiles.[43]

> The loss of a single carrier could conceivably lead to about twice as many US fatalities as in the entirety of the war in Afghanistan . . . For this reason, the modern carrier violates a core principle of war: Never introduce an element that you cannot afford to lose.[44]

So it doesn't really make sense in today's world. But do you think that will stop them from ordering more of them? With that much money at stake? Think again.

Then there is the Air Force's F-22 Raptor fighter plane. As Senator John McCain pointed out—even though he is a former combat pilot himself and a strong supporter of the military—the plane is ridiculously expensive and serves no purpose.[45] We have had F-22s for about a decade, they cost $420 million each.[46] They had been sitting around for about ten years before even being used in actual combat—they finally saw action in Syria in 2015—leading Senator McCain to call it "an expensive, corroding hangar queen."[47]

The F-22 has also had a lot of safety issues, but that didn't stop the program.[48] They just kept on ordering them—$79 billion worth of 'em.[49] And the spending spree isn't over, by any means. They "cost $49,000 an hour to operate" and "the Pentagon plans to spend another $9.7 billion on upgrades to the planes that the manufacturer and the military had never planned on needing."[50]

But all of that is a drop in the bucket compared to the big granddaddy of all military programs—the place where dollars pour in like a fire hose and companies are getting filthy rich off our taxpayer dollars. You'll *wish* they were only wasting billions of dollars when you hear the details about this one! Because now we're talking about the F-35 fighter plane, so now we're talking *trillions*.

The F-35 is often referred to as "The Pentagon's $1.5 Trillion Dollar Mistake"[51] and described with the worst of all military acronyms, "FUBAR"—Fucked-Up Beyond All Repair.[52] An entire book could be written about all of its problems, some of which are mind-bogglingly bad too—like "Unsafe at any speed."[53] Or how about this one? How's this professional assessment for a good indication of where that $1.5 trillion of *our* money is going:

> The aircraft can barely do anything: it has trouble flying at night, its engines have exploded during takeoff, and early models suffered structural cracks. There's no end in sight, either.[54]

And they still haven't "ironed out" its problems, either. "The last time the next-generation fighter jet was matched up to an older plane, it failed to live up to its expensive promise."[55]

But the Pentagon has got so much invested in the project that the Air Force says the F-35 program is "too big to fail."[56] Sound familiar? When will these bums get cured of giving our tax dollars away to huge corporations?

So, the evidence is abundant that a combination of corporations and the US military has virtually taken over the reins of true leadership of our Republic. Many are now convinced that a cabal of corporate and military leaders is actually running America's policy-making decisions. Witness Barack Obama, the 44th President of the United States. It honestly seemed, at the time of his election, that Obama was a real signal for a major change in our country. If you recall, he was elected on a campaign platform of peace. That was the basic tenet of his entire campaign. Peace, not war. He promised to get our troops out of the Middle East. To bring them home from Iraq immediately. And what happened after he was elected, dare one ask? Did he follow up on that campaign platform of his? Well, not exactly. In fact—exactly *the opposite*. He left our troops in Iraq in a protracted, unwinnable war, thus beginning a new and even larger war in Afghanistan, and a secret war in Pakistan with illegal drone strikes on the civilian population of a nation with whom we were not at war. He drastically *expanded* foreign military incursions, rather than eliminating them, as he had proposed during his campaign to run for president.

Is that because he was evil? It does not seem so. He seemed like a decent man who actually wanted peace. And maybe he did. But that's not really the point. The point is that—even if he or she truly wants to (and Obama seemingly did)—the President of the United States no longer seems capable of acting independently of some shadowy ruling system that is obviously controlling their actions, as well as the course of this country. Some hidden force is apparently deciding US policy now—*not* the President of the United States. And that hidden force that determines America's international policies is clearly based on *corporate* interests, *not* upon the true wishes of American citizenry. That much appears crystal clear now, folks. And that seems to finally be getting clear to everybody. Our would-be leaders only pay polite lip service to what the American people really want. And then they go off and do precisely what *they* want instead and, inevitably, it ends up being based on *corporate* interests rather than upon the wishes of the American people.

This is all nothing new. The United States intervened militarily in Central America decades ago, and it turns out it was to protect the corporate interests of an American company. The United Fruit Company (which became today's Chiquita Brands International) used the CIA and the mercenary army it developed, by order of the President of the United States, for the specific purpose of protecting its vast investments in foreign banana plantations.[57] Those actions actually gave rise to the phrase "banana republic."[58] It bears noting that people "in the know," have observed these same things for a long time. CIA pilot Francis Gary Powers was held captive by the Soviets from 1960 to 1962. During that time he wrote many letters while in captivity. Listen closely to the wisdom in his words, and how closely it directly parallels our political enslavement today. And this was in 1961! This is direct from one of his letters about the obvious problems concerning the ongoing Cold War with the Soviets, as well as the real reasons for the US invasion of Cuba:

> It certainly does look as if there is no desire on the part of the US Government to stop the arms race and the production of arms which is very profitable to a small percentage of the US Citizens and very costly to the majority.

Why do we citizens of the United States put up with all this? I personally think it is because we do not bother to think about it at all ... For instance, if the motive "profit" is substituted as a major reason for many of the questionable actions of the Government it becomes clear why we have many policies that do not seem to be for the country as a whole.[59]

Powers also saw what the real reason for going into Cuba was:

Was it to help the Cuban people that the United States backed the invasion of or was it on the behalf of the large corporation which had been nationalized? Would it have helped all the American citizens who paid for the invasion if it had accomplished its purpose or would it have helped only a few corporations?

In my opinion only a few people would have profited by a successful invasion of Cuba, but all American taxpayers would have and did pay for it. To me this indicates that our government does not always have the benefit of all citizens of the United States in mind when it makes its very expensive decisions.

Does the arms race benefit all the American people who pay for the arms or does it only benefit the makers of the arms?[60]

Nowadays, another problem is the privatization of war—using private corporations to act as paid mercenaries in America's conflicts. You may have heard a bit about the company, Blackwater, used a lot for those purposes, in Iraq, Afghanistan, and Pakistan:

Blackwater is the most powerful mercenary firm in the world, with 20,000 soldiers, the world's largest private military base, a fleet of twenty aircraft including helicopter gunships, and a private intelligence division. The firm is also manufacturing its own surveillance blimps and target systems.[61]

To say that they are well-connected conservatives is putting it very mildly:

Run by a multimillionaire Christian conservative who bankrolls President Bush and his allies, its forces are capable of overthrowing governments, yet most people have never heard of Blackwater.[62]

Since those words, immediately above, were written, Blackwater has metamorphisized, or tried to, at least. First it was known as "Blackwater Worldwide," then it was shortened to simply "Blackwater," then after scandals involving the murder of Iraqi civilians, they changed their name to "Xe Services"; but since folks usually called Xe "the company formerly known as Blackwater," they ditched that too and went for the soft and harmless-sounding "Academi" (nice touch, don't you think?) so that, technically, it was now the "company formerly known as Xe" and Blackwater was a bit farther behind them, or so they hoped.[63] Then, it became "Constellis Group," and has changed its spots yet again, to wit, as of this writing, it has now acquired "Triple Canopy" and "Olive Group," yet is apparently sticking with the name Constellis, at least for now (but don't bet the ranch on that, kids). By the time you read this, who knows, it may be going by a different name again. Call it what you will—their track record speaks for itself, and it is not a pretty story.

After four American soldiers were killed and made an example of in Iraq—their burned corpses were hung from a bridge over the Euphrates River—it was the Blackwater Army, *not* the US Army, that was reportedly responsible for the mass slaughter including Iraqi civilians in Fallujah "that would fuel the fierce Iraqi resistance that haunts occupation forces to this day."[64]

As author Naomi Klein warned of this new and lethal development, "the Bush administration has spent hundreds of millions of public dollars building a parallel corporate army, an army so loyal to far right causes it constitutes nothing less than a Republican Guard," in "the death throes of US democracy."[65] CIA veteran Ray McGovern called it "a US government–outsourced Frankenstein . . . that poses a grave and gathering danger to the future of our Republic."[66]

And, as we said, they can change their name all they want—actions speak louder than words. According to some sources, they were not only being used in Iraq and Afghanistan as a private army, they were also in Pakistan:

Blackwater's operations in Pakistan, he adds, are not done through State Department contracts or publicly identified defense contracts. "It's

> Blackwater via JSOC (Joint Special Operations Command, the military HQ for black ops), and it's a classified no-bid (contract) approved on a rolling basis."[67]

JSOC contracts are shielded from public oversight, top secret stuff.[68] Working with JSOC, Blackwater was at the center of a program in Karachi, Pakistan, in which they helped "direct a secret US military drone bombing campaign."[69]

> The program puts Blackwater at the epicenter of a US military operation within the borders of a nation against which the United States has not declared war. . . . Officially, the United States is not supposed to have any active military operations in that country.[70]

But we *do* run military operations in Pakistan, and everybody knows it, especially the families of civilians who have died in our drone strikes there—and Blackwater (by any name) has worked with both the CIA and the JSOC on those drone strikes *inside Pakistan*, as reported in *The Nation*.[71] The *New York Times* also reported that, in addition to being used in an assassination program, Blackwater has also worked with the CIA on its drone-bombing program inside Pakistan.[72] So, companies like Blackwater not only operate in a highly questionable manner—they even operate where it is illegal to be operating at all.

Many have pointed out that the actual reason for the Iraq War was economic interest, primarily oil.[73] Companies like Halliburton also made a fortune from that war.[74] In Afghanistan, that country just happens to be sitting smack-dab in the middle of the best route for a crucial pipeline for the US energy giants and, as documented in the *New York Times*, the announcement of the discovery of a trillion dollars' worth of critical metals;[75] not to mention control of the world's largest opium production, which—very oddly, one would surmise—has been *expanding* amidst the US military occupation there, not contracting.[76]

We began this chapter with General Butler's quote. We will end it with Presidents Eisenhower's very direct warning, from his Farewell Address to the nation, about the dire dangers of huge defense corporations working together with the Pentagon:

This conjunction of an immense military establishment and a large arms industry is new in the American experience . . . In the councils of government, we must guard against the acquisition of unwarranted influence, whether sought or unsought, by the military–industrial complex. The potential for the disastrous rise of misplaced power exists and will persist.

We must never let the weight of this combination endanger our liberties or democratic processes. We should take nothing for granted. Only an alert and knowledgeable citizenry can compel the proper meshing of the huge industrial and military machinery of defense with our peaceful methods and goals, so that security and liberty may prosper together.[77]

We've shown you numerous examples of the profit, greed, and corruption of corporations when it comes to the pursuit of war. So now, the message is clear:

We have got to take the profit out of killing people!

And as you can see, from just a handful of the examples in this chapter, we could literally cut many hundreds of billions of dollars from the Pentagon's budget *without* even affecting our nation's actual security.

FURTHER RESEARCH:

Butler, Smedley D., Major General, USCM (ret.). *War Is a Racket*. Port Townsend, WA: Feral House, 2003. https://archive.org/stream/WarIsARacket/WarIsARacket_djvu.txt.

Vidal, Gore. *Perpetual War for Perpetual Peace: How We Got to Be So Hated*. New York: Nation Books, 2002.

Johnson, Chalmers. *Dismantling the Empire: America's Last Best Hope*. New York: Metropolitan Books, 2010.

Scahill, Jeremey. *Blackwater: The Rise of the World's Most Powerful Mercenary Army*. New York: Nation Books, 2007.

Hobbs, Andrew, Brittney Gates, and Kelsey Arnold. "Blackwater (Xe): The Secret US War in Pakistan." October 2, 2010, in Huff, Mickey, Peter Phillips, and Project Censored, eds. *Censored: The News That Didn't Make the News—The Year's Top 25 Censored Stories—2011.* New York: Seven Stories Press, 2010. http://www.voltairenet.org/article175040.html.

Scahill, Jeremy. "The Secret US War in Pakistan: Inside sources reveal that the firm works with the US military in Karachi to plan targeted assassinations and drone bombings, among other sensitive counterterrorism operations." *The Nation* (November 23, 2009). http://www.thenation.com/article/secret-us-war-pakistan/.

Scahill, Jeremy, Sverre Tysl and Noel Byrne, PhD. "Behind Blackwater Inc." January 26, 2007, in Phillips, Peter, Andrew Roth, and Project Censored, eds. *Project Censored: The News That Didn't Make the News—The Year's Top 25 Censored Stories—2007.* New York: Stories Press, 2007. http://www.projectcensored.org/7-behind-blackwater-inc/.

Mazzetti, Mark and Mat Apuzzo. "Deep Support in Washington for CIA's Drone Missions" *New York Times* (April 25, 2015). http://www.nytimes.com/2015/04/26/us/politics/deep-support-in-washington-for-cias-drone-missions.html.

Joynar, James. "How Perpetual War Became U.S. Ideology." *The Atlantic* (May 11, 2001). http://www.theatlantic.com/international/archive/2011/05/how-perpetual-war-became-us-ideology/238600/.

Solomon, Norman. "Perpetual war creates endless consequences: Democrats who once spoke out against Bush's militarism have enabled Obama's." *Al Jazeera America* (July 13, 2015). http://america.aljazeera.com/opinions/2015/7/perpetual-war-creates-endless-consequences.html.

Lyster, Lauren. "Want to Cut Government Waste? Find the 8.5 Trillion the Pentagon Can't Account For." *Yahoo Finance: Daily Ticker* (November 25, 2013). http://finance.yahoo.com/blogs/daily-ticker/want-cut-government-waste-8-5-trillion-pentagon-142321339.html.

Paltrow, Scot J. "Behind the Pentagon's doctored ledgers, a running tally of epic waste." *Reuters.com* (November 18, 2013). http://www.reuters.com/investigates/pentagon/#article/part2.

Fallows, James and Jackie Lay. "The Pentagon's $1.5 Trillion Mistake." *The Atlantic* (December 29, 2014). http://www.theatlantic.com/video/index/384088/the-pentagons-15-trillion-mistake/.

Fischer, Brendan. "A Banana Republic Once Again?" The Center for Media and Democracy's *PR Watch* (December 27, 2010). http://www.prwatch.org/news/2010/12/9834/banana-republic-once-again.

Juhasz, Antonia, Special to CNN. "Why the War in Iraq was fought for Big Oil." *CNN.com* (April 15, 2013). http://www.cnn.com/2013/03/19/opinion/iraq-war-oil-juhasz/.

"Why we are in Afghanistan." *The Charleston Gazette. Global Exchange.org*. http://www.globalexchange.org/news/why-we-are-afghanistan.

Martin, Abby. "How Opium is Keeping US in Afghanistan: CIA's Shady History of Drug Trafficking." *MediaRoots.org* (January 3, 2014). http://mediaroots.org/opium-what-afghanistan-is-really-about/.

Grant, Zalin. "WHO MURDERED THE CIA CHIEF? William E. Colby: A Highly Suspicious Death." *Zalin Grant's War Tales*. Pythia Press. http://www.pythiapress.com/wartales/colby.htm.

CHAPTER FIVE

LEGALIZED SLAVERY: THE PRISON–INDUSTRIAL COMPLEX

This is the crime of which I accuse my country and my countrymen, and for which neither I nor time nor history will ever forgive them; that they have destroyed and are destroying hundreds of thousands of lives and do not know it and do not want to know it.[1]

—James Baldwin

Even conscientious people tend to get blurry, obscured vision when looking at the American correctional system. For openers, that's what it's actually called, folks—the *correctional* system. It's supposed to *correct* bad behavior, not enhance it.

Our entire system of incarceration is appallingly bad and—as it's being privatized now to corporations—it's in the process of getting appallingly worse. Did you know that many more Americans are raped *inside* our prisons, jails, and juvenile detention centers, than outside them? The Justice Department estimates that well over 200,000 people are "sexually abused in prisons and jails"—and that's quite probably a very low estimate.[2] That's about 600 people a day who are raped while they are in custody.[3] Many of those are juveniles and inmates accused—not even convicted, simply *accused*—of *non*violent crimes.[4] But that subject tends to make us uncomfortable. Therefore, we, as a society, tend to look the other way. And *worse*—we even tend to joke about it, in a feeble effort to allay our discomfort. One needs to look no further than television and movies to see a constant stream of questionable jokes about the certainty of gang rape in jail and in prison. Seemingly, folks consider it somehow "okay"— even funny—that a person incarcerated by the State will also be subjected to sexual violation during their incarceration. "Don't bend over to pick up the soap" and other such "one-liners" are part of a regular diet of attempted humor about a very unfunny topic: rape. But it's *still* rape. How can we joke about that?

We, as a society, seem to have a brutal double standard on that subject. If it becomes known that church altar boys—who are in a relatively helpless position—are sodomized by a priest, then there is a massive public outcry. But if prisoners or detainees—in *completely* helpless situations—are regularly sodomized, while under the auspices of the poorly termed "correctional system," the great majority of people pay no attention to it whatsoever. Is that acceptable? Is that morally just? Is there anybody who actually believes that isn't really rape?

Why do we tolerate that? We don't tolerate rape if it happens to a jogger running through a city park. Why do we tolerate it in our correctional system? Isn't it still rape? Of course it is. But we, as a society, somehow seem conditioned to lessen the importance of things like rape—even extremely brutal gang rapes—if they happen to people who have been incarcerated. It's something we don't completely understand, or *want* to understand, so we look the other way. And we tolerate jokes about it. Shame on us! *Really*. It's a shameful development. When you look at the extent of it and the devastating human impact on millions of lives, it's not just a human rights violation—it's an atrocity; a series of many *ongoing* atrocities, actually.

And while we've all been looking the other way on points like that, the entire correctional system has been hijacked, to a large extent, by some profiteering, self-centered folks who couldn't really care less about what happens to the millions of human beings now enslaved in that system. Unbeknownst to most Americans, our prison system has virtually been taken over by private corporations and turned into a business. While we've all been busily working away to make ends meet and making an effort to stay informed in what little spare time we have, a revolution has taken place behind our backs. It's a development that has largely escaped public attention, and media scrutiny; an "under the radar" issue. And it's a *big* problem.

We're very quick to note racism when a white police officer shoots an unarmed person of color. But it's a much different scenario when racism is institutionalized. That's what has happened in our so-called correctional system. When racism seems to be occurring on a massive scale—the virtual enslavement of millions of young adults of color—it somehow seems to escape the attention of mass media and the public at large. We can't see the forest because all those damn trees are in the way. Well, we're going to focus on those trees in that forest very clearly in this chapter and we're going to show you some numbers that are truly shocking.

You probably thought some communist country or "Third World" country has the highest percentage of its people locked away behind bars. China, or Uganda; someplace like that, right? Wrong. The level of incarceration in the United States *far* surpasses any other country in the world. The United States is by far the "world leader"—in a *bad* way—when it comes to the percentage of its people locked away behind bars. The United States only has 5 percent of the world's population but has "25 percent of the people in the entire world who are in jail or prison."[5] A recent study by the London School of Economics "points to the enormously high incarceration rate in the United States as evidence that it is time for a new strategy."[6] An article at *CBS Chicago* cites that study as merely one example of a system that is blatantly racist and in need of reform.

Think about that for a second. Isn't there something terribly wrong about those numbers? "That's half a million more than China, which has a population five times greater than the US. Many are incarcerated for nonviolent crimes, like the use or possession of marijuana, and other problems that would be far better served through a rehabilitation or education program."[7] Whereas, in other countries, unilateral drug decriminalization policies—even for narcotics like heroin—have proved to reduce addiction levels, reduce crime, and dramatically reduce the societal costs of drug use.[8]

America's "War on Drugs"—which one of the above-referenced articles rightly refers to as America's "Failed Drug Policies"—"has produced enormous negative outcomes and collateral damage," that same study concluded.[9] While it's true that drug offenders—and usually *non-violent* drug offenders—are a huge part of those large numbers for the United States, that only tells *part* of the story. The real tragedy is that minorities being housed in correctional institutions has become commonplace nationwide. As a Chicago official said recently regarding incarceration levels in his county: "86 percent of the people in my jail are black and brown."[10] Those alarming points have caused many observers to label incarceration as just a new form of slavery—because it unfairly punishes minorities.

In historical perspective, the whole scenario is even scarier. And political analyst Noam Chomsky puts it into perspective, detailing how the whole so-called "War on Drugs" is inherently racist:

> It's called the Drug War, and it's a racist war. Ronald Reagan was an extreme racist—though he denied it—but the whole drug war is designed, from policing to eventual release from prison, to make it impossible for black men and, increasingly, women to be part of society.[11]

That is the actual *design* of the system—to enslave minorities and limit their possibilities, just as it was when Africans were brought to America and sold as slaves.[12] The new system of enslavement is now less overt, but no less horrific. If you don't believe that, then you probably have not visited a prison recently.

> They have been re-criminalized and turned into a slave labor force— that's prison labor. This is American history. To break out of that is no small trick.[13]

We know that African-Americans are often targeted and literally even "set up" on false charges by police departments—that has been very well documented.[14] But the inherent racism systemic to our culture is even more overt and difficult to shed. This is an important distinction because— contrary to the accepted social precept of simply taking responsibilities for one's actions as a solution to the problem—it documents an ongoing *historical assault upon the freedom of black people specifically.*

Harsher sentencing guidelines—like mandatory prison sentences for drug offenders—unfairly punish those who cannot afford adequate legal representation, especially minorities: "The rise in incarceration has been even more striking than the decline in crime, leading to growing agreement on both the right and the left that it has gone too far. From the early 1970s to 2009, mainly because of changes in sentencing, the share of

American residents in state or federal prison multiplied fourfold, reaching 1.5 million on any given day, with hundreds of thousands more held in local jails . . . "[15] And that number, by the way, is now well over *2 million*— actually about 2.3 million prisoners.[16] And if you include all the nation's jails, that number rockets to almost *twelve million* Americans!

> Despite the country growing safer—with violent crime down 49 percent and property crime down 44 percent from their highest points more than 20 years ago—annual admissions to jails nearly doubled between 1983 and 2013 from 6 million to 11.7 million, a number equivalent to the combined populations of Los Angeles and New York City and nearly 20 times the annual admissions to state and federal prisons.[17]

While some saw that as injustice, others apparently saw it as *opportunity*— an increase in a potential labor source. As unbelievable and inhumane as it may seem, many corporations—and even elected officials—see prisons as a business. And they're making fortunes from it too, as unconscionable as that is.

The above accusation—that mass incarceration in the United States has reached a point where it's now legalized slavery—is made even more poignant by the point that the *labor* and even the *mere presence* of those convicts is being used to enrich some very unsavory folks who benefit from the massive number of incarcerated Americans. The book *Prison Profiteers: Who Makes Money From Mass Incarceration* is a collection of efforts that has extensively documented the widespread abuses of a system employing incarceration for profit. As that book points out, there is a "motley group of perversely motivated interests" that clearly *benefits* from mass incarceration.[18] And making money off of other people's misery is generally regarded as a pretty un-American thing to do. So if you want to call them scumbags, you go right ahead. And now we're going to show you who they are.

It starts—believe it or not—right at the level of the prisons and jails themselves. You probably think that the states and counties, or the Justice Department or other official entities like that, are the only ones entrusted with running our prisons and jails. Wrong, Wyatt Earp! Our state and federal politicians—God bless their souls (and God knows those souls of theirs are in need of blessing)—have been secretly "farming out" that responsibility to private corporations, for many years now. They refer to that as outsourcing. And they've been doing it for so long now that two large corporations have actually grown into gigantic multibillion-dollar corporations that are even listed on major stock exchanges, all from their profiteering on the prison sentences of millions of Americans, many of whom could not afford adequate legal representation. When they say that capitalism has its weak spots, we think it's fair to point out that this is no doubt one of the biggest.

Two companies you may have never even heard of—The Geo Group and Corrections Corporation of America—have amassed a combined market value of approximately $8 billion from their ambitious profiteering in human misery.[19] And some of their biggest shareholders—propagating the whole despicable system of making profit from human beings being locked up in cages on a massive scale—are the retirement funds of people like teachers and government employees who are completely unaware that they're financing a continuous money machine that feeds off human misery.[20] These type of corporations make huge donations to the political campaigns of state and federal politicians who, in turn, keep sending hundreds of thousands of predominantly minority offenders into a "correctional" system that houses them at a high price, and also benefits from their forced labor.[21] Good Lord Almighty, folks! What century did you say this was happening in? Because it sounds like Ancient Rome—or *worse*.

Like many corporations, Corrections Corporation of America has changed its name to one that is more euphemistic in an attempt to disassociate itself from ethically questionable issues like profiting from prison sentences. They are currently known as CoreCivic, Inc. And politicians give these companies "sweetheart deals" to make sure they get their contracts to build their prisons too; in exchange, of course, for a little corporate bribery in the form of ongoing campaign contributions that amount to the purchase of political influence.[22] "Some of the worst examples of juvenile injustice arise in this context, including the nepotistic dealings of Louisiana politicians willing to sell off the state's financial credibility and its imprisoned youth's safety for sweetheart deals and state-backed bonds. In exchange for selling off the rights to its juvenile facilities to the highest bidder, Louisiana's privately run juvenile facilities produced horror stories of Dickensian proportion . . . "[23] Great, huh? Like we said: What century did you say we're supposed to be living in?

And they're not the only ones. A whole slew of other companies—in fact, entire industries—have sprung up to take their share of the pie. Who *are* they? They are corporations that make everything from Taser stun guns to pharmacy prescription plans for inmates. Other examples of financial feasting on the human misery of others include a wide variety of companies and services:

- Manufacturers of helmets, shields, batons, stab-proof vests, Tasers, and chemical agents—known as the Law Enforcement Industry, with billions of dollars in sales, annually;
- Providers of medical and prescription services, a lucrative franchise that is auctioned off;
- Private prisoner transportation companies;
- Phone service providers;
- Food service contracts.

The whole thing seems to be getting dramatically out of control. "Even one-year-olds have been shocked, according to records Taser International supplied to the Associated Press. The company also told the *San Jose Mercury News* that its Taser can be used safely on toddlers."[24] *Can you believe* these people? Apparently, the newspaper failed to ask Taser International just how exactly they *know* that Tasers work fine on toddlers—and whose toddlers they had tried it on! But that's the mindset of these maniacs, just so you know.

They also make tons of money by "farming out" prison labor to big companies (as well as the US military), sometimes at a rate of pay to prisoners at less than $1 per day! One dollar per inmate, for a full day's work— that's right, you read correctly. The Minimum Wage Law is exempted in the prison business, courtesy of those same scumbag politicians. "When you can get that kind of labor for less than a dollar a day, it's hard to see the government's motivation for incarcerating fewer people. And it's all done at the taxpayer's expense."[25]

And you're not going to like the answer to this next question either. "Why has the number of children in private juvenile facilities increased by 95 percent in the past decade, *despite* a downward turn in juvenile crime in the same time period?"[26] Because there's <u>money to be made</u>, that's why! Lots of it too. The "prison industry" makes a whopping $4 billion dollars in profit a year and that's on the increase![27] And that $4 billion in profits is just from the companies who run the prisons. If you include the peripheral businesses making money from this horror story, that's many billions more. So <u>crime *does pay*</u>—just not for the people we thought. All serving to support a system in which the federal and state governments are actually motivated to incarcerate *more* Americans, not less.

Because *incarceration is now a business and prisoners are its product*! In fact, as a vivid example of that, a 2013 report revealed that "private prison companies are striking deals with states that contain clauses guaranteeing high prison occupancy rates—sometimes 100 percent. This means that states agree to supply prison corporations with a steady flow of residents—whether or not that level of criminal activity exists. Some experts believe this relationship between government and private prison corporations encourages law enforcement agencies to use underhanded tactics—often targeting minority and underserved groups—to fill cells."[28]

Minorities are targeted to *become* the product of the prison industry through a process known to criminal justice experts as "Million-Dollar Blocks"; where residents of the poorest urban centers are looked at as the gold mine for prison spending.[29] The book *Prison Profiteers* "investigates the phenomena of 'million-dollar blocks,' as illustrated by maps representing prison spending by neighborhood. The maps make clear that people in the poorest urban neighborhoods often have the highest 'price tags' per block, with an average of $30,000 per resident per year being spent to incarcerate a large percentage of these blocks' populations."[30]

The demographic norms simply don't hold up when you look at prison populations. They are blatantly racist. "Ninety-two percent of people incarcerated in federal and state prisons are men. Blacks and Latinos are only a quarter of the US population, but are almost 63% of the nation's incarcerated."[31] That's a pretty astounding inequity. *African-Americans and Latinos are not inherently more violent than whites. They are, however, subjects of a system which is inherently racist in respect to the rate at which it incarcerates Blacks and Latinos.*

The Feds created a corporation—Federal Prison Industries, also known as UNICOR—which employs tens of thousands of prisoners and only pays them between 23 cents and $1.15 per hour.[32] That company has used its captive labor pool to make a fortune. In 2002, they sold $687,700,000 in products to the US government.[33] How's that for "one hand washing the other"? They had $400 million in sales to the Defense Department![34] "In the past decade, the annual growth rate of increased private facilities has steadily risen by about 45 percent, with a bustling $33 billion annual profit."[35]

> Among the prominent companies that use or have used prison labor are Dell Computers, the Parke-Davis and Upjohn pharmaceutical companies, Toys R Us, Chevron, IBM, Motorola, Compaq, Texas Instruments, Honeywell, Microsoft, Victoria's Secret, Boeing, Nintendo, and Starbucks." Microsoft uses prison labor to ship its Windows software. "Honda pays $2 an hour to prisoners in Ohio to do the same job that members of the United Auto Workers union were once paid $20 an hour to do.[36]

Prison officials in some states such as Washington even advertised their prisoners by asking, "Are you experiencing high employee turnover? Worried about the cost of employee benefits? Getting hit by overseas competition? Having trouble motivating your workforce? Thinking about expansion space? Then the Washington State Department of Corrections Private Sector Partnerships is for you."[37] Yeah, right. What they're really sayin' is "Give it to *our* 'employees'—cause we'll use Tasers to make *sure* that they're motivated!"

And that cheap prison labor translates into fat corporate profits for these sleazebags too. While these prisoners are made to toil away in sub-human conditions, these bastards are making a fortune off of their forced labor:

> Meanwhile, America's prisons constitute a multibillion-dollar industry. UNICOR, also known as the Federal Prison Industries, reported net sales from prisoner-made products and services of $472 million in 2015, and this is only for federal institutions. Federal and state prisons combined are estimated to produce at least $2 billion in goods and services.[38]

Inhumane conditions abound in US prisons. For example, despite concerns stemming from a mass 60-day hunger strike by 30,000 inmates at the supermax Pelican Bay and elsewhere in the California prison system over two years ago—conditions are now getting even worse.[39] Now, in addition to being kept in *solitary confinement for 23 hours a day*—it is proposed that inmates can be punished extra just for participating in protests of any kind—like hunger strikes, for example.[40] And yes, we know—you probably haven't heard about any of this in the media. Neither have we. But that doesn't make it any less real.

Connecticut is one state that's *finally* doing something about the systematic levels of mass incarceration. "To shrink the prison population, they adopted several strategies, including reducing the number of people sent to prison for violating probation rules."[41] Connecticut used those savings to help programs that curbed the cycle of people returning to prison: especially mental health and drug treatment programs. It's highly commendable and it's working. As Michael Jacobson, former commissioner of the New York City Department of Corrections, observed: "It's the first state that through legislation has simultaneously done a bunch of things that will intelligently lower its prison population, and then reinvest a significant portion of that savings in the kind of things that will keep lowering its prison population."[42] That's clearly what's sorely needed. But you can bet that the prison-industrial complex is lobbying hard against it in every state. The prison industry is a $50 billion per year business in America.[43] It should be controlled, not allowed to run wild in a system that makes the original practice of slavery in this country seem almost mild in comparison.

The degree to which that system is unethical is laid bare by the words of the very companies that profit from it and seek to continue to profit from their heartless train of human misery. The following is straight out of the annual report of Corrections Corporation of America:

> The demand for our facilities and services could be adversely affected by the relaxation of enforcement efforts, leniency in conviction and sentencing practices, or through the decriminalization of certain activities that are currently proscribed by our criminal laws. For instance, any changes with respect to drugs and controlled substances

or illegal immigration could affect the number of persons arrested, convicted, and sentenced, thereby potentially reducing demand for correctional facilities to house them.[44]

So the prison industry lobbies for laws and practices that maximize punishment and create massive imprisonment.[45] What a nasty bunch of people, huh?

Unconscionable is the word that best describes this whole blood-for-money saga. At this point, it is a question of how much longer we can allow a system to be unethically misused simply for unconscionable corporate gain. Forty-three US Catholic bishops issued a formal statement raising the immoral issues of the privatization of prisons. It reads as follows:

> We believe that private prisons confront us with serious moral issues, demanding a gospel response. To deprive other persons of their freedom, to restrict them from contact with other human beings, to use force against them up to and including deadly force, are the most serious of acts. To delegate such acts to institutions whose success depends on the amount of profit they generate is to invite abuse and to abdicate our responsibility to care for our sisters and brothers.[46]

We sure do say Amen to that.

In August 2016, the US Department of Justice announced an "initiative" with which they were going to try to begin to "phase out" private contractor prisons.[47] It is an "attempt to cease its use of for-profit prisons, in the wake of a scathing inspector general investigation that found privately run detention centers are more dangerous and inefficiently run than public sector counterparts."[48]

But that's not as progressive as it sounds, because the phasing out—if it actually happens—is only for *federal* prisons. In reality, most of the prison contracts are with *non*-federal institutions, including immigrant detention centers where abuses abound. "The vast majority of the incarcerated in America are housed in state prisons—rather than federal ones—and Yates's memo does not apply to any of those, even the ones that are privately run."[49]

So they make it sound like some wide-sweeping change but it's not. "The directive is instead limited to the 13 privately run facilities, housing a little more than 22,000 inmates, in the Federal Bureau of Prisons system." But at least it's finally a step in the right direction.[50]

> Most private prison companies contract with the Department of Homeland Security (DHS), not the DOJ, to keep thousands of immigrants, including mothers and their children fleeing violence in Central America, in the same substandard, inhumane conditions the DOJ just denounced. Immigrant detention has exploded under the Obama administration, with conditions and treatment so horrific that the federal courts have stepped in.[51]

Describing the conditions in those privately run detention centers as horrific would be a massive understatement:

> Privately run facilities don't have the same legal obligation to provide information about their facilities as federally run prisons do, so most of what happens behind closed doors is a mystery. But we know it's bad. Detention centers hold nearly twice the number of inmates in solitary confinement as other federal facilities. Medical neglect is rampant and has contributed to many of the deaths of immigrants in DHS custody."[52]

And worse yet—it's we, the taxpayers, who are financing those abuses. These private prison corporations are making a fortune off the suffering of immigrant families, just like they rake in profits from the systematic persecution of minorities trapped within the "justice system"—what a name to give that Dickensian horror! And those grossly unjust corporate profits are all being paid for with tax dollars from all of us, folks.

The whole US prison system—and that includes jails, juvenile facilities, and immigrant detention centers—is a real nightmare. And it's a nightmare that it's high time we, as a society, finally wake up from.

If you'd like a great three-minute lesson on the travesty of the US prison system, just go online and listen to "San Quentin" by Johnny Cash.[53]

Search "Johnny Cash San Quentin" or go to: https://www.youtube.com/watch?v=1zgja26eNeY

That song says it all.

The system is not just "corrupt" or "broken" or in "disrepair." It is obscenely inhuman and requires dramatic correction.

FURTHER RESEARCH:

Herivel, Tara and Paul Wright, eds. *Prison Profiteers: Who Makes Money from Mass Incarceration*. New York: The New Press, 2007.

Alexander, Michelle. *The New Jim Crow: Mass Incarceration in the Age of Colorblindnes*s. New York: The New Press, 2010. http://www.kropfpolisci.com/racial.justice.alexander.pdf.

Winant, Howard. *The World is a Ghetto: Race and Democracy Since World War II*. New York: Basic Books, 2001.

Mauer, Marc. *Race to Incarcerate*. New York: The New Press, 1999.

Beckett, Katherine. *Making Crime Pay: Law and Order in Contemporary American Politics*. Oxford University Press, 1999.

Wilson, William Julius. *When Work Disappears: The World of the New Urban Poor*. New York: Vintage, 1997.

Beckett, Katherine and Theodore Sasson. *The Politics of Injustice: Crime and Punishment in America*. Thousand Oaks, CA: Sage Publications, 2004.

Greenwald, Glenn. *Drug Decriminalization in Portugal: Lessons for Creating Fair and Successful Drug Policies*. Washington, DC: Cato Institute, 2009. www.cato.org/pubs/wtpapers/greenwald_whitepaper.pdf.

Hatton, Barry and Martha Mendoza. "Portugal's Drug Policy Pays Off; US Eyes Lessons." Associated Press (Dec. 26, 2010). http://www.washingtontimes.com/news/2010/dec/26/portugals-drug-policy-pays-off-us-eyes-lessons/?page=all.

Kaiser, David and Lovisa Stannow. "Prison Rape and the Government." *The New York Review of Books* (March 24, 2011). http://www.nybooks.com/articles/ archives/2011/mar/24/prison-rape-and-government/.

Mauer, Marc. "Two-Tiered Justice: Race, Class and Crime Policy." Hartman, Chester and Gregory Squires, eds. *The Integration Debate: Competing Futures for American Cities*. London: Routledge, 2005.

Kaufman, Scott. "Noam Chomsky: Reagan was an 'extreme racist' who re-enslaved African-Americans." *Raw Story* (December 11, 2014). http://www .rawstory.com/2014/12/noam-chomsky-reagan-was-an-extreme-racist-who-re-enslaved-african-americans/.

Ingraham, Christopher. "The U.S. has more jails than colleges. Here's a map of where those prisoners live." *The Washington Post* (January 6, 2015). http://www. washingtonpost.com/blogs/wonkblog/wp/2015/01/06/the-u-s-has-more-jails-than-colleges-heres-a-map-of-where-those-prisoners-live/.

Subramanian, Ram and Ruth Delaney, Stephen Roberts, et al. "Incarceration's Front Door: The Misuse of Jails in America." The Vera Institute of Justice, Center on Sentencing and Corrections (July 29, 2015). http://www.vera.org/ sites/default/files/resources/downloads/incarcerations-front-door-report_02. pdf.

Buczynski, Beth. "Shocking Facts About America's For-Profit Prison Industry," *Truth-out.org* (February 6, 2014). http://www.truth-out.org/news/item/21694-shocking-facts-about-americas-for-profit-prison-industry.

Gonnerman, Jennifer. "Million-Dollar Blocks: The Neighborhood Costs of America's Prison Boom." *The Village Voice* (November 9, 2004). http://www. villagevoice.com/2004–11–09/news/million-dollar-blocks/.

Downs, Ray. "Who's Getting Rich off the Prison-Industrial Complex?" *Vice. com* (May 7, 2013). http://www.vice.com/read/whos-getting-rich-off-the-prison-industrial-complex.

Law, Victoria. "Two Years After Pelican Bay Hunger Strike, What's Changed for People Inside the Prison?" *Truth-out.org* (July 8, 2015). http://www.truth-out.org/news/item/31778-two-years-after-pelican-bay-hunger-strike-what-s-changed-for-people-inside-the-prison.

Knight, Sam. "Justice Department Announces Initiative to End Use of For-Profit Prisons." *The District Sentinel* (August 18, 2016). http://www.truth-out.org/news/item/37292-justice-department-announces-initiative-to-end-use-of-for-profit-prisons.

Preston, Julia. "Judge Orders Release of Immigrant Children Detained by U.S." *New York Times* (July 25, 2015). http://www.nytimes.com/2015/07/26/us/detained-immigrant-children-judge-dolly-gee-ruling.html?_r=0.

CHAPTER SIX:

BIG PHARMA: "SIDE EFFECTS" (SUCH AS ROBIN WILLIAMS'S SUICIDE) MAY VARY

What would you say if you knew someone had killed 60,000 people? Would you call it a felony of the worst kind, times 60,000? If you totaled up the value of all those lives in criminal court, what would you say they're worth? Billions? Trillions? Or—how about a measly $321 million in exchange for a guilty plea to a misdemeanor? When you consider that this involves the second-largest drug maker in the US—Merck—and its deadly drug Vioxx, then you'll probably agree that a misdemeanor and a 321-million-dollar fine amounts to nothing more than a slap on the wrist.[1]

—Dr. Joseph Mercola

Here's a news flash for you:
Robin Williams was murdered.

That's right. That's what happened, in our opinion—and in the opinions of many others too.[2] But he wasn't murdered by a thief in the night that killed him and made it look like a suicide. He was murdered by a system in which multi-billion-dollar corporate conglomerates disguise the fact that their drugs kill many thousands of people every single year. Could his prescription drugs have been the cause of his sudden increased paranoia that drove him to take his own life? That is probably what actually *did* happen to the great comedian and actor Robin Williams. That's why those huge drug companies spend fortunes on public relations to make it appear that they are not technically responsible for those tragedies.[3] But you sure as hell won't see that on the nightly news because, as you've probably noticed, Big Pharma commercials are their biggest corporate sponsors. We will show you the exact details of that case in just a minute. But first, a bit of history.

The *known* evils of the pharmaceutical industry are almost too numerous to mention. And when it comes to corrupted ethics, Big Pharma is evil "on steroids." They engage in activities that, for us, would be criminal. For them, it's just business as usual. "Pfizer, the world's largest drug maker, operates 151 subsidiaries in tax havens and officially holds $74 billion in profits offshore for tax purposes, the fourth highest among the Fortune 500."[4] If *you* do that, it's tax evasion and the IRS will come after you. When *they* do it, it's politically protected profit enhancement.

The drug business is the most profitable in the entire world of capitalism.[5] Total pharmaceutical revenue worldwide has now reached over one trillion US dollars per year.[6]

> US consumers are so price-gouged by pharmaceutical corporations that a well-known cancer drug costs $159 to produce and distribute a one-year supply. But in the UK, people are charged $30,000 and in the US, individuals must pay $106,000 for the same one-year supply."[7]

Large pharmaceutical firms spend hundreds of millions of dollars on political operations every year.[8] That's why they have so much clout on Capitol Hill—they *buy* it. That's how they get their tax breaks. That's how they keep a revolving door between Big Pharma and government agencies that are *supposed* to be watching out for consumers.[9] The result is utter disaster, as you will see in the following chart that we put together to display just a few of their epic failures:

Vioxx:	The drug giant, Merck, spent millions on the marketing and wide-scale promotion of their pain reliever, Vioxx. It was prescribed to over 20 million people.[10] Eventually, it became apparent that their drug was killing people—in fact, over 60,000 people.[11] And some investigators place the true figure of premature deaths from the drug at over half a million people.[12] It ended up being the biggest drug recall in history.[13] *Then* internal information from Merck,

	in documents that were leaked, not shared, revealed that the company actually *knew—for years*—about the dangers of their drug, but they promoted it to the unknowing public anyway and hid those dangers from the public.[14] That's the kind of ruthless greedy killers that we're talking about here. Both Merck and the FDA were criticized for their failure to the public in "ignoring evidence of the dangers of Vioxx before its eventual recall."[15]
Celebrex:	After Merck's fellow drug giant, Pfizer, marketed Celebrex, another pain-relieving prescription, to as many as 45 million users, it finally issued a recall on their drug.[16] The stated reason was a "link between the drug and serious cardiovascular problems including heart attack and stroke."[17]
Prozac:	Antidepressant marketed to millions by the gigantic pharmaceutical manufacturer, Eli Lilly. Many lawsuits have been filed for suicides or homicides by patients. "The lawsuits claim that the companies knew about, but hid the documents which showed increased risk of akathisia, a form of agitation causing suicide and violence. Payouts by Lilly estimated to be over $50 million to quietly settle more than 30 of those Prozac lawsuits."[18]
Paxil:	An antidepressant that was prescribed to millions of teenagers. "Paxil causes serious side effects, agitation, violent or suicidal behavior, painful withdrawal and addiction problems. It may cause birth defects in pregnant women. Both children and adults taking Paxil have demonstrated suicidal tendencies during treatment, while trying to quit and during withdrawal."[19] Paxil was a very dangerous drug that was *way* overprescribed—and incorrectly, at that. "According to a reanalysis of the original data from a 2001 study of paroxetine (Paxil) for teens with major depression, the drug was not effective and led to serious side effects, which is not how the results were presented 14 years ago."[20] But there are many billions of dollars at stake with the release

	of these drugs and the Big Pharma folks slant the results in their favor through rhetoric, misinterpretation, and skewing of the scientific interpretation of the data, plus good public relations work, in order to get to those big profits: "The drug never should have been prescribed in teens to treat depression, as it was through the first decade of the 2000s, according to a new study."[21] It was no more effective than a placebo (sugar pill) for any measure of depression.[22] Which is a fancy way of saying that tests showed the drug actually did nothing beneficial whatsoever. Yet they still managed to get it approved by the FDA and prescribed—very inappropriately—to millions of young users.
Risperdal:	Johnson & Johnson—a company with a market value of over $250 billion—was hiding the dangerous side effects of one of its major prescription drugs, Risperdal.[23] It excluded results from a 2003 study showing harmful effects from using their drug.[24] So they *knew* that—since at *least* 2003—and they hid that from the public, intentionally, and criminally. The public was not told about the harmful effects until 2015—and not because the manufacturer warned them—but because an erstwhile journalist obtained the results of the 2003 study.[25] Johnson & Johnson lost its case in trial in 2015, citing "grave mistreatment of children."[26] The company also "paid $2.2 billion two years ago to resolve criminal and civil allegations of illegally marketing Risperdal to children and the elderly."[27]

This stuff is still going on, *now, today*. And it seems like it will *keep* going on. And those are just the most famous cases. There are—literally—scores more of these murderous horror stories.

Now—the great Robin Williams, and the tragedy that took his life. We have all seen those prescription drug advertisements on television that have all the warnings at the end of the commercial for their latest "wonder drug." You know the ones we mean—where they name off ten or twenty possible "side effects" that come with the drug, and they sound a lot worse than whatever complaint the person might be taking the drug for, to begin with! They say things like, "Stop taking this drug immediately if your depression worsens or if you experience an increase in thoughts of suicide," and similar warnings. First of all, they should not even be called *side* effects—that is what the drug actually does to a person when they put it into their body. But they use semantics to make it sound like that's just something *else* that could happen. It's just a *side* effect.

And when we hear all those warnings at the end of their commercials, we tend to think "Yeah, but that probably hardly ever really happens," right? Or *so we hope*, at least. Well, we've got a news flash for you, folks. It happens *a lot*! In fact, let's take a closer look at that very high-profile Robin Williams case where it is very likely to have happened.

The media immediately proclaimed *en masse* that it was depression that drove Robin to suicide.[28] Mass media also informed us that no drugs were found in his body at autopsy: "These headlines couldn't be more wrong."[29] Lest we believe the polished innuendos of the Big Pharma media machine, let's take a close look at the facts of this case. Robin Williams had dealt with drug problems and depression issues for *decades*, and—it is important to note—he dealt with them *successfully*.[30] Robin was "receiving mental health 'treatment,' he was under the supervision of a psychiatrist, he was not abusing illegal drugs and he had not 'fallen off the wagon.'"[31] His struggles with cocaine and alcohol are well-documented *as are* his successful efforts to keep them under control. He had an established track record of achieving sobriety, including successful stints in rehab institutions.[32] "He had always been very open about his addiction, depression and stints in rehab, but his wife said he'd gotten his life back on track. They even celebrated on July 11, his sobriety date."[33]

That's actually more noteworthy concerning the man's true character than it probably sounds. To place it in proper perspective, cocaine was so prevalent in Hollywood in the 1970s and early 1980s, that more people were doing it at that time than were *not* doing it. Robin used to tell a story about when his managers began getting concerned that it might be a problem and suggested that he go see a doctor. The doctor asked him how much coke he was doing and Robin answered that he did about a gram of it every couple of days. "Then you don't have a problem," was basically that doctor's response because, back in those days, it was only considered habit forming, not addictive.[34]

But then, when the famous *Saturday Night Live* comedian John Belushi died of a drug overdose in 1982, it sent shock waves through the entertainment industry and, for some, it was a real "wake-up call."[35] For Robin Williams, who was expecting a child with his wife, it was a clear choice of which path his life was going down. He made that choice, quitting coke—and quitting it cold turkey too. And much to his credit, he succeeded and never went back—and that was way back in 1982. Alcohol posed a more complicated problem for him though, probably because of its wider use and acceptance. But, although he struggled with not using alcohol—he had a brief relapse in 2003 when he started drinking again for a period, while depressed on a movie-shoot up in Alaska—he successfully dealt with that issue again also.[36] Robin went into rehab, got sober, and stayed that way. He was, in fact, so diligent about staying sober that he even checked himself into a special program specializing in sustaining and maintaining long-term sobriety.[37]

Robin's wife substantiated that: "He was completely clean and sober when he died. And he had eight years of sobriety," she said, adding that he was happy.[38] So he was certainly more serious than most about maintaining his sobriety. And that also provides us with a good view of his mental fortitude concerning that issue—that he apparently had quite a bit of inner strength and personal resolve. So remember that important fact—he was clean and living sober in the period leading up to his death.[39] He was clean and living sober, we *should* say, except for the newly-prescribed pharmaceuticals which he was directed to take.

Why then, did he suddenly dissolve into deep depression, extreme paranoia, and suicidal action? Because *that's* the operative question. It wasn't illegal drugs—there were none found in his system.[40] It was not alcohol—there was none of that in his body either.[41] Therefore, *logically*, we should ask a very important question. What *was* found in his body?

Well, if you believe the crap that you hear on the news in this country, then you probably incorrectly believe that "no drugs were found" in the body after his suicide. That is simply and categorically not correct. Contrary to very misleading and incorrect reports in the mainstream media that "no drugs or alcohol" were found in Robin's body, very strong prescription drugs *were* present.[42]

If you read the original mainstream news reports about his suicide, they leave you with the impression that you'd have to be crazy to think that's what drove him to suicide.[43] Well, surprise, surprise, friends! You wouldn't be crazy *at all* to think that! Just keep reading. Because we are going to take a much *closer* look at that and believe you will be surprised at where it all leads.

Robin had been recently diagnosed with Parkinson's disease. Robin's wife concurred that his depression started to come on with the strong prescription drugs that he was being given for Parkinson's disease. "The depression didn't start to come on until about April or May, she said. That's when he started on antidepressants."[44] Robin's wife attributed his odd behavior to the start of the prescription drugs: "Robin's wife had told authorities shortly after his death he had been complaining about the meds and the way they made him feel," according to official court documents.[45]

Shortly after Robin's death, his old friend and fellow comedian, Rob Schneider, made statements on Twitter that directly blamed Big Pharma for the tragedy:

> Now that we can talk about it, #RobinWilliams was on a drug treating the symptoms of Parkinson's. One of the SIDE-EFFECTS IS SUICIDE!"[46]

A very interesting thing then happened:

> Supporters of Big Pharma quickly tried to deflect the accusation, suggesting that Robin Williams may have died from mixing his doctor-prescribed drugs with illegal drugs or even alcohol.[47] His wife Susan immediately jumped to her husband's defense, Tweeting, "Robin's sobriety was intact. And he was brave as he struggled with his own

battles of depression, anxiety, as well as early stages of Parkinson's disease, which he was not yet ready to share publicly."[48]

The media made it seem as though Mr. Schneider was an alarmist who was speaking without merit and Big Pharma's public relations people really came out swinging:

> It didn't take long for Wall Street's pharmaceutical corporations to enlist their high-priced advertising and PR agencies to go after Rob Schneider for his accusatory Tweets. The pharma giants also enlisted some of their highest paid news companies to inform the American people that prescription drugs had nothing to do with the suicide of Robin Williams.[49]

Can you believe that crap? Isn't that outrageous?

> Consider these facts when listening to people debate the safety and suicidal risks of so many Big Pharma drugs these days. Nobody paid comedian Rob Schneider a single cent to say what he did about the 100,000 preventable deaths caused by prescription drugs in America and their link to suicides . . . Rob Schneider simply said what he truly believes—pharmaceutical drugs are murdering more Americans every year by accident than any other cause, including car accidents and firearms.[50]

Take a look at who ganged up on Rob Schneider:

> Now look at who's on the other side of the prescription drug debate. America's broadcast media networks like ABC News that immediately jumped to Big Pharma's defense were paid a combined $27 billion in 2012 by the very same pharmaceutical corporations. The allegedly impartial "doctors" the corporate news outlets like to hold up as unbiased experts were themselves showered with a combined $24 billion in "promotional" spending by pharmaceutical corporations in 2012.[51]

And get a load of *this*:

Lies and propaganda, but not from Rob Schneider

Showing how determined Big Pharma is to distance themselves from Robin Williams's violent suicide, they enlisted no less than *Good Morning America* to defend the world's pharmaceutical corporations. GMA is a property of ABC News, which is a property of ABC, which is owned by The Walt Disney Company—one of the largest recipients of Big Pharma money each year.[52]

Are you beginning to understand what a rigged game the whole thing is?

GMA quickly blasted comedian Rob Schneider yesterday writing, "Parkinson's disease experts say Schneider is out of line." The corporation's hand-picked expert was Dr. Irene Richard, a professor of neurology and psychiatry at the University of Rochester and an adviser to the Michael J. Fox Foundation for Parkinson's Research. She told *Good Morning America*, "Suicide is of no more concern in patients with Parkinson's versus those who don't have Parkinson's." Notice Rob Schneider never said Robin Williams's suicide was caused by his Parkinson's disease, like the doctor attempted to refute. Instead, Schneider blamed Williams's suicide on the prescription drugs he was taking."[53]

So, the Big Pharma media machine will tell you that the above conclusions are just an alarmist opinion by "nonprofessionals" like Robin's Hollywood friends. But—properly analyzed—it should not be a minority opinion, folks. The evidence is overwhelming:

"23,755 suicides are attributed to psychiatric drugs each year in the US alone."[54]

And the number of preventable deaths from prescription drugs annually is an absolutely *astounding* figure that we never hear about:

The *Journal of The American Medical Association* published papers which indicated that approximately 106,000 Americans die from pharmaceutical drugs each year. Now, these are drugs that are properly prescribed, not physician errors. And these are side effects that are normally expected. And these are people who took the medication as directed. This doesn't count overdoses or misuses.[55]

That is *mass murder*, if you ask us, folks. Rob Schneider was right.
 Let's look at the drugs that *were* present in Robin's body.

The medical examiner's report cites an antidepressant drug was in Williams's system at the time of his death. The particular antidepressant, Mirtazapine, (also known as Remeron) carries 10 international drug regulatory warnings on causing suicidal ideation.[56]

Remeron is an extremely dangerous prescription drug:

Remeron Drug Warnings:

There have been 18 drug regulatory agency warnings from four countries (United States, Australia, United Kingdom, and Canada) and the European Union. These include the following (note that some warnings cite more than one side effect, so the list below may not be equal to the total number of warnings):

10 warnings on Remeron causing suicidal thoughts/behavior/risk;
4 warnings on Remeron causing hostility/aggression;
3 warnings on Remeron causing anxiety;
2 warnings on Remeron causing birth defects;
1 warning on Remeron causing hallucination.[57]

Moreover, as proof of the potential severity of these dangers, the FDA issued the necessity of a "black box warning"—for <u>increased suicidality</u>— for Remeron: "Black-box warnings are the strictest warning that can be carried by a drug."[58] It reads:

WARNING: Suicidality and Antidepressant Drugs
    Antidepressants increased the risk compared to placebo of suicidal thinking and behavior (suicidality) in children, adolescents, and young adults in short-term studies of major depressive disorder (MDD) and

other psychiatric disorders. Anyone considering the use of REMERON®
(mirtazapine) Tablets or any other antidepressant in a child, adolescent,
or young adult must balance this risk with the clinical need. Short-
term studies did not show an increase in the risk of suicidality with
antidepressants compared to placebo in adults beyond age 24; there was
a reduction in risk with antidepressants compared to placebo in adults
aged 65 and older. Depression and certain other psychiatric disorders
are themselves associated with increases in the risk of suicide. Patients of
all ages who are started on antidepressant therapy should be monitored
appropriately and observed closely for clinical worsening, suicidality, or
unusual changes in behavior. Families and caregivers should be advised of
the need for close observation and communication with the prescriber.
REMERON® is not approved for use in pediatric patients.[59]

And guess what? It gets worse. A *lot* worse:

In the surrounding area of Williams's home, a prescription for
the antipsychotic Seroquel was also found. It is known that many
antipsychotics can significantly alter healthy brain functioning and
impair overall cognition. Based on information available to those
who surveyed the suicide, it appeared as though Williams had taken
Seroquel. Since it wasn't in his body, he may have been going through
early stages of Seroquel withdrawal, which may account for increased
depression and/or agitation.[60]

Would you like to know—having read the above—the specific Seroquel
withdrawal symptoms possibilities? Well, drum roll, please—here they are!

Suicidal thoughts: Many people take this medication to help with
suicidal thoughts and depression. When you quit taking it, you may
feel more suicidal than you have ever felt. This is due to the fact that
your neurotransmitter levels are out of balance and you are no longer
receiving the drug to help.[61]

Health officials have been worried about Seroquel's side effects for quite
some time and have expressed those concerns publicly.[62] "Federal health

experts said overwhelmingly Wednesday (September 30, 2009) that the side effects of AstraZeneca's schizophrenia drug Seroquel are too worrisome to make it a first choice against depression."[63]

"Increased paranoia" is a very accurate description of Robin Williams's behavior immediately prior to his suicide. Until his prescription drugs had started bothering him, which he had complained about to his wife, he had been exercising, and was in control of his demons—he was drug-free except for his medical prescriptions.[64]

The Coroner's Investigative Report specifically noted "a recent increase in paranoia."[65] It also found that there were no illicit drugs or alcohol in his body, and noted regular levels of his prescription drugs."[66] As noted, for many decades, Robin successfully dealt with more serious problems than he was facing at the time of his death, depression-wise, drug-wise, alcohol-wise, and career-wise. In fact, he was recently signed up for a sequel to the big movie hit, *Mrs. Doubtfire*, the most popular film of his career. The *one* denominator that was different was that he was now taking prescription drugs for Parkinson's disease.

A documentary examining the suicide produced some important observations:

> A coroner's report determined he was likely suffering from Lewy body dementia—which Dr. Shepherd believes may have triggered his unusual behavior, as his online activity prior to taking his own life insinuates the father of three knew "there was something else wrong with him," he explains in the controversial program.[67]

Those types of actions are consistent with Seroquel withdrawal symptoms.[68]

> His wife, Susan Schneider, has said the Academy Award winner—who was suffering from Parkinson's disease at the time of his death—was acting very paranoid when he crammed his collection of watches into a sock and took it to a friend for safekeeping. Pathologist Richard Shepherd explains, "This is a very peculiar incident that his wife describes as typically increasing paranoia that he had been suffering."[69]

It was not until April 2014 that they started Robin on antipsychotic drugs. After he had suffered a panic attack in April, his doctor began prescribing him antipsychotics:[70]

> Susan would later find out, months after her husband's death, that antipsychotics can cause severe reactions in people with LBD (Lewy body dementia), and in some cases even worsen their cognitive and physical symptoms.[71]

It was not until May that Robin was officially diagnosed with Parkinson's; his doctors changed his medication again in July and by August, his symptoms seemed to be improving—until his sudden suicide on August 11.[72]

Robin's wife also informed us that it was "nearing the end of July," during the last couple weeks prior to his death, when Robin's Parkinson's medication was changed from Mirapex to Sinemet.[73] Sinemet is from Big Pharma giant, Merck, and is known for some very bizarre "side effects" in patients.[74] For example, in some patients Sinemet has caused an overpowering "out-of-control" urge to gamble or engage in sexual activity to the extent that it becomes obsessive and self-destructive.[75] Moreover, one of the many warnings on what "side effects" to watch out for when taking the drug Sinemet are the following: "confusion, hallucinations, anxiety, agitation, depressed mood, thoughts of suicide or hurting yourself."[76]

> For example, the US Food and Drug Administration warns that patients taking either levodopa or Sinemet, two drugs commonly used to treat Parkinson's, "should be observed carefully for the development of depression with concomitant suicidal tendencies."[77]

Merck, the manufacturer of Sinemet, makes billions of dollars from selling prescription drugs. And if you go to the "Side Effects Center" at the "Patient Monograph" for that drug, the folks there supposedly protecting our health actually have the nerve to say on their warning list that "Many people using this medication do not have serious side effects."[78] Well, as anyone who has ever taken a class in logic can deduce from that statement, that also means that many people using that medication *do* have serious side effects.

So there were probably at least four different powerful prescription drugs that Robin had apparently been given by doctors in his final months:

- Mirtazapine, also known as Remeron, was found in his body at the time of death and it carries 10 international drug regulatory warnings on causing suicidal ideation.[79]
- Seroquel is an antipsychotic that "can significantly alter healthy brain functioning"—it was not in his body at the time of death but it was reportedly found in his home and the withdrawal symptom warning when a person *stops* taking Seroquel is dramatically increased suicidality.[80]
- Mirapex, known to cause "mental/mood changes (e.g., confusion, depression, hallucinations, memory problems), unusual strong urges (such as increased gambling, increased sexual urges)."[81] It should also be noted that a study determined that "Parkinson's disease itself doesn't seem to raise a person's risk for compulsive addictions to things like gambling, shopping, or sex," it's the *treatment* of Parkinson's with drugs that seems to cause it.[82] Adverse reactions to Mirapex include *Hallucinations and Psychotic-like Behavior* in many patients.[83] Robin was apparently taken off Mirapex shortly before his death.[84] Stopping Mirapex can result in mental confusion.[85]
- Sinemet was prescribed for Robin shortly before his death.[86] It is known to cause "confusion, hallucinations, anxiety, agitation, depressed mood, thoughts of suicide or hurting yourself," as well as "out-of-control" urges.[87]

The combination of powerful drugs that Robin had taken after his diagnosis of Parkinson's three months prior to his death apparently had an intense effect upon his mental condition, just as they have for millions of others. Remember that number: 106,000. That's the number of Americans who die from "properly prescribed" pharmaceutical drugs each year and their "side effects that are normally expected."[88]

Therefore, after what we have learned from looking closer than mainstream media did into the *real* situation surrounding the death of Robin

Williams—from now on, any time you hear some weird story in the news about some crazy parent doing some outrageous act to their children (which is the strongest bond in the world) or some other bizarre act, you have to wonder if the *real* blame is actually the "side effects" of some mind-blowing pharmaceutical drug.

But hey, the big public relations firms that handle the spin for Big Pharma were technically correct. As the big PR people put it in mainstream media: Parkinson's disease wasn't responsible for Robin Williams's suicide. But, as we just showed you, the *drugs* that he was *prescribed* for Parkinson's disease very likely were responsible for his suicide. And we hope that really pisses you off. Because *it should*!

And who do you think controls the medical literature? And censors what they don't like in the medical literature? If you guessed the drug companies, you're right. If an established medical journal like the *Journal of Orthomolecular Medicine* (nutritional therapy) publishes a study proving that high doses of nutrients actually can cure disease, guess what happens? You're not going to hear about it. Because that study will not be indexed by the US National Library of Medicine.[89] So you won't hear it on the news. The medical literature, if it is alternative to the mainstream, is effectively censored.[90]

> So that what looks like pure, scientific, academics researching journals publishing on the whole edifice of science has actually been turned by the drug companies into an arm of their marketing department.[91]

Most people don't even come close to realizing the extent of the damage that Big Pharma does. Did you know that many of the mass shootings that have plagued the American landscape of late are the apparent result of legal pharmaceutical prescriptions?[92] But whenever there is another mass shooting, the traditional media focus has been on the debate for gun control. Yet, as we have learned from extensive research for this book, that is *not* all that is really going on. America's historical problems with gun use and availability have worsened into an explosion of violence linked to prescribed psychiatric drugs. It is now evolved into a problem that is like a national psychosis on steroids. Why do you think America has so many of these mass shooting incidents, to begin with?

Other countries don't—not like us. The apparent reason is <u>psychiatric prescription drugs</u>. That is often the underlying cause.[93] And with 1 in 4 Americans taking one or more psychiatric drugs, and 183 million people taking them worldwide—it's a problem of dramatic proportions that is not going away anytime soon unless we take measures to address it.[94]

> **Fact**: At least 35 school shootings and/or school-related acts of violence have been committed by those taking or withdrawing from psychiatric drugs resulting in 169 wounded and 79 killed (in other school shootings, information about their drug use was never made public—neither confirming or refuting if they were under the influence of prescribed drugs).

> **Fact**: Between 2004 and 2012, there have been 14,773 reports to the US FDA's MedWatch system on psychiatric drugs causing violent side effects including: 1,531 cases of homicidal ideation/homicide, 3,287 cases of mania, and 8,219 cases of aggression. Note: The FDA estimates that less than 1 percent of all serious events are ever reported to it, so the actual number of side effects occurring are most certainly higher.[95]

The drug companies and the government agencies who you would *think* would investigate such matters, to date, very sadly, have not—but private researchers have documented the cases linking mass shootings with psychiatric drugs.[96] In fact, an excellent article—"Another Mass Shooting, Another Psychiatric Drug? Federal Investigation Long Overdue"—is available online and it details the drug links and the specific incident details with 35 mass shootings and 25 additional murders and murder-suicides that resulted in 251 dead and 134 wounded (that's in addition to the 35 mass shootings).[97] They were *all* prescription-related.[98] You can access that article at:

http://www.cchrint.org/2012/07/20/the-aurora-colorado-tragedy-another-senseless-shooting-another-psychotropic-drug/

Research studies back those findings up too. Here are the conclusions of one British study exploring the phenomenon of mass shootings:

We did a whole study on those school shootings over in America. And we studied a number of these incidents. And in most cases—in most cases the shooter is either *on* or withdrawing *from* these types of psychiatric medications at the time that they commit these offenses. And yet none of this stuff really comes out in the trials at all.[99] The numbers are incredible: "One hundred million people worldwide are on psychiatric drugs."[100]

You can also download an excellent study online, free from *Whistleblower Magazine*, called "MANIA: The shocking link between psychiatric drugs, suicide, violence and mass murder":

http://www.wnd.com/2007/07/42434/

And if you haven't heard about those studies then we're not really that surprised! And you shouldn't be either. But eventually, we often learn that the shooter's doctors had him drugged-up to the gills on concoctions of psychiatric prescription drugs. Another guy gets turned into a drug-crazed nut-job by some crazy combination of strong mind-altering prescriptions and then *boom*, he goes off the edge and we have yet another mass shooting.

> There is overwhelming evidence that psychiatric drugs cause violence. Twenty-two international drug regulatory warnings cite violence, mania, hostility, aggression, psychosis, and even homicidal ideation . . . Recent examples of individuals under the influence of such drugs including Navy Yard shooter Aaron Alexis and Fort Hood shooter Ivan Lopez.[101]

So let's put it plainly:

Access to guns is not the only cause of mass shootings. Access to psychiatric prescription drugs often is. And that's why researchers have called upon law enforcement and policy makers to *address the link* between Big Pharma's drugs and the violence they apparently incite: "Law enforcement must finally acknowledge the very real threat of violence that is unquestionably associated with psychiatric treatment and drugging . . . " or we may never see an end to all these mass shootings.[102]

We also currently face an epidemic of returned veterans who are dying young from suicides and drug interactions:

"Antipsychotics and antidepressants have been linked to many of the deaths."[103]

A clear link has been established between the suicides of returning veterans and combinations of prescribed antidepressants.[104] Health journalist Martha Rosenberg has documented how deadly mixes of "prescription cocktails" to treat PTSD (post-traumatic stress disorder) have been linked to the sudden deaths of soldiers returning from war.[105]

The autism epidemic is another recent phenomenon and the drug industry and government agencies are in denial of it. But it is very real. For over five decades, the rate of autism in the United States was only 1 in 10,000 but in the past twenty years it has recently skyrocketed to 1 in 68.[106] That's a staggering increase and a graph depicting that is a moving sight, detailing a steady and dramatic rise.[107] It is now of epidemic proportions: Autism now affects 2 percent of children in the United States, one child in every fifty.[108] And it just keeps going up—the 2015 findings were that it is now 1 in 45.[109] "A once rare disorder is now so common that everyone knows someone with an affected child. Yet neither mainstream doctors nor government officials can tell the American public what is behind the staggering rise in diagnoses."[110]

The common link that can and should no longer be ignored is the increased number of childhood vaccines—a multibillion-dollar industry—during the exact same period. Jim Moody, an attorney well versed on the issue, spells it out point blank:

It's unquestionably environmental. The science points to vaccines.[111]

And medical experts who actually know what they are talking about do back up that conclusion. Boyd Haley, PhD, is former Chairman of the Department of Chemistry at the University of Kentucky. His research clearly points in the exact same direction:

It's got to be the vaccines. It's the only thing that went up in all fifty states at the same time.[112]

The mercury-based preservative, Thimerosal, invented by the drug giant, Eli Lilly and Company, was added to vaccines increasingly during the time period that autism rates skyrocketed. As Dr. Haley put it:

> Everyone knows that genetics can't cause an epidemic . . . You have to have the toxin.[113]

Thimerosal is not even a necessary component of the vaccines, it's just a preservative to make them easier to handle. But there are a lot of profits in its production. Vaccines are big, big business. Thimerosal adds to the life span of the vaccines, making them a more profitable product; it gives Big Pharma companies "a very cheap option to give vaccines more shelf life."[114] It's the cheapest option available to vaccine producers.[115] The work of environmentalist Robert F. Kennedy, Jr. establishes a clear case of Thimerosal being the toxin that is to blame for a health epidemic and he considers the issue so important that he wrote a book about it.[116] The title of that book says it all: *Thimerosal: Let the Science Speak: The Evidence Supporting the Immediate Removal of Mercury—a Known Neurotoxin.*

Thimerosal has a very high level of toxicity. A great documentary, *Trace Amounts: Autism, Mercury and the Hidden Truth*, establishes—scientifically—that Thimerosal is one of the deadliest chemicals ever invented and is extremely toxic *even* in dosage so low that it is not grams, or milligrams, or micrograms, but *nanograms*, which are a few *parts per billion*.[117]

That documentary also points out that the huge risks associated with the use of Thimerosal are considered acceptable in the drug industry for one reason and one reason only: *profit*.[118] As usual, it's all about the money, even if the health problems concurrent with its use are devastating. Vaccines are over a $25-billion-per-year business and their revenue keeps going up.[119]

> It has nothing to do with the greater good. It has everything to do with the greater greed.[120]

The lethal effects of Thimerosal have been evident for decades, cited in many published papers on the chemical's dangers—but Eli Lilly and Company continued its mass use.[121] And, tragically—as of the publication date of this book—it is still being used in vaccines. If you had a regular flu shot, it had a large amount of Thimerosal.[122] Even a Congressional study by Chairman Dan Burton concluded that "Thimerosal used as a preservative in vaccines is likely related to the autism epidemic."[123] The solution is so obvious and simple that it's astounding that it has taken this long to make it an issue:

If in doubt, take it out!
Stop putting the damn mercury in the vaccines you make for our children! Or in anybody else, for that matter. It's so crazy that it's hard to believe that has not been done yet. It's so obvious, it's ridiculous. And get all the toxicity out of *all* vaccines. The vaccine industry is even pushing "mercury-free" vaccines that are injections where the Thimerosal is replaced with dangerous levels of aluminum—as a "preservative"—which could even be worse than the mercury in Thimerosal![124] Are these people insane, or what? But the beat just goes on and on and on. "Beam me, up, Scotty."

If in doubt, take it out!
And stop telling lies to people! The CDC (Centers for Disease Control and Prevention) has rigged the research to cover up the established links between vaccines and autism.[125] It's hard to believe these maniacs who are determining what is put into our children's bodies, in fact, *don't*! Don't blindly believe them when it comes to your child's health.

Vaccines with trace amounts of Thimerosal are labeled "preservative-free." But, as the CDC openly admits, even the vaccines being touted as "preservative-free" actually contain "trace amounts" of Thimerosal, which they define as less than .3 micrograms. But .3 micrograms of Thimerosal is still toxic to the human body.[126] If they tell you it has "trace amounts" then that is an unacceptable health risk, as the film *Trace Amounts* clearly establishes.[127] So pay attention to this important differentiation:

> Vaccines with trace amounts of Thimerosal are labeled "preservative-free." Vaccines that do not contain any thimerosal are labeled "Thimerosal-free."[128]

You have the right to always insist on vaccinations that are totally free of mercury and aluminum and they *can* be obtained.[129] But most of the flu vaccines distributed in the United States, and many other vaccines as well, still contain Thimerosal as a preservative.[130] And that is a fact that should scare you.

And speaking of vaccines—be very careful about your sources of information. The CDC manipulates data to justify the mass use of vaccines and enrich the drug companies.[131] But you won't read about that in mainstream media, because it was a censored story, so you will have to get the book *Project Censored: The News That Didn't Make the News*. Also, just so you are aware of it, the US government has paid out $3 billion to vaccine-injured Americans since 1989.[132] So it would be extremely naive to blindly accept them as safe.

The *British Medical Journal's* Roy Moynihan has made an astounding observation about the latest spin of the pharmaceutical industry: "There's a lot of money to be made telling healthy people they're sick."[133] They are literally convincing people that they are diseased, so that they can sell them more pharmaceuticals.[134]

A perfect example of that "disorder creation"—and its mainstream acceptance—is the fact that FSD (female sexual dysfunction) is now to be classified as a specific disease. The reason is to create the need to "treat" FSD with every kind of drug imaginable, especially what has been called "female Viagra."[135] The big drug giant, Valeant Pharmaceuticals recently spent a billion dollars to acquire a company that has been rumored to have what could be the female version of Viagra.[136] But, as the excellent documentary, *Orgasm Inc.*, drives home, female sexuality is not as simple a matter as taking a little pill to enhance their drive, nor does it actually work in such a way—it's all an invention for drug companies to create another multibillion-dollar marketing opportunity.[137] In fact, as that documentary observes, the best way they could help women sexually would be to give men (and even some women) a map leading to the clitoris!

But the drug companies don't make their billions of dollars every year by teaching men how to stimulate their lovers—they make billions by selling people drugs. So instead, they needed to be able to get women to take prescription drugs to *sell* them a happy sex life—and to be able to do that, they needed to reclassify ordinary sex life imperfections as a new disease. A big stir was caused by a great article in the *British Medical Journal* about that—and the title says it all: "The making of a disease: female sexual dysfunction—*Is a new disorder being identified to meet unmet needs or to build markets for new medications?*" That article makes some huge points:

> The corporate-sponsored creation of a disease is not a new phenomenon, but the making of female sexual dysfunction is the freshest, clearest example we have. A cohort of researchers with close ties to drug companies are working with colleagues in the pharmaceutical industry to develop and define a new category of human illness at meetings heavily sponsored by companies racing to develop new drugs.[138]

The conflicts of interest are almost as obvious as the issues with ethics and facts of the matter:

> Researchers with close ties to drug companies are defining and classifying a new medical disorder at company-sponsored meetings;
> The corporate-sponsored definitions of "female sexual dysfunction" are being criticized as misleading and potentially dangerous;
> Commonly cited prevalence estimates, which indicate that 43% of women have "female sexual dysfunction," are described as exaggerated and are being questioned by leading researchers;
> Controversy surrounds current attempts to medicalize sexual problems and establish "normative data" for a range of physiological measurements of female sexual response;
> The role of drug companies in the construction of new conditions, disorders, and diseases needs more public scrutiny.[139]

It has been established that the research is very slanted. Moynihan further observed that "The key meetings, through the mid to late 1990s and onward, the key medical and scientific meetings, where this new condition called Female Sexual Dysfunction was being debated, and defined, and refined, *all* of them were sponsored by the drug industry."[140] Now it is a case of "We, the drug company, define the disease. Why, on earth would we want a drug company involved in developing or defining a disease? Clearly they have a vested interest in maximizing the numbers of people they target with their drugs, so they'll define the disease as big and broad and wide as possible."[141] And that's exactly what they did with FSD. In fact, they defined it so broadly that 43% of all women can be targeted with their new drugs to address it.

> If they can transform very common female sexual difficulties into Female Sexual Dysfunction and treat it with a pill, then that's a bonanza for their shareholders . . . There's a lot of money to be made telling healthy people that they are sick.[142]

Further research established that the figure of 43% for women with FSD was broadly misdiagnosed. Even the sociologist who surveyed the women for that study making the claim that it applied to 43% of all women, said himself that "A lot of these 43% of women are perfectly normal. And a lot of their problems arise out of perfectly reasonable responses of the human organism, to challenges and stress."[143] But if you think the drug companies are going to tell you that, the answer is *Hell no, they're not!* They're going to tell you over and over and over again on their commercials that 43% of all women suffer from female sexual dysfunction. Because they want to sell them drugs! So they take it to the airwaves and they sponsor "medical experts" to go on television and parrot the views that market their own corporate scenario: "Medical experts pushed the concept of Female Sexual Dysfunction."[144] But get a load of this: "Most of the medical experts had financial ties to the pharmaceutical industry, but did not disclose them."[145]

> The pharmaceutical industry—through a whole range of very sophisticated PR and marketing strategies is actually changing how we all think about our bodies, about our health, and about our diseases.[146]

And just because their mass marketing works—and makes them *billions* in the process—does not translate into people actually being healthier. It just means that they *sell* more: "The USA makes up just 5% of the world's population but it accounts for 42% of the world's spending on prescription drugs. And yet we don't live any longer than others."[147]

Only a very small percentage of so-called "new drugs" are really new—most are just new issues and combinations of existing compounds, which industry people call "Me Too" drugs.[148] Nexium, the "healing purple pill," was the successor to Prilosec, the original "purple pill." They're the same drug (they just added a yellow stripe!). There is little or no difference between Nexium and Prilosec, but it created a new market and Nexium *costs seven times as much*.[149]

When a billion-dollar drug like Prozac went generic, its manufacturer, Eli Lilly and Company, simply repackaged the *exact same drug and dosage of the exact same compound* and introduced it as the "new" drug, Sarafem.[150] It's bullshit beyond belief! The "fem" part of that name is because they *also* invented a "new disorder" to go along with their "new" drug and, therefore, through the magic of US medical legislation, Eli Lilly holds a patent on their "new" drug that is the only thing that can be prescribed for the new disorder.[151] By the way, the "new disorder," PMDD (premenstrual dysphoric disorder), is actually something that has been around ever since human beings have walked the earth.[152] You may know it as PMS, or monthly premenstrual syndrome. So women were being prescribed "Sarafem" like crazy, but they had no idea that it was really just Prozac renamed. It's amazing, the games that these bastards play with our health is absolutely disgraceful. The message for We, The People is very, very clear:

Don't Buy Into Their Bullshit!

Dr. Marcia Angell was editor in chief of the *New England Journal of Medicine* and then Senior Lecturer in the Department of Global Health and Social Medicine at Harvard Medical School. She has written critically acclaimed books, lectured around the country, and was named one of the "25 Most Influential Americans" by *TIME Magazine* in 1997.[153] So she's been around the medical block more than most and is very aware of what is happening on that playing field. And listen to her conclusion about those drug commercials, the influence of Big Pharma, and what they say about their prescription drugs:

> It is self-evidently absurd to look to a company for impartial, critical education about a product it sells.[154]

Dr. Angell and other medical critics explored the whole disorder-creation-and-medication for the documentary, *Big Bucks, Big Pharma: Marketing Disease and Pushing Drugs*. Here's a short excerpt:

DR. ANGELL: What Eli Lilly was very successful in doing to expand its market on Prozac, was to essentially recolor it, instead of a green capsule, made it pink, rename it, Sarafem, and get approval to market it for premenstrual tension, which it called Premenstrual Dysphoric Disorder.

ABC News: Drug manufacturer Eli Lilly launched a $30 million marketing campaign to inform women about their new drug that promises relief. The problem is, Sarafem is not new, and the condition it's being advertised to treat may not even exist.

LARRY SASICH (Doctor of Pharmacy): Prozac and Sarafem are exactly the same thing, it's all a matter of image.

SARAFEM ADVERTISEMENT: The first and only prescription medication for PMDD.

LARRY SASICH: Once again, the pharmaceutical industry, through its advertising ingenuity is able to sell us almost anything, even old drugs as new drugs.

DR. ANGELL: A lot of women would really be outraged if they knew that they were just taking good old Prozac—same dose, same dose—but priced, at my drug store anyway, over three times as much as generic Prozac.

ABC NEWS: Fueling the debate, Sarafem's marketing blitz started just before Eli Lilly lost its exclusive patent to sell Prozac, a drug that generates $2 billion in sales each year. With Sarafem, the company obtained a new patent, and for now, they are the only company that can market a treatment for PMDD.

KATHERINE GREIDER (author of *The Big Fix: How The Pharmaceutical Industry Rips Off American Consumers*): The whole process of creating disease awareness is controversial, and I think it's sort of a question that we should decide as a society. And what bothers me about it is it's being promoted by an industry that has its own motivations, which have nothing to do with our culture or our physical well-being, or really our health as a society.

DR. ANGELL: I can't help but think that there are millions of Americans who are taking drugs that they probably don't need and may even be harmful. That they're being convinced, and their doctors are being convinced that they should take life-long drugs that probably are of no net benefit and may be of net harm.

So the reason that Sarafem was the only medication for PMDD is because the drug company created the disease: "Premenstrual Dysphoric Disorder" didn't exist before they needed to re-market Prozac.[155] As Dr. Bob Goodman of Colombia University Medical Center puts it:

> Of all the things that industry does, this is probably the one thing that I think could be labeled as evil—that in order to make a profit, you're disease-mongering . . . medicalizing something that is just really part of everyday life. So, in other words, a person who is not yet a patient, who is actually feeling quite good, sits down to watch the evening news, and after seeing a few commercials, says to him or herself, "You know, I'm not quite as healthy as I thought." What's happened now is, you've taken a healthy person and medicalized something that was not medical, and this person may very soon end up on prescription medication.

The FDA (Food and Drug Administration) has been widely called a "servant of the drug industry."[156] Dr. Marcia Angell points out how even though it is supposed to be the other way around—the FDA is supposed to control the drug companies—in reality, Big Pharma controls Congress *and* the FDA:

> That's one of the things that the industry does with its vast wealth, it buys influence and it also uses its wealth to co-opt any institution that might be expected to stand in the way of its drive for profits. So it co-opts, first of all the US Congress, it gives generously to political campaigns, it has the largest lobby in Washington. Nothing goes through Congress that it hasn't approved. So it begins with US Congress and then through the US Congress and the administration, it controls to a remarkable extent, the FDA.[157]

Health author Jacky Law makes a great point: How can the medical system function properly when the regulating agencies in charge of protecting public health interests are inexorably tied to the pharmaceutical industry? How can it be healthy when it is the drug companies that pick and choose which clinical tests of new drugs will be made public—when market considerations, not medical need, are what determines the research agenda?[158]

So Big Pharma lies about the *literally* murderous effects of its drugs and vaccines, manipulates the media "spin" on the *actual* effects of its drugs to intentionally confuse the public, spends massive amounts on its political programs to shield its unethical behavior, makes billions and billions in profits from these actions, and does not pay its fair share of taxes on those profits. *Great* bunch of folks.

Food Matters is an excellent documentary that everyone should watch. It explains how the game is rigged *away* from the natural things that really help us, and *into* a system where pharmaceutical drugs are used *en masse* and profits are flowing toward the corporations that mass-produce them. "We have been taught our whole lives to be consumers—mostly consumers of modern medicine, which is pharmaceutical medicine."[159] And if you think about it, that's really true.

> The pharmaceutical industry is the BIGGEST political lobby in the US. There should be no doubt about the power the drug industry wields in shaping the US health-care system and all the laws relating to the industry. Political lobbying is one of the primary reasons why the drug companies control nearly the entire health industry, and why alternative medicine is under such constant legislative attack.[160]

It has been *proved* that nutritional dietary changes can literally reverse serious conditions, even cardiovascular disease—but instead, doctors just prescribe drugs for it, and bypass surgeries.[161]

> We've still got a health system which really is a disease-care system and dominated by doctors and hospitals, pathologists, and pharmacologists. And that sort of a system is going to look after itself. It wants more work

and is truly not interested in reducing the amount of illness and disease. The more work they get, the more profit there is.[162]

So the message of all this information is clear and the solution is simple. Reject the norms of that system, at least as far as its unhealthy effects. If you have a broken bone then, of course, you need a doctor. But you *also* have the power to take back control of your health; through diet, through exercise, through nutrition, through knowledge—and through *not* buying into the whole *Big Pharma bullshit* that there's a pill for everything and everything requires a pill. That's what we *all* need to do, because that's actually the *right* prescription.

FURTHER RESEARCH:

Prakash, Snigdha. *All the Justice Money Can Buy: Corporate Greed on Trial*. New York: Kaplan Publishing, 2011.

O'Meara, Kelly Patricia. *Psyched Out: How Psychiatry Sells Mental Illness and Pushes Pills that Kill*. Bloomington, IN: AuthorHouse, 2006.

Moynihan, Ray and Alan Cassels. *Selling Sickness: How the World's Biggest Pharmaceutical Companies Are Turning Us All Into Patients*. New York: Nation Books, 2006).

Law, Jacky. *Big Pharma: Exposing the Global Healthcare Agenda*. New York: Carroll & Graf, 2006.

Kennedy, Robert F. Jr. *Thimerosal: Let the Science Speak: The* Evidence *Supporting the Immediate Removal of Mercury—a Known Neurotoxin—from Vaccines*. New York: Skyhorse Publishing, 2015.

Barry, Kevin. *Vaccine Whistleblower: Exposing Autism Research Fraud at the CDC*. New York: Skyhorse Publishing, 2015.

Dachel, Anne. *The Big Autism Cover-Up: How and Why the Media Is Lying to the American Public*. New York: Skyhorse Publishing, 2014.

Rohde, Wayne. *The Vaccine Court: The Dark Truth of America's Vaccine Injury Compensation Program.* New York: Skyhorse Publishing, 2014.

Gladen, Eric and Shiloh Levine, directors. *Trace Amounts: Autism, Mercury and the Hidden Truth.* Gathr Films, 2015. DVD.

Colquhoun, James and Laurentine Ten Bosch, directors. *Food Matters: Prevent Illness, Reverse Disease & Maintain Optimal Health…Naturally.* Australia: Permacology Productions, 2008. DVD.

Ridberg, Ronit, producer. *Big Bucks, Big Pharma: Marketing Disease and Pushing Drugs,* Media Education Foundation: 2007). DVD. https://www.youtube.com/watch?v=lAzh28nEoWU.

Canner, Liz, director. *Orgasm Inc.* New York: First Run Features, 2011. DVD.

Burwell, Toby and Randall Stith, directors. *Making a Killing: The Untold Story of Psychotropic Drugging.* Los Angeles: Citizens Commission on Human Rights, 2008). DVD. https://www.youtube.com/watch?v=qHlLRge45sg.

Sheehan, Bobby, director. *BOUGHT: Your Health Now Brought to You by Wall Street—The Truth Behind Vaccines, Big Pharma & Your Food.* Jeff Hays Film: 2015. DVD.

Seneff, Stephanie, PhD. "Roundup and GMO and the Rise of Modern Disease," (April 28, 2014). https://people.csail.mit.edu/seneff/Oahu2015.pdf.

Wachtler, Mark. "Rob Schneider says Big Pharma killed Robin Williams." *Whiteout Press* (August 20, 2014). http://www.whiteoutpress.com/articles/2014/q3/rob-schneider-says-big-pharma-killed-robin-williams/.

Neporent, Liz. "Doctors Blast Rob Schneider's Parkinson's Drug Twitter Rant," *ABC News* (August 19, 2014). http://abcnews.go.com/Health/experts-blast-rob-schneiders-parkinsons-drug-twitter-rant/story?id=25041317.

O'Meara, Kelly Patricia. "Contrary to News Headlines, Robin Williams Was on Drugs at the Time of His Death—Antidepressant Drugs." *CCHR International (Citizens Commission on Human Rights)—The Mental Health Watchdog* (November 10, 2014). http://www.cchrint.org/2014/11/10/robin-williams-was-on-drugs-at-the-time-of-his-death-antidepressant-drugs/.

"Robin Williams Suicide Causes: Dementia or Antidepressants to Blame?" *MentalHealthDaily.com* (2015). http://mentalhealthdaily.com/2014/12/24/robin-williams-suicide-causes-dementia-or-antidepressants-to-blame/.

Larimer, Sarah. "Robin Williams coroner's report: Paranoia, depression and Parkinson's, but no alcohol or illegal drugs." *The Washington Post* (November 7, 2014). https://www.washingtonpost.com/news/style-blog/wp/2014/11/07/robin-williams-autopsy-no-alcohol-or-illegal-drugs-in-his-system/.

Almendrala, Anna. "Robin Williams' Widow Writes A Devastating Account Of His Final Year." *The Huffington Post* (September 30, 2016). http://www.huffingtonpost.com/entry/inside-robin-williams-devastating-final-year-of-life_us_57eee8ace4b024a52d2f25be?ncid=engmodushpmg00000006.

Schneider Williams, Susan. "The terrorist inside my husband's brain." *Neurology* 87 no. 13 (September 27, 2016): 1308–1311. http://www.neurology.org/content/87/13/1308.full.

Ludwig, Mike. "How Much of Big Pharma's Massive Profits Are Used to Influence Politicians?" *Truth-out.org* (September 30, 2015). http://www.truth-out.org/news/item/33010-how-much-of-big-pharma-s-massive-profits-are-used-to-influence-politicians.

Adams, Mike. "Yet another psych drug shooter: Oregon gunman Christopher Mercer was taking five types of medication, likely vaccine-damaged with autism spectrum disorder." *Natural News* (October 6, 2015). http://www.naturalnews.com/051453_Christopher_Mercer_psychiatric_medications_autism_spectrum_disorder.html.

"MANIA: The shocking link between psychiatric drugs, suicide, violence and mass murder," *Whistleblower Magazine* (July 6, 2007). http://www.wnd.com/2007/07/42434/.

"Psychiatric Drugs & Violence—The Facts," *CCHR International (Citizens Commission on Human Rights—The Mental Health Watchdog* (2013) http://www.cchrint.org/psychiatric-drugs/drug_warnings_on_violence/.

"Another Mass Shooting, Another Psychiatric Drug? Federal Investigation Long Overdue," *CCHR International (Citizens Commission on Human Rights)—The Mental Health Watchdog* (2012). http://www.cchrint.org/2012/07/20/the-aurora-colorado-tragedy-another-senseless-shooting-another-psychotropic-drug/.

O'Meara, Kelly Patricia. "Are Psychiatric Drugs, Documented to Cause Violence, Fueling the Increase in Murders That is Puzzling Criminal Experts?" *CCHR International—The Mental Health Industry Watchdog* (September 30, 2016). https://www.cchrint.org/2016/09/30/are-psychiatric-drugs-fueling-increase-in-murders/.

Rosenberg, Martha. "Are Veterans Being Given Deadly Cocktails to Treat PTSD? A potentially deadly drug manufactured by pharmaceutical giant Astra-Zeneca has been linked to the deaths of soldiers returning from war. Yet the FDA continues to approve it." *AlterNet* (March 5, 2010). http://www.alternet.org/story/145892/are_veterans_being_given_deadly_cocktails_to_treat_ptsd.

Mercola, Joseph, DO. "The 6 Types of Pills Big Pharma Wants You Hooked on for Life." *Mercola.com* (May 14, 2012). http://articles.mercola.com/sites/articles/archive/2012/05/14/mercks-adhd-drugs-unsafe.aspx.

Veracity, Dani. "Leaked documents show Merck knew of Vioxx dangers, yet hid them for years," *NaturalNews.com* (August 6, 2005). http://www.natural-news.com/010613.html.

Moynihan, Ray. "The making of a disease: female sexual dysfunction—*Is a new disorder being identified to meet unmet needs or to build markets for new medications?" British Medical Journal* 326 no. 45 (2003): 45–47. http://www.ncbi.nlm.nih.gov/pmc/articles/PMC1124933/.

Rebensdorf, Alicia. "Sarafem: The Pimping of Prozac for PMS: Sarafem, a new FDA-approved treatment from Eli Lilly, promises to make you 'more like the woman you are.'" *AlterNet* (June 11, 2001). http://www.alternet.org/story/11004/sarafem%3A_the_pimping_of_prozac_for_pms.

Higdon, Nolan, Michael Smith, and Mickey Huff. "The H1N1 Swine Flu Pandemic: Manipulating Data to Enrich Drug Companies." *Project Censored*

(October 2, 2010). http://www.projectcensored.org/the-h1n1-swine-flu-pandemic-11-manipulating-data-to-enrich-drug-companies/.

Dane, Lily. "The US Government Has Paid Out $3 Billion To Vaccine-Injured Americans Since 1989. " *Activist Post* (February 5, 2005). http://www.activistpost.com/2015/02/the-us-government-has-paid-out-3.html.

Rosenberg, Martha. "Disgraced FDA Official Goes Back to Big Pharma: Former FDA number two is doing what he did best on the FDA—push for the sale of unsafe drugs on the market." *AlterNet* (January 8, 2008). http://www.alter-net.org/story/72513/disgraced_fda_official_goe.

CHAPTER SEVEN

CHEMICAL WARFARE: THE AGRI-CHEM GIANTS' ASSAULT UPON OUR FOOD & HEALTH

Former Texas Agriculture Commissioner Jim Hightower told me, "They've eliminated the middleman. The corporations don't have to lobby the government anymore. They are the government." Hightower used to complain about Monsanto's lobbying the Secretary of Agriculture. Today, Monsanto executive Ann Veneman is the Secretary of Agriculture.[1]

—Greg Palast, 2004

Some people will believe almost anything:

Once an industrial-chemical titan, GMO seed giant Monsanto has rebranded itself as a "sustainable agriculture company." Forget such classic post-war corporate atrocities as PCB and dioxin—the modern Monsanto "uses plant breeding and biotechnology to create seeds that grow into stronger, more resilient crops that require fewer resources," as the company's website has it.[2]

Well, we're here to tell you—it's utter *bullshit*, folks! *Do not* believe it for a second. We have *lots* of information for you about that—in just a minute.

Sandra Steingraber is a scientist who has documented the environmental links to cancer and human health and the case for banning the poisons that are now pervasive in our air, soil, and food.[3] And "pervasive" is the right word too. You can add water to that list as well:

Today more than 40 percent of US waterways are unsafe for swimming and fishing, and, as shown by the PIRG (Public Interest Research Groups, a nonprofit group of public interest advocacy organizations) study, industrial pollution of the nation's waters persists—despite the goals of the 1972 Clean Water Act to make all US waters safe for fishing, swimming, and other uses by 1983, and to eliminate the discharge of pollutants into waterways by 1985.[4]

And—as megamergers now set the stage for a pesticide-soaked future— it is a good time to re-examine the seeds of greed that have polluted our environment in pure pursuit of profit, and in a shamefully blatant negligence of the health of our children and the world we will leave them.[5] So, with that in mind, would you like to hear what people think about Monsanto? Listen up:

Of all the megacorps running amok, Monsanto has consistently outperformed its rivals, earning the crown as "most evil corporation on Earth!" Not content to simply rest upon its throne of destruction, it remains focused on newer, more scientifically innovative ways to harm the planet and its people.[6]

Nice, huh? It makes you scared to even wonder what they've done to attract *that* kind of attention. Well—*quite a bit*, would be the right answer.

Just take a look at a partial list of Monsanto's products—it's a cornucopia of cancer-causing chemicals.	
1. **Saccharin**:	The artificial sweetener used in thousands of products has been shown to cause cancer, but massive pressure from manufacturers of artificial sweeteners and diet sodas managed to get the product taken off of the NIH's (National Institutes of Health) Carcinogen List.[7]
2. **PCBs**:	(polychlorinated biphenyls): "PCBs were considered an industrial wonder chemical, an oil that wouldn't burn, impervious to degradation and had almost limitless applications."[8] After mass producing the chemical additive for fifty years, studies revealed that it causes cancer.[9]

	"Today PCBs are considered one of the gravest chemical threats on the planet."[10] Internal company memos revealed that Monsanto was well aware of the serious health risks but hid them from the public.[11]
3. **DDT:**	Highly toxic pesticide. "Despite decades of Monsanto propaganda insisting that DDT was safe, the true effects of DDT's toxicity were at last confirmed through outside research and in 1972, DDT was banned throughout the US"[12] Monsanto actually had the nerve to run advertisements proclaiming "*DDT is good for me!*"[13]
4. **Agent Orange:**	Monsanto and Dow Chemical Company mass produced the herbicide/defoliant that was used for chemical warfare during the Vietnam War. It is known to have caused hundreds of thousands of serious birth defects and "thousands of US military veterans suffering or dying from its effects."[14] "Internal Monsanto memos show that Monsanto knew of the problems of dioxin contamination of Agent Orange when it sold it to the US government for use in Vietnam. Despite the widespread health impact, Monsanto and Dow were allowed to appeal for and receive financial protection from the US government against veterans seeking compensation for their exposure to Agent Orange."[15] An internal company memo admitted that "the evidence proving the persistence of these compounds and their universal presence as residues in the environment is beyond question."[16]
5. **Aspartame** (*NutraSweet*/*Equal*):	With saccharin use declining, Monsanto introduced a new artificial sweetener that was even more questionable. "The FDA's own scientific research clearly reveals that aspartame causes tumors and massive holes in the brains of rats, before killing them."[17] But the additive was approved anyway. "Twenty years later, the US Department of Health and Human Services released a report listing 94 health issues caused by aspartame."[18]

6. **Bovine Growth Hormone** (rBGH):	This "genetically modified hormone was developed by Monsanto to be injected into dairy cows to produce more milk." In addition to causing excruciating pain to the cows, it is linked to causing cancer in humans.[19]
7. **GM (Genetically Modified) Crops:**	"Because these GM crops have been engineered to 'self-pollinate,' they do not need nature or bees to do that for them."[20] "When bees attempt to pollinate a GM plant or flower, it gets poisoned and dies. In fact, the bee colony collapse was recognized and has been going on since GM crops were first introduced."[21]
8. **Terminator Seeds:**	Monsanto developed the ability to produce sterile grains which are unable to germinate. "The goal of these 'Terminator Seeds' was to force farmers to buy new seeds from Monsanto year after year, rather than save and reuse the seeds from their harvest as they've been doing throughout centuries."[22] Though it never came to market, "Monsanto managed to accomplish the same thing by requiring farmers to sign a binding contract agreeing that they will not save or sell seeds from year to year, which forces them to buy new seeds and preempts the need for a 'terminator gene.'"[23]
9. **Roundup:**	Be advised that—as much as Monsanto has told us that it isn't dangerous—its popular herbicide Roundup is highly toxic. It contains high levels of glyphosate. "The cancer-research arm of the World Health Organization last week announced that glyphosate, the world's most widely used herbicide, is probably carcinogenic to humans."[24] Yet Monsanto is still in denial—they're busily cashing in their profits: "Glyphosate is the world's most widely produced herbicide."[25] The problem is now pervasive in our food supply. "Between 75% to 80% of the processed food you consume every day has GMOs inside, and residues of Monsanto's Roundup herbicide outside."[26] The health aspects of this issue will probably

	continue to be staggering: "There is a direct correlation between our genetically engineered food supply and the $2 trillion the US spends annually on medical care, namely an epidemic of diet-related chronic diseases."[27]
"Monsanto's history reflects a consistent pattern of toxic chemicals, lawsuits, and manipulated science."[28]	
So make no mistake—*no one* has done a better job of earning a bad reputation than Monsanto!	

Monsanto's pesticides have become so prevalent that glyphosate (a highly toxic ingredient of Monsanto's popular Roundup product) is now being found at dangerous levels in vaccines being given to children. It's "due to the fact that certain vaccine viruses including measles in MMR and flu are grown on gelatin derived from the ligaments of pigs fed heavy doses of glyphosate in their GMO feed."[29]

As Dr. Toni Bark, medical director of the Center for Disease Prevention and Reversal and co-producer of the documentary *BOUGHT: The Truth Behind Vaccines, Big Pharma & Your Food*, warns:

> I am deeply concerned about injecting glyphosate, a known pesticide, directly into children. Neither Roundup nor glyphosate has been tested for safety as an injectable. Injection is a very different route of entry than oral route. Injected toxins, even in minute doses, can have profound effects on the organs and the different systems of the body.[30]

Then there is a whole new matter of *owning* the new seeds and everything in their path:

> What often gets lost in the GMO controversy is how Big Ag has managed to obtain patented "intellectual property rights" on seeds, and when these patented seeds, which are genetically modified to resist herbicides, literally trespass on another's land, Big Ag is allowed to pursue legal action against the true victims of its polluting seeds. This brand of legal terrorism also extends to those who "clean" seeds.[31]

Cleaning seeds has been a common agricultural practice, almost since farming began. But the Agri-Chem giants are changing that tradition now:

> Cleaning is a mechanical process that separates debris from seeds, enabling small farming enterprises to sell seeds to other farmers for future use. Big Ag has targeted seed cleaning businesses in an effort to break the ability of small family farms to market seeds. Collecting seeds has been a part of farming for thousands of years, but big agricultural global powerhouses want the world dependent on their "patented" seeds.[32]

So, as food expert Michael Pollan puts it, "When you genetically modify a crop—*you own it*. We've never had this in Agriculture."[33]

It's not just Monsanto. Now Dow Chemical has teamed up with fellow giant corporation, DuPont, in a megamerger that makes it one of the world's most powerful companies.[34] And it is also one of the most *dangerous* companies.[35]

> Dow Chemical, the same company that brought us Dursban, napalm, and Agent Orange, is now in the food business and is pushing for an unprecedented government approval: genetically engineered (GE) versions of corn and soybeans that are designed to survive repeated dousing with 2,4-D, half of the highly toxic chemical mixture Agent Orange. Do you trust Dow Chemical with your food?[36]

These toxic pesticides and GMOs are now everywhere. They're the rule, not the exception:

> A startling **82 percent** of cotton planted is herbicide-resistant, genetically-modified organisms (GMOs).
> Corn? **85 percent**.
> Soybeans? **93 percent**.
> In fact, the United States leads the world in planting GMO crops.[37]

Taken together, these massive changes to our food and soil have a potentially life-altering combined effect on our health, on our environment—on the very survival of our planet. The situation was summarized very eloquently in a book examining the hidden atrocities of changing agriculture, *Facing Hawai'i's Future: Essential Information About GMOs*:

> Today, we can see an approaching food and farming tsunami. The revolution occurring in agriculture has the potential to forever change the basic genetic structure of the food we eat, as well as the soils, the plants, and the animals that form the delicate balance in our ecosystem. Multinational corporations and universities with the full support of federal and state governments are altering the genetic structure and nutritional content of the foods we eat, patenting the seed, preventing farmers from saving seed, and changing the course of 10,000 years of agriculture. Genes of different species are being combined in food crops at the molecular level without knowledge of their effects on ecosystems or human health.[38]

GMO safety studies were found to have significant flaws.[39] That's not really too surprising considering the country's huge commitment to GMO farming and the massive influence wielded by giant corporations like Monsanto.[40] Jeffrey Smith is author of *Seeds of Deception*, in which he warns us about a GMO future: "Jeffrey M. Smith reveals in shocking detail the biotechnology industry's laundry list of perpetual crimes against humanity via its propagation of genetically modified organisms (GMOs). Smith explains how biotech giant Monsanto, in particular, has rigged the entire system to push its deadly products on the populations of the world."[41]

As the following chart vividly highlights, that damage is already very visible.

The economic damage from mass GMO farming is obvious—unhealthy fast food is now cheaper than fresh healthy produce, and megacorporations thrive as small farmers have been driven out of business. But the devastating results of the Agri-Chem giant's deplorably toxic assault on our environment and on our health are even more abominable:

Dwindling Bee Population:	"Just about every fruit and vegetable you can imagine is dependent on the pollinating services of bees."[42] That bee population so crucial to our survival is now in danger of disappearing. Bees are leaving hives due to the poisons in the ecosystem from the massive use of pesticides toxic to them, especially glyphosate, in Monsanto products like Roundup.[43] "These critical pollinators are dying at some of the highest rates ever recorded—a whopping 42 percent of US bee colonies collapsed in 2015."[44] "And if CCD (colony-collapse disorder) continues, the consequences for the agricultural economy—and even for our ability to feed ourselves—could be dire."[45] In one CCD incident alone, 40,000 hives were lost—that means *2 billion bees*.[46] And the problem is now worldwide. The same phenomenon occurred in France in the 1990s and it was found that the use of "systemic pesticides" (of the Roundup variety) was the cause. But massive protests by French beekeepers—*they don't put up with that shit in France!*—caused *their* Minister of Agriculture to officially *ban* systemic pesticides, and guess what happened then? *Healthy bees*.[47]
Dwindling Monarch Butterfly Population:	"As recently as 1996, there were close to 1 billion monarchs across the US. Today, their numbers have dwindled by *90 percent*."[48] Pesticides-primarily the glyphosate found in Roundup—are wiping out the monarchs' primary food source, the milkweed plant.[49] For example, 99 percent of the milkweed has been destroyed in Iowa corn and soybean fields.[50]

Soil Toxicity:	"Residues left in the field contain the active *Bacillus thuringiensis* (Bt) toxin. The long-term, cumulative effects of growing Bt maize are of concern."[51] Monsanto's highly toxic chemical, DDT, and other pesticides, are *still* present in our soil because DDT has a half-life of close to 50 years.[52]
Water Toxicity:	On many farms, no one can drink the water. The wells have been poisoned by pesticides and are too dangerous to drink. And the same thing can happen to ground water.[53]
Food Toxicity:	The DDT and other toxic chemicals that were in mass use are *still* in your organic carrots, and just about everything, because that DDT is still in the soil that grows most of them. Even farms that have been organic for years still have plenty of toxic residues.[54]
Early Onset Diabetes:	"It used to be that type 2 diabetes only affected adults. And now it's affecting children at epidemic proportions. One in three Americans born after 2000 will contract early onset diabetes. Among minorities the rate will be 1 in 2." That's because minorities are less able to afford healthy foods. And our food seems to be the cause of the problem; particularly processed foods with high fructose corn syrup and other GMOs.[55] "This diet of high-fructose corn syrup and refined carbohydrates leads to these spikes of insulin and gradually a wearing down of the system by which our body metabolizes sugar."[56]
Childhood Obesity:	"Child obesity is a modern-day epidemic. The last 30 years have been especially devastating as the percentage of obese children skyrocketed to more than double what it was in the 80s."[57] If you want to see the terrifying effects of a processed fast food diet, all you have to do is watch Morgan Spurlock's great documentary, *Super Size Me*. It gets to the point where his doctor pointedly warns him that he literally *may not live* through his 30-day experiment to eat nothing but fast food.[58] "Why is it that you can buy a double cheeseburger at McDonald's for 99 cents and you

	can't even get a head of broccoli for 99 cents? We've skewed our food system to the bad calories and it's not an accident. The reason that those calories are cheaper is because those are the ones we're heavily subsidizing. And this is directly tied to the kind of agriculture that we're practicing and the kind of farm policies we have. All those snack-food calories are the ones that come from the commodity crops—from the wheat, from the corn, and from the soybeans. By making those calories really cheap, that's one of the reasons that the biggest predictor of obesity is income level."[59]
Liver Toxicity:	Toxicity to the liver from GM foods has already been established.[60] And who knows what further health risks from pesticides and genetic alteration will be discovered as time passes and the linkage eventually becomes apparent? The toxicity in livers *reverses when switched to a non-GM diet.*[61]
Cancer:	"Pesticides can cause many types of cancer in humans. Some of the most prevalent forms include leukemia, non-Hodgkin's lymphoma, brain, bone, breast, ovarian, prostate, testicular, and liver cancers. In February 2009, the Agency for Toxic Substances and Disease Registry published a study that found that children who live in homes where their parents use pesticides are twice as likely to develop brain cancer versus those that live in residences in which no pesticides are used. Studies by the National Cancer Institute found that American farmers, who in most respects are healthier than the population at large, had startling incidences of leukemia, Hodgkin's disease, non-Hodgkin's lymphoma, and many other forms of cancer. There is also mounting evidence that exposure to pesticides disrupts the endocrine system, wreaking havoc with the complex regulation of hormones, the reproductive system, and embryonic development."[62] "Chronic health effects may occur years after even minimal exposure to pesticides in the environment, or result from the pesticide residues which we ingest through our food and water."[63]

Autism:	Cutting-edge research indicates that glyphosate, the toxic chemical found in Monsanto's Roundup, _causes autism_.[64] That's been the conclusion of several studies: "A July 2007 study conducted by researchers at the Public Health Institute, the California Department of Health Services, and the UC Berkeley School of Public Health found a sixfold increase in risk factor for autism spectrum disorders (ASD) for children of women who were exposed to organochlorine pesticides."[65]

And that's even _more_ disturbing now, because it was recently learned that the same toxic glyphosate is now present at dangerous levels in vaccines that are being given to our children![66]

But—even with all the evidence of the possible dangers—we cannot even seem to be able to get government to force the labeling of GMO foods. Other countries—most of Europe, in fact—passed laws requiring labeling. But in America, their lobbyists are so influential that politicians have failed to serve the prevailing interest of the people they supposedly represent:

> Polls show that the vast majority of consumers say they support labeling products that contain GMOs, even though regulators—and established scientific organizations—have declared such modifications safe. Big food companies, however, have poured millions of dollars into overturning state initiatives that require labeling.[67]

It should be pointed out that the "established scientific organizations" that _Fortune Magazine_ so glowingly refers to above are actually staffed by former executives of the very same big food companies they are supposedly empowered to police.[68] It's all part of the revolving door policy between big business and government, whether it is the food industry, the armaments industry, the drug industry, or you name it, folks! The foxes have been put in charge of the hen house, and you can guess how the story plays out.

After a study by scholarly researcher Gilles-Eric Séralini showed negative effects from Monsanto's herbicide Roundup, its author was mercilessly attacked in a highly organized industry assault upon his work—and very unfairly, at that:

> A sustained and vitriolic attack on Séralini's paper began within hours of publication . . . The quality of Séralini's work aside, the process by which his paper was retracted reeks of industry pressure . . . There are hundreds of studies that should be permanently removed from the scientific literature, but the Séralini study is not one of them . . . The media coverage in the United States has been one-sided; criticism of Séralini's study has been widely covered in mainstream press, while information about the conflicts of interest of critics have remained in the alternative press.[69]

Then, the plot thickened. After being implicated in the recent phenomenon of bee colony collapse, Monsanto bought out the research firm making the accusation so that they could take control of its research![70] Can you believe the *audacity* of that? "To counter the accusations that they deliberately caused this ongoing genocide of bees, Monsanto devilishly buys out Beeologics, the largest bee research firm that was dedicated to studying the colony collapse phenomenon and whose extensive research named the monster as the primary culprit!"[71]

"Monsanto is not alone in trying to silence its critics."[72] A clear history of marginalizing the damage of its controversies has run rampant throughout the whole Agri-Chem power structure.[73]

It was recently revealed that "the sugar industry funded research that downplayed the risks of sugar" back in the 1960s to trick American consumers into unsafe, high-sugar habits such as soda drinks and other "snacks" to which many millions became addicted.[74]

There are only three macronutrients—protein, fat, and carbohydrates:

> Nearly everything you eat or drink contains one or more of these. And if you followed the government's advice to eat less fat, it's inevitable that your carb consumption would shoot up . . . That's just what happened at a population level during the 1980s and 90s.[75]

So the results of that blatant conspiracy by the sugar industry are both obvious and tragic: "As Americans eat more sugar, diabetes and obesity have soared."[76] The American people were the guinea pigs in a failed experiment—and paid for it with soaring rates of heart disease, diabetes, and obesity:

> This advice [to avoid fat] allowed the food industry to go hog-wild promoting low-fat, carb-heavy packaged foods as "light" or "healthy," and that's been a disaster for public health.[77]

In the United Kingdom they followed America's lead on diet and suffered the same horrendous health results in their society as well.[78] To illustrate the problem, in Scotland, only 2.7 percent of men and women were obese in 1972. But by 1999, the obesity rate skyrocketed to 26 percent.[79] The National Obesity Forum recently released a scathing report condemning government guidelines for food. As a British cardiologist who was consulted in that obesity report concluded:

> The change in dietary advice to promote low-fat foods is perhaps the biggest mistake in modern medical history.[80]

And it all traces back to the change in guidelines that resulted from the very self-serving "research" by American corporations who benefited financially; once again, placing corporate profits above public health. The sugar industry funded a study that "suggested there were major problems with all the studies that implicated sugar, and concluded that cutting fat out of American diets was the best way to address coronary heart disease."[81] There is "evidence that the interests of the sugar lobby shaped the conclusions of the review" and the sugar consumption of consumers in America—and those around the world who followed the same wrong advice—rose dramatically as a result.[82]

That sugar industry "research"—if it should even be termed such—even had the gall to suggest that other more professional and valid dietary research in the past was what was flawed: "In some cases the scientists alleged investigator incompetence or flawed methodology."[83]

That corporate promotion disguised as credible research dramatically affected the health of hundreds of millions of people: "The review minimized the significance of research that suggested sugar could play a role in coronary heart disease."[84]

And guess what? It's *still happening*. Corporate America *continues* to corrupt the research that directly affects our health:

> Is it really true that food companies deliberately set out to manipulate research in their favor? Yes, it is, and the practice continues. In 2015, the *New York Times* obtained emails revealing Coca-Cola's cozy relationships with sponsored researchers who were conducting studies aimed at minimizing the effects of sugary drinks on obesity. Even more recently, the Associated Press obtained emails showing how a candy trade association funded and influenced studies to show that children who eat sweets have healthier body weights than those who do not.[85]

As just about everybody is now aware, the consumption of soda drinks is related to a lot of health issues:

> Sugary drink consumption has become a major public health concern in recent years, with links to obesity, diabetes, and heart disease.[86]

But the big soft drink companies really know how to throw money at health organizations in an effort to influence the marketing of their products:

> Talk about a conflict of interest: A new study published in the *American Journal of Preventive Medicine* reveals that at least 96 health organizations received funding from either one or both of the country's largest soda companies between 2011 and 2015.[87]

And to make matters worse, that was "during the same five-year period when the soda companies were lobbying against at least 28 public health bills intended to reduce soda consumption or improve nutrition."[88] Independent researchers point out that "big drink companies are hampering efforts to improve health and nutrition in the United

States, and they call for health organizations to refuse funding from these companies."[89]

Put bluntly:

Big Soda has been serving up big helpings of dirty money.[90]

In fact, a "report from the *American Journal of Preventive Medicine* likened the soft drink giants to tobacco companies that have tried to hide harsh health truths from their consumers."[91] And that's some very nasty company to find yourself near, isn't it, Big Soda?

Anyone who watches network television can learn a lot just by paying close attention to the corporate commercials we are bombarded with on a daily basis regarding pharmaceuticals, junk food, soda drinks, and "fast food." It's almost as if the drug companies are telling us what to purchase to treat the health problems that are caused by consuming all the junk foods, soda drinks, and fast foods being pushed at us in the *other* commercials. When will we get it through our collective heads as a society, that corporate interests will do *anything* to make money? The record clearly shows that our health is not as important to them as their profits.

What has already happened to the bees and butterflies from the reckless disregard of these corporate maniacs is totally unforgivable. Let alone what has been happening to *us*! Do we really want the image of an obese child with early-onset diabetes as the new poster child of America? We don't think so. We sure as hell don't. And there's still time to do something about it. Hawai'i and other states are making genuine efforts to enhance our health with Farm-to-School programs that reach students with "fresh, nutritious food in order to encourage healthy eating habits and strengthen local economies."[92] Getting healthy, locally grown foods into school cafeterias, classrooms, and gardens is a huge step in the right direction. Ninety-one percent of Americans do not eat healthily.[93] Studies have identified the stages of change required to encourage people to acquire a healthier diet—and a lot of people are ready to make those changes.[94] The awareness is out there, but now we need to make healthy food *accessible* and *affordable*. Because, especially now, small-scale, sustainable agriculture and the healthy food it produces *really makes sense*.

So keep reading, keep learning, and keep caring.

FURTHER RESEARCH:

Steingraber, Sandra. *Living Downstream: An Ecologist's Personal Investigation of Cancer and the Environment.* Boston: Addison-Wesley, 1997.

Robi, Marie-Monique. *The World According to Monsanto: Pollution, Corruption, and the Control of the World's Food Supply.* New York: The New Press, 2010.

Louv, Jason. *Monsanto vs. The World: The Monsanto Protection Act, GMOs and Our Genetically Modified Future.* Las Angeles: Ultraculture Press, 2013.

Facing Hawai'i's Future: Essential Information About GMOs. Koloa, HI: Hawai'i SEED: 2013. *http://www.hawaiiseed.org/resources/articles/facing-hawaiis-future-book/.*

Oberhauser, Karen S., Kelly R. Nail, and Sonia Altizer, eds. *Monarchs in a Changing World: Biology and Conservation of an Iconic Butterfly.* Sacramento: Comstock Publishing, 2015. http://www.centerforfoodsafety.org/issues/311/ge-foods/fact-sheets/3096/infographic-monsanto-vs-monarchs.

Smith, Jeffrey M. *Seeds of Deception: Exposing Industry and Government Lies About the Safety of the Genetically Engineered Foods You're Eating.* Portland, ME: Yes! Books, 2003.

Langworthy, George and Maryam Henein, directors. *Vanishing of the Bees.* Dogwoof Pictures, 2009. DVD.

Sheehan, Bobby, director. *BOUGHT: Your Health Now Brought to You by Wall Street- The Truth Behind Vaccines, Big Pharma & Your Food.* Jeff Hays Film, 2015. DVD.

Kenner, Robert, director. *Food, Inc.* Home Entertainment, 2009. DVD.

Spurlock, Morgan. *Super Size Me.* Virgil Films, 2010. DVD.

"Dow: Destroying Our World," Center For Food Safety (2016). http://www.centerforfoodsafety.org/video/2519/cfs-videos/dow-destroying-our-world/3005/dow-destroying-our-world.

Ventura, Jesse. "WTF Monsanto?" *Off the Grid—Ora. TV.* https://www.you-tube.com/watch?v=XJXafJXcRyk.

Seneff, Stephanie, PhD. "Roundup and GMO and the Rise of Modern Disease." (April 28, 2014). https://people.csail.mit.edu/seneff/Oahu2015.pdf.

"Monsanto's Dirty Dozen." GMO Awareness (May 12, 2011). http://gmo-awareness.com/2011/05/12/monsanto-dirty-dozen/.

A Sheep No More. "The Revolving Door Between Monsanto, the FDA, and the EPA: Your Safety in Peril." *Sheep Media* (January 15, 2014). http://asheepnomore.net/2014/01/15/revolving-door-monsanto-fda-epa-safety-peril/#arvlbdata.

Honeycutt, Zen. "Glyphosate Found in Childhood Vaccines." *Ecowatch.com* (September 10, 2016). http://www.ecowatch.com/glyphosate-vaccines-1999343362.html.

"Briefing: Environmental and health impacts of GM crops - the science," *Greenpeace.org* (September 2011). http://www.greenpeace.org/australia/PageFiles/434214/GM_Fact%20Sheet_Health_%20and_Env_Impacts.pdf.

Zeese, Kevin and Margaret Flowers. "The Growing Global Challenge to Monsanto's Monopolistic Greed." *Truth-out.org* (May 22, 2013). http://www.truth-out.org/opinion/item/16516-the-growing-global-challenge-to-monsantos-monopolistic-greed.

Cressey, Daniel. "Widely used herbicide linked to cancer: As the World Health Organization's research arm declares Glyphosate a probable carcinogen, *Nature* looks at the evidence." *Nature* (March 24, 2015). http://www.nature.com/news/widely-used-herbicide-linked-to-cancer-1.17181.

Capetta, Amy. "Soda Companies Funded Nearly 100 Health Organizations Despite Conflict of Interest, According to Investigation." *Yahoo!* (October 10, 2016). https://www.yahoo.com/beauty/soda-companies-funded-nearly-100-health-231231055.html.

Rettner, Rachel. "Most Americans Still Don't Eat Their Fruits & Veggies." *Live Science* (July 09, 2015). http://www.livescience.com/51500-fruit-vegetable-consumption-united-states.html.

Kittinger, D.S., S.T. Mayet, S. Niess, et al. "Examining the predictive value of the Theory of Planned Behavior and stages of change on fruit and vegetable intake." *Hawaii Journal of Public Health* 1 (2008): 45–51. https://fsu.digital.flvc.org/islandora/object/fsu:204633/datastream/PDF/view.

"Local Foods in Hawai'i's Schools: A report on the challenges to local food procurement in Hawai'i and the opportunities to advance beyond them." The Kohala Center (September 2015). http://kohalacenter.org/docs/reports/2015_LocalFoodHawaiiSchools.pdf.

Séralini, GMO "Séralini retraction is black mark on scientific publishing—Georgetown professors." (January 13, 2014). http://www.gmoseralini.org/seralini-retraction-is-black-mark-on-scientific-publishing-georgetown-professors/.

Parks, Katelyn and Kenn Burrows. "Agribusiness Giants Attempt to Silence and Discredit Scientists Whose Research Reveals Herbicides' Health Threats." *Project Censored* (October 1, 2014). http://www.projectcensored.org/19-agribusiness-giants-attempt-silence-discredit-scientists-whose-research-reveals-herbicides-health-threats/.

Benson, Johnson. "Monsanto buys leading bee research firm after being implicated in bee colony collapse." *NaturalNews.com* (April 26, 2012). http://www.naturalnews.com/035688_Monsanto_honey_bees_colony_collapse.html.

Mercola, Joseph, DO. "New Study Shows Bee Research Tainted by Corporate Funding." *Mercola.com* (August 12, 2014). http://articles.mercola.com/sites/articles/archive/2014/08/12/neonicotinoids-bee-deaths.aspx.

CHAPTER EIGHT

BIG OIL, KING COAL, & (UN)NATURAL GAS: STILL THE SCUM OF THE EARTH— AND *FRACK YOU*!

When the United States invades another country, our leaders tell us the invasion is necessary for "humanitarian" reasons, or to bring "democracy" to the people in the target country, or to protect US "national security." But in Afghanistan, Iraq and Libya, geopolitical interests—including access to Middle Eastern oil—were the primary motivations. We came dangerously close to invading Syria as well, until 63 percent of Americans—and active-duty US military personnel by a margin of three to one—opposed the invasion, and Russian president Vladimir Putin worked out a deal to dispose of Syria's chemical weapons.[1]

—Professor Marjorie Cohn
Thomas Jefferson School of Law

The well-established energy lobby—which is petroleum, natural gas, and coal—has played a dominant role in the shaping of US foreign policy.[2] At the start of the Iraq War, an old hippie sat at a big street intersection with a sign that read "NO BLOOD FOR OIL"—aand most people, when they saw that, probably thought, "Could it really be that simple?" And guess what? Proof comes out—decades later—that's *exactly* what it was.[3] Even at CNN and at the Pentagon, that point is now conceded: "Yes, the Iraq War was a war for oil, and it was a war with winners: Big Oil."[4]

From ExxonMobil and Chevron to BP and Shell, the West's largest oil companies have set up shop in Iraq. So have a slew of American oil service companies, including Halliburton, the Texas-based firm Dick

Cheney ran before becoming George W. Bush's running mate in 2000. The war is the one and only reason for this long-sought and newly acquired access.[5]

Of course, that's not what they told *us*—or the US servicemen and women whom they sent directly into harm's way for their corporate motivations—but hey, who the hell are we? We're just the people they supposedly represent—a group whose interests are now very low on the whole geopolitical agenda.

And the War in Afghanistan? Different, you say? Sorry, Charlie—*same story* there:

> The reasons for our military commitments are complex, but one explanation can be summed up as: pipelines, geography, and energy reserves. Afghanistan sits smack in the middle of a pipeline route that would bring the control of future energy to whoever can install "friendly governments" in the area. Afghanistan's gas reserves are largely unexplored, but expected to be vast (the World Bank is funding a study of those reserves). But the key is the region itself. Afghanistan lies south of Turkmenistan, Kazakhstan, and Uzbekistan. These three countries have known gas reserves that place each of them among the top 20 nations with the most natural gas.[6]

And while we send men and women to their deaths to fight for the energy industry, what are they doing for us, one might ask? Well—they've been very busy for the past few years, denying the existence of climate change, hiding its well-known link to fossil fuel use, and effectively lobbying hard against the best interests of the planet that gives us life to begin with. Another *wonderful* group of human beings!

Internal Exxon documents prove that the company knew—way back in the 1970s—about "the dangers of the greenhouse gases we were spewing into the atmosphere" and instead of alerting anyone to the vast problem, they instead concealed the information from both the public and government agencies.[7] In fact, they not only concealed what they knew to be the unfortunate truth; they consciously—and *abominably*—acted to disguise those facts and perversely alleged them to be untrue:

The company fired most of its climate scientists and started doing everything it could to cast doubt on the scientific consensus about the causes and dangers of man-made climate change. Exxon helped to organize the "Global Climate Coalition," which fights to block any efforts to address global climate change. And the company worked with groups like the American Petroleum Institute (API) and the American Legislative Exchange Council (ALEC) to get fossil fuel–friendly climate deniers into every level of government. In 1997, Exxon chairman and CEO Lee Raymond argued against the Kyoto Protocol, using the logic that we don't really know what's going to happen with the climate, so why bother? That pattern of denial and deception has continued to this day.[8]

Meanwhile, no less an institutional icon than Citibank recently warned that the *cost* of our inaction over global warming is now estimated at a whopping 44 trillion dollars; so *thank you ExxonMobil!*[9]

Former California Governor Arnold Schwarzenegger posed some excellent questions to the audience at the Paris climate talks in 2015:

First—do you believe it is acceptable that 7 million people die every year from pollution? That's more than murders, suicides, and car accidents—combined. Every day, 19,000 people die from pollution from fossil fuels. Do you accept those deaths? Do you accept that children all over the world have to grow up breathing with inhalers? Now, my second question: Do you believe coal and oil will be the fuels of the future? Besides the fact that fossil fuels destroy our lungs, everyone agrees that eventually they will run out. What's your plan then? I, personally, want a plan. I don't want to be like the last horse-and-buggy salesman who was holding out as cars took over the roads. I don't want to be the last investor in Blockbuster as Netflix emerged. That's exactly what is going to happen to fossil fuels.[10]

People can argue about it if they elect to argue. But the facts are in—global warming is a *reality*.

Senator Bernie Sanders put it point-blank:

"The debate is over. Sixteen of the last 18 years have been the hottest ever recorded. This planet is in trouble."[11]

Professor Marjorie Cohn of Thomas Jefferson School of Law believes that ExxonMobil's crimes are so grave that the courts should take action against them to revoke their public charter, dissolve their corporation, and seize and sell off their assets:

> As calls for reductions in carbon dioxide from fossil fuels increased in the United States and around the world, Exxon realized the severity of the threat to its bottom line. Brian Flannery, Exxon's climate expert, wrote in an internal newsletter that such regulations would "alter profoundly the strategic direction of the energy industry." Exxon made a strategic decision to publicly sow seeds of doubt about climate change while internally confirming it.
>
> Exxon was not alone in its deception. Mobil, Texaco, Shell, Standard Oil of California, Gulf Oil, and other behemoths joined together in the GCC (Gulf Cooperation Council) to protect their enormous profits.[12]

Before their anti-everything approach to the known facts about climate change, the big energy giants were very busy—and still *are*—polluting our planet with a long series of environmentally catastrophic events:

The environmental costs of the energy industry are mind-boggling:	
1989:	*Exxon Valdez*: "An **Exxon** oil tanker crashed into Bligh Reef on March 24, 1989 and unleashed 11 million gallons of crude oil into Alaska's pristine Prince William Sound. Wildlife in the surrounding area was severely impacted—oil-covered dead birds, fish, and mammals washed ashore."[13]
2000:	"The **Exxon** refinery released 1.68 million pounds of toxic chemicals into the air and water [in Houston] in 2000 by accident. According to ExxonMobil records, if the pentane on site vaporized and ignited, it would burn human skin within 1.8 miles: 7,300 people live in that zone."[14]
2010:	"18,000 gallons of crude oil spilled from a **Chevron**-operated pipeline in the Delta National Wildlife Refuge in southeastern Louisiana."[15]

2010:	Gulf of Mexico Oil Spill: "The largest blowout in thirty years of an oil and gas well in the Gulf of Mexico killed eleven people and saturated the surrounding areas in a blanket of oily destruction. The rig was owned and operated by **Transocean**."[16] It "spilled millions of gallons of oil into the Gulf of Mexico . . . The devastating environmental impact is still being evaluated."[17]
2010:	"**Duke Energy** is the third largest emitter of carbon dioxide in the United States at 112,000,000 tons per year and the number 11 emitter worldwide. According to a 2010 study by Clean Air Task Force, Duke's coal fleet collectively causes more than $7 billion dollars' worth of health impacts annually . . . Duke Energy owned ten of the EPA's 44 'high hazard potential' coal impoundment ponds, toxic dams full of watered-down byproducts from burning coal. In North Carolina, 13 coal ash ponds owned by Duke and Progress were found to be leaking neurotoxins and carcinogens into the surrounding groundwater. Levels of arsenic, lead, cadmium, and chromium were sometimes found to be more than 380 times greater than state-approved limits."[18]
2011:	The **ExxonMobil** Baytown Refinery in Texas "tops all 155 upset emitters, spitting out 3.8 million pounds' worth from 2007 to 2011."[19] Those are very toxic emissions that go directly into the air, then atmosphere. "The Exxon complex ranks among the state's biggest upset emitters involving carcinogens and noxious gases."[20]
2015:	California oil spill: A leak from oil distributor, **Plains All American Pipeline**, "released up to 101,000 gallons" of oil, much of it spilling into the Pacific Ocean off the California coastline.[21] Oil continued pumping for three hours before it was finally shut off but, by that time, a thick oil slick had already stretched nine miles out into the ocean.[22] It will take *years* to assess the full damage to marine animals and the ecosystems of the ocean.[23]

2016:	Aliso Canyon Gas Rupture: "The single biggest contributor to climate change in California is a blown-out natural gas well" of **Southern California Gas Company** which "has released more than 77,000 metric tons of the powerful climate pollutant methane." "Methane is a fast-acting climate pollutant—more than 80 times more powerful than carbon dioxide over a 20-year time frame . . . A byproduct of the oil and gas industry and agriculture, methane accounts for about a quarter of the world's warming . . . The Aliso Canyon well failure was widely seen as the climate equivalent of the BP disaster in the Gulf of Mexico . . . R Rex Parris, who is suing the gas company on behalf of Porter Ranch residents, said the site should have been shut down long ago. He faulted the company for removing a blow-out preventer at the bottom of the well in 1979. 'They deliberately took the brakes off the car and continued to drive it. That's the best metaphor I can come up with,' he said. 'They are saying it's an accident that they ran into somebody. I'm saying: "No, it was inevitable."'"[24] Though the leak was "spewing 50 tons per hour of the potent greenhouse gas methane" into the atmosphere, SoCalGas said it would take two months before they could stop it.[25] The company website reads: "Southern California Gas Company (SoCalGas®) delivers safe, reliable natural gas to 20.9 million consumers throughout Central and Southern California."[26] "The safety and security of our pipeline system is our top priority."[27]

Those are merely a few of the horrendous environmental impacts—to list all would fill up a book.

And you can also add the Agri-Chem corporations to the list of big problem polluters:

> Monsanto is a major threat to climate change due to its energy-intensive agricultural model and promotion of ethanol as a fuel source. The Organic Consumers Association adds it all up: "All told, the production and processing of Monsanto's GMO crops, from deforestation to fossil

fuel–based pesticides and fertilizers, polluting factory farms, and fuel-intensive food processing and distribution, is estimated to produce up to 51% of global greenhouse gas emissions."[28]

If you watch the documentary *Gasland*, it does a great job of explaining the problems with fracking (hydraulic fracturing, the process by which they drill deep into the earth and shoot a mixture of high-pressure water, chemicals, and sand into the rock to release deep sources of gas).[29] *National Geographic*—hardly known as a wildly alternative media source—also documented some of the dangers of fracking, years ago.[30] Often, ranchers and farmers "own their land but not the mineral rights, so they had no say in the placement of the wells."[31] They put the damn things wherever the companies want to, and if that happens to be close to families who breathe it in, they do it anyway.

Halliburton are the freaking folks who invented fracking:

> Halliburton developed the process in 1949 and utilized the technology for decades with oil and gas wells to increase production, as they began to run dry. In conventional fracking, the well is stimulated by pumping in water at high pressure. But hydraulic fracturing used for shale rock is a relatively new process and the one we hear most about today.[32]

"The US currently has 500,000 active gas wells, which require 72 trillion gallons of water and 360 billion gallons of chemicals to run." One might say: So *that's* where all our water is going. In other words: We've Been *Fracked*, Folks!

So there are *hundreds of thousands* of fracked wells stretching across America and their environmental impact has never been properly assessed.[33] It began in the Bakken formation of North Dakota,[34] then on to the prairies of Wyoming, and has now spread like a wildfire out of control.[35] A majority of states are now fracking and the big companies are in a state of denial about its dangers.[36] But the toxic gases from those wells deaden a person's sense of smell and "can be poisonous, even lethal."[37] Other independent news reports have verified that the ground water underneath those wells also gets contaminated with natural gas.[38]

The *Gasland* documentary also shows how the bastards at these giant corporations have the nerve to sit in front of Congress and lie through their teeth, testifying that there are no environmental dangers from fracking at all.[39] And *then*, that same documentary shows the people who live near a well, <u>lighting their tap water on fire</u>—*literally*. Their water has so much gas and so many chemicals in it that it <u>ignites in their sink and explodes</u>![40] But it's safe to drink, right? Yeah, *sure* it is.

The fracking fluid consists of "a mix of at least 596 chemicals (many of them toxic), from the unpronounceable, to the unknown, to the too well known. The brew is full of corrosion inhibitors, gellants, drilling additives, biocides, shale control inhibitors, liquid breaker aids, viscosifiers, liquid gel concentrates."[41] And, oh yeah—many of them are known to be cancer-causing chemicals.[42] But since those chemicals and the combinations of them that are used are legally considered proprietary information, those companies don't even have to divulge to anyone what they are injecting into our planet![43]

Documentarian Josh Fox did some digging and came up with some very interesting facts:

> What I didn't know was that the 2005 energy bill, pushed through Congress by Dick Cheney, exempts the oil and natural gas industries from the Safe Water Drinking Act. They were also exempt from the Clean Air Act, the Clean Water Act, the Superfund Law and about a dozen other environmental and democratic regulations.[44]

And, as you may remember, the illustrious Mr. Cheney just happened to be the former CEO of Halliburton. Well, guess who reaped a fortune from that bill? You *got* it—*Halliburton*.[45] They even call that game-changer the "Halliburton loophole."[46] Mr. Cheney was CEO of that company from 1995 until he became Vice President in 2000, and one of the first things he did in Washington was to form the Energy Task Force, which lobbied almost exclusively for energy interests.[47] It was largely that group and a 100-million-dollar lobbying effort—or, as we call it in the first chapter of this book—*buying votes*—that got the 2005 energy bill passed by Congress.[48] That bill authorized "oil and gas drillers, exclusively, to inject known hazardous materials, unchecked, directly into or adjacent to underground drinking water supplies."[49]

It gets worse! They even took over huge land areas for fracking that are in the public trust—in other words, they actually belong to us as part of the Bureau of Land Management (BLM)—lands open to the public at all times. Vice President Cheney started pushing the BLM to lease those public lands of ours for fracking and, "in what some call the greatest transfer of public lands to private hands in history, Dick Cheney persuaded the BLM to lease millions of acres to gas companies for exploration and drilling."[50]

> When the 2005 energy bill cleared away all the restrictions, companies like Encana, Williams, Cabot Oil & Gas, and Chesapeake began to use the new Halliburton technology (fracking) and it began the largest and most extensive domestic gas drilling campaign in history, now occupying 34 states.[51]

So these big companies go in and suck all the gas they can out of the ground but if they contaminate people's drinking water, they stonewall the people who get sick and make them take them to court before they can get anything resolved. Dr. Theo Colburn is a distinguished medical expert who has investigated the effects of fracking and has concluded that "Every environmental law we wrote to protect public health is ignored. But the neurological effects are very insidious."[52] The symptoms of the exposure to those toxic chemicals develop and "eventually you may feel what is called peripheral neuropathy and when you get to this stage, you have irreversible brain damage."[53]

> The corporate business model is to come into an area, develop it as fast as you can and if you trash anything, you make the people who you impact prove it, you make them argue it in a court of law, and the last person standing is bought off and you move on.[54]

And meanwhile, your drinking water is flammable! The results? Contaminated ground water and air, chronically ill residents—and pushing animals already on the endangered species list like the pronghorn ante-lope, mule deer, and sage grouse closer to the brink of extinction.[55]

Great, huh? So hey, all you big fat cat executives at Big Energy compa-nies—this is direct from us to you, for once and for all—*Frack You!*

And above all: *Frack Off!*

Another great documentary called *Pump* is also very enlightening. It explains how the US mass transit system of electric trolley cars was very successful and highly functional: "Once upon a time, we had the best and cheapest public transportation in the world."[56] *Until* a corporate con-spiracy of oil-related companies bought up all the trolley cars, destroyed them, and replaced them with city bus systems that ran on gasoline in-stead.[57] We're not making this up! It's not *us* saying it was a corporate conspiracy. Those corporations were indicted, tried in a court of law, and found guilty of conspiracy! Their names were Standard Oil, Phillips Pe-troleum, General Motors, Firestone, and Mack Trucks, Inc.:

> Eventually, the federal government discovered that this was a conspiracy to subvert mass transit. All five corporations were indicted, they were tried, they were found guilty. A corporate conspiracy was responsible for destroying the trolleys in America.[58]

They had formed a secret company to do their dirty deed, were caught and convicted—but their plan succeeded.[59] Our national system of electric trolley cars was destroyed, the national highway system was constructed, and our reliance upon an oil economy was established.

The smear campaign against ethanol and biofuels was also financed by the oil industry. It was said, and put all over mainstream media, that the use of bio fuels endangered the world's food supplies—which is patently false![60]

But instead of *penalizing* the huge, irresponsible companies, we, as tax-payers, actually help these corporate monsters. Against all common sense and thousands of protests—now we are letting them drill in precious eco-systems like the Arctic. That just happened in 2015. It's madness!

> The Interior Department decision angered environmentalists who for years have demanded that the administration reject offshore Arctic

drilling proposals. They fear that a drilling accident in the treacherous Arctic Ocean waters could have far more devastating consequences than the deadly Gulf of Mexico spill of 2010, when the Deepwater Horizon rig explosion killed 11 men and sent millions of barrels of oil spewing into the water.[61]

And then on top of all that, we actually *subsidize* their corporate crimes!

In 2015, the International Monetary Fund reported that global energy subsidies for that year will amount to 5.3 trillion dollars, with the United States providing $700 billion in subsidies to big oil.[62] As Robert F. Kennedy, Jr. observed, they are already "the richest industry in the history of the planet."[63] And Kennedy really blew their doors off with the truth, full throttle:

> "Why would we be doing that?" he asks. "The only reason we'd give subsidies to a century-old industry with the biggest profits in human history is because the oil barons own our government. There is no economic reason. Carbon's economic model is looking at the same bleak future as the horse and buggy industry faced in 1903. So what do you do when your profits rely on a fading economic model? You use your money and use the campaign finance system that consists of legalized bribery to get your hooks into a public official who allows you to privatize the commons, dismantle the market place and rig the rules to give you monopoly control," Kennedy explained.[64]

So why in hell are we giving them subsidies? Why would we subsidize *anything* for those companies? *Why* are we doing that? Are we insane? It only happens because the Big Energy fat cats buy their extensive influence in Washington with donations and gifts—what one would call flat out bribery—and they find ways to suppress the true facts of it all in the media. Because if people knew it was happening they would be in an uproar—as they *should* be! But we're here to tell you folks, it is happening! We're giving them billions of our tax dollars! It's *happening*, now, today.

And it's not just folks like us saying that—it's even huge established organizations like the International Monetary Fund. Even the IMF recommends reducing or eliminating those obscenely huge energy subsidies and observes that the reform gains would be large—large enough, for example in the United States, to "cover one-quarter of public health spending."[65] This is right out of the 2015 IMF Report:

> Eliminating global energy subsidies could reduce deaths related to fossil fuel emissions by over 50 percent and fossil fuel–related carbon emissions by over 20 percent. The revenue gain from eliminating energy subsidies is projected to be US $2.9 trillion (3.6 percent of global GDP) in 2015. This offers huge potential for reducing other taxes or strengthening revenue bases in countries where large informal sector constrains broader fiscal instruments.[66]

And the crap from these corporations just keeps on coming. In September 2016 it was revealed that the fossil fuel industry was working secretly behind the scenes in an attempt to undermine and kill the federally proposed Clean Power Plan addressing the dangers of climate change.[67] It begs the question:

When will these corporate scumbags give up trying to destroy our planet?

One thing that becomes crystal clear as all of these corporations' smokescreens dissolve around us is that we all need to become involved in these issues. The speech on the subject by Robert F. Kennedy, Jr. clearly laid out the enemy we face:

> Whether we recognize it or not, we are all locked in a life-and-death struggle with these corporations over control of our landscapes and political sovereignty. If a foreign nation did to our country what the coal and oil barons do every day, we would consider it an act of war! They poison our rivers and aquifers, steal our fish, flood our cities, and trample our democracy. They are pilfering our values, robbing our culture, impoverishing our lives, sickening our children, and stupefying our minds with pollution. They subvert our heritage by privatizing our patrimony. They are turning America into a colonial economy.[68]

All around the country, people are grouping together to fight the energy industry and their poisoning of our communities.[69] People have _had_ it with the reckless disregard of the fossil fuels industry for human health—and that of our planet—and they're finally doing something about it too.

> The bulk of the chemicals that cause cancer are derived from fossil fuels, petrochemicals. Moving our economy away from fossil fuels is already something we need to do because of climate change. Even though the environment and cancer seems like this big, overwhelming and depressing problem, in fact its root causes are the same as the causes that are killing the planet.[70]

As biologist Sandra Steingraber eloquently puts it:

> We are all musicians in this great human orchestra. It really *is* time now to play the "Save The World" symphony. None of us has to play solo, but we do have to know which instrument we hold and play it as well as we can . . . What we love, we must protect.[71]

And, as Margaret Mead—a sociologist who really *did* change the world, said:

Never doubt that a small group of thoughtful, committed citizens can change the world. Indeed, it's the only thing that ever has.[72]

It's time we *all* join that effort to change our world:

> We are killing ourselves with coal, with chemicals, with carelessness, and with greed. The people behind all this don't care, and won't care until they are made to. Navajo Nation activists literally chased a sitting US senator down the road and off their lands in an attempt to force the issue.
>
> What will you do?[73]

There are still over 500 coal-fired power production plants in the United States and that is unacceptable, given what we now know about their poisonous emissions into our atmosphere and their contribution to global warming.[74] They have stagnant capacity and declining output yet they continue polluting our planet day and night with deadly toxins that threaten the very survival of our planet.[75] They should be closed—*now*!

In 2016, US Senator Jeff Merkley petitioned Congress to "end all new leases for coal mining, oil drilling, tar sands extraction, and fracking on our public lands, stop all new leases for drilling off the Pacific, Atlantic, and Gulf of Mexico coastlines, and prohibit offshore drilling in the Arctic."[76] We can start by all signing that petition; it's online at:

http://www.jeffmerkley.com/petition/keep-it-in-the-ground

Senator Merkley is right on target! We need to just totally *end* our reliance on all fossil fuels, for once and for all. It's a blind date with disaster. We *have* to focus on alternative energy with all our resources— electric, solar, wind—everything. *But*—we also have to learn from our mistakes of the past and not let the alternative energy industry lapse into a state of political gamesmanship, corrupt lobbying, corporate handouts, and being subsidized with billions of taxpayer dollars. We will make them do it right this time! If there's one thing you can count on in this country, it's that if they *make* alternative energy attractive, people *will* buy it. And American innovation *can* achieve that.

We *can* prevail against these maniacs if we stay informed and act with integrity.

But, like we said at the start:

If you're not pissed off, then you're not paying attention . . .

FURTHER RESEARCH:

Steingraber, Sandra. *Living Downstream: An Ecologist's Personal Investigation of Cancer and the Environment*. Boston: Addison-Wesley, 1997.

Black, Edwin. *Internal Combustion: How Corporations and Governments Addicted the World to Oil and Derailed the Alternatives*. Washington DC: Dialog Press, 2008.

Colburn, Theo. *Our Stolen Future: Are We Threatening Our Fertility, Intelligence and Survival? A Scientific Detective Story*. New York: Plume, 1997.

Fox, Josh, director. *Gasland*. Docurama (2010). DVD.

Tickell, Joshua and Rebecca Harrell, directors. *Pump: The Movie*. Submarine Deluxe (2014). DVD.

Cohn, Marjorie, JD. "Human Rights and Global Wrongs." *Truth-out.org*. http://www.truth-out.org/news/item/24035-human-rights-and-global-wrongs.

Colburn, Theo, Carol Kwiatkowski, Kim Schultz, et al. "Natural Gas Operations from a Public Health Perspective." *Human and Ecological Risk Assessment: An International Journal* 17 no. 5 (2011):1039–1056. http://www2.cce.cornell.edu/naturalgasdev/documents/pdfs/fracking%20chemicals%20from%20a%20public%20health%20perspective.pdf.

Colborn, Theo, Kim Schultz, Lucille Herrick, et al. "An Exploratory Study of Air Quality Near Natural Gas Operations." *Human and Ecological Risk Assessment: An International Journal* 20 no.1 (2014):86–105. http://www.tandfonline.com/doi/full/10.1080/10807039.2012.749447.

Juhasz, Antonia. "Why the war in Iraq was fought for Big Oil," *CNN.com* (April 15, 2013). http://www.cnn.com/2013/03/19/opinion/iraq-war-oil-juhasz/.

"Why we are in Afghanistan." *The Charleston Gazette*. *Global Exchange.org*. http://www.globalexchange.org/news/why-we-are-afghanistan.

Dobb, Edwin. "The New Oil Landscape: The fracking frenzy in North Dakota has boosted the U.S. fuel supply- but at what cost?" *National Geographic* (March 2013):28–59.

Wright, Carolanne. "The Fracking Industry's Answer to Toxic Wastewater: Spray It On Public Roadways." *Wake Up World* (January 16, 2016). http://wakeup-world.com/2016/01/16/the-fracking-industrys-answer-to-toxic-wastewater-spray-it-on-public-roadways/.

Zaino, Kelley, Stephanie Dyer, and Sascha von Meier. "The True Cost of Chevron." *Project Censored* (October 2, 2010). http://www.projectcensored.org/the-true-cost-of-chevron/.

Oreskes, Naomi. "Exxon's Climate Concealment." *New York Times* (October 9, 2015). http://www.nytimes.com/2015/10/10/opinion/exxons-climate-concealment.html.

The Daily Take Team. "Exxon's Climate Cover-Up." The Thom Hartmann Program. *Truth-out.org* (October 20, 2015). http://www.truth-out.org/opinion/item/33311-exxon-s-climate-cover-up.

Hartmann, Thom. "Citibank warns about the cost of climate inaction." *Thom Hartmann Program* (September 10, 2015). http://www.thomhartmann.com/blog/2015/09/citibank-warns-about-cost-climate-inaction.

Thomsen, Simon. "'I don't give a f—if we agree': Arnold Schwarzenegger just gave a climate-change speech that will give you chills." *Business Insider Australia* (December 8, 2015). http://www.businessinsider.com/arnold-schwarzeneggers-went-on-an-epic-rant-about-climate-change-2015-12.

Lombardi, Kristen. Center for Public Integrity. "'Upsets': Chemical releases disrupt lives but rarely result in punishment." *NBC News* (May 21, 2013). http://investigations.nbcnews.com/_news/2013/05/21/18401250-upsets-chemical-releases-disrupt-lives-but-rarely-result-in-punishment.

Goldenberg, Suzanne. "A single gas well leak is California's biggest contributor to climate change." *The Guardian* (January 5, 2016). http://www.theguardian.com/environment/2016/jan/05/aliso-canyon-leak-california-climate-change.

Pitt, William Rivers. "Greed Dies Hard in a Poisoned Land." *Truth-out.org* (August 18, 2015). http://www.truth-out.org/opinion/item/32389-greed-dies-hard-in-a-poisoned-land.

Koch, Blair. "Communities Push for Legal Rights to Regain Power Over Fracking Companies." *Truth-out.org* (October 24, 2015). http://www.truth-out.org/news/item/33322-communities-push-for-legal-rights-to-regain-power-over-fracking-companies.

Lee, Matilda. "Sandra Steingraber: There's a taboo about telling industry and agriculture that practices must change to prevent cancer." *The Ecologist* (November 30, 2010). http://www.theecologist.org/Interviews/687501/sandra_steingraber_theres_a_taboo_about_telling_industry_and_agriculture_that_practices_must_change_to_prevent_cancer.html.

"Counting the Cost of Energy Subsidies," International Monetary Fund (July 17, 2015). http://www.imf.org/external/pubs/ft/survey/so/2015/new070215a.htm.

Merkley, Jeff, Senator. "TELL CONGRESS: KEEP FOSSIL FUELS IN THE GROUND!" *CREDO Mobilize* (December 6, 2015). http://www.jeff merkley.com/petition/keep-it-in-the-ground

Spear, Stefanie. "RFK, Jr. Calls Koch Brothers 'Deadly Parasites on American Democracy.'" *The Ring of Fire Network* (September 13, 2015). http://ringoffire-radio.com/2015/09/13/rfk-jr-calls-koch-brothers-deadly-parasites-on-american-democracy/.

Afterword

You have seen some amazing examples of corporate corruption in the chapters of this book and you may be wondering what can possibly be done about it. The answer to that question is: a lot.

Many of the abuses of Corporate America would not be possible without our silent cooperation. Most of Congress has to stand up for re-election every two years. If we participate fully, working together, we can force them to be transparent and equitable. We have to end fossil fuels *before they end us*. In 2016, US Senator Jeff Merkley petitioned Congress to "end all new leases for coal mining, oil drilling, tar sands extraction, and fracking on our public lands, stop all new leases for drilling off the Pacific, Atlantic, and Gulf of Mexico coastlines, and prohibit offshore drilling in the Arctic." We can start by all signing Senator Merkley's online petition.

There are many things we can each do to help end our slavery to these corporate masters and return our republic back to We, The People in an *actual* democracy instead of the corporate oligarchy that currently rules our country. Become your *own* lobbyist. Email your representatives in Washington—you have two Senators, one Representative in the House, and the President, who are *supposed* to be representing *you*. Tell them it's a priority to you to redirect our focus from fossil fuels to alternative energy. Also contact them regarding the following:

- Force corporations to pay their fair tax share by totally eliminating the elaborate tax breaks like deferrals and offshoring capital, that politicians are always giving them, while they promise to us (at election time) that they will close them, but never actually do.
- Make the wealthiest Americans pay their fair share of tax.
- Enhance and enforce environmental policies that get co-opted by the political influence exerted by corporate lobbying and the revolving door between Washington and corporate boardrooms. We should *close* that revolving door and make it illegal for officers of corporations

to receive positions at government agencies that are responsible for the oversight of those *same* corporations.

- Make banks play by the rules by closing the loopholes for Wall Street and returning to the safeguards that were in place prior to the repeal of the Glass-Steagall Act.

- Send the message that our democracy is *not* for sale! Return to reasonable limits on campaign contributions, such as $10,000 to any campaign—whether it is by an individual, a corporation, or a committee; limit total contributions from any one organization or individual to $100,000; limit spending by candidates from personal funds to $50,000.

- Stop the self-serving "pork barrel" projects that proliferate in Congress, and reign in excessive military spending on ridiculously expensive programs that are often deemed superfluous before they are even produced.

- Petition Congress for an immediate 25 percent reduction in the defense budget, followed by another 5 percent reduction every year for the next five years. And we know what you're thinking, but *believe this,* we will *still* have the strongest military in the world—and by using that money for a strong economy, we will actually be *more* secure, not less. With those funds, we can create *millions* of jobs and rebuild America's crumbling infrastructure in the process.

- Totally eliminate private corporations from profiting on what is currently a prison–industrial complex that actually promotes a blatantly racist system of encouraging the incarceration of minorities.

- Reinforce the fact that the airwaves belong to the public—and require access to mainstream radio and TV stations that is representative of alternative and minority interests.

- Petition and force the CDC and FDA to recognize the valid research concerning the links between the high mercury and aluminum levels in vaccines and the skyrocketing rates of autism and immediately ban them from all vaccines.

- Direct the FDA to ban all toxic pesticides and dangerous prescription drugs, require the labeling of all GMO ingredients, and redirect our priorities *away* from GMO crops.

- Use the court system in favor of We, The People: "Lawbreaking corporations can be dissolved, put out of business and their assets sold pursuant to a judge's order. Corporations have no inherent right to exist. Since corporations are created by states, the states possess the power to dissolve them. Every state and the District of Columbia have a procedure by which citizens, through their attorney general, can go to court to revoke the charter of a corporation that violates the law." That's what law professor Marjorie Cohn suggests we do to ExxonMobil and here's why: "Exxon made a strategic decision to publicly sow seeds of doubt about climate change while internally confirming it."

- Use the policies of shareholder activism and promoting SRI (Socially Responsible Investing) to hit these greedy corporations right where they live—in the dollar signs. We urge you to support the elimination of the use of public monies and pension funds to effectively encourage investment in corporate corruption and the poisoning of our precious environment in pursuit of profit. We can force their hand by blacklisting—and even boycotting—companies with unethical business practices. We have the choice to Go Green with our investment dollars, or to continue supporting state-sponsored corporate crimes—it's as simple as that. Isn't it time that we wake up? Clearly, it is now time that we all make the conscious move to Go Green.

So we're *not* powerless. We have many democratic vehicles at our disposal. Let's *use them*. Let's *take back* control of this Republic—take it *out* of the hands of the megacorporations who now can literally buy their influence from the politicians—and put it back *into* the hands of *We, The People* where it belongs.

NOTES

Introduction

1 Charlie Derber, *Regime Change Begins at Home: Freeing America from Corporate Rule* (Oakland, CA: Berrett-Koehler Publishers: 2004).

2 Ibid.

3 Prof. James F. Tracy, "'Conspiracy Theory': Foundations of a Weaponized Term; Subtle and Deceptive Tactics to Discredit Truth in Media and Research," Global Research, January 22, 2013, http://www.globalresearch.ca/conspiracy -theory-foundations-of-a-weaponized -term/5319708.

4 Kelly Patricia O'Meara, "Contrary to News Headlines, Robin Williams Was on Drugs at the Time of His Death– Antidepressant Drugs," CCHR International, November 10, 2014, http://www.cchrint.org/2014/11/10 /robin-williams-was-on-drugs-at-the -time-of-his-death-antidepressant-drugs/.

5 Nicole Flatow, "The United States Has the Largest Prison Population In The World— And It's Growing," *ThinkProgress*, September 17, 2014, http://thinkprogress. org/justice/2014/09/17/3568232/the -united-states-had-even-more-prisoners -in-2013/.

6 New York Indymedia, "The pulling down of the Statue was a staged media event," *Global Research*, April 11, 2003, http:// www.globalresearch.ca/articles/NYI304A .html.

7 Thom Hartmann, "Citibank Warns About the Cost of Climate Inaction," Spunik News, September 11, 2015, http://sputniknews .com/radio_thom_hartmann_show /20150911/1026879714.html.

8 Tom Hays and Tom Krisher, "GM Pays to Settle Ignition Switch Cases," Associated Press, September 17, 2015, http://www.usnews.com/news/business /articles/2015/09/17/gm-said-to-settle -criminal-case-over-ignition-switches.

9 Hays and Krisher, "GM Pays to Settle Ignition Switch Cases."

10 John Perkins, *Confessions of an Economic Hit Man* (Oakland, CA: Berrett-Koehler, 2004).

11 Charles Lewis, *935 Lies* (New York: Perseus Books, 2014), 83.

12 Abigail Field, "Justice Denied: Why Countrywide Chief Fraudster Isn't Going to Prison," AOL.com, February 23, 2011, http://www.dailyfinance.com /2011/02/23/countrywide-mozilo-fraud -no-prison-trial-sec-mortgage-meltdown -deal-crisis/.

13 Stefanie Spear, "RFK, Jr. Calls Koch Brothers 'Deadly Parasites on American Democracy,'" The Ring of Fire Network, September 13, 2015, http://ringoffireradio .com/2015/09/13/rfk-jr-calls-koch -brothers-deadly-parasites-on-american- democracy/.

14 Tom Stites, "How corporations became 'persons,'" *UU World*, May/June 2003, http://www.uuworld.org/articles/how -corporations-became-persons.

15 Spear, "RFK, Jr. Calls Koch Brothers 'Deadly Parasites on American Democracy.'"

16 Ibid.

17 Cost, *A Republic No More: Big Government and the Rise of American Political Corruption*, 204–205.

18 David Cay Johnston, *Perfectly Legal: The Covert Campaign to Rig Our Tax System to Benefit the Super Rich—and Cheat Everybody Else* (New York: Portfolio, 2003), 41.

19 Ibid., 49.

20 Spear, "RFK, Jr. Calls Koch Brothers 'Deadly Parasites on American Democracy.'"

21 Ibid.

22 Joshua Holland, "The Fascinating History of How Corporations Became 'People'—Thanks to Corrupt Courts Working for the 1%," *AlterNet*, November 23, 2001, http://www.alternet.org/story/153201/the_fascinating_history_of_how_corporations_became_%22people%22_—_thanks_to_corrupt_courts_working_for_the_1.

23 Jenifer Whitten-Woodring and Patrick James, "Fourth Estate or Mouthpiece? A Formal Model of Media, Protest and Government Repression," *Political Communication* 29 no. 2 (April 26, 2012): 113–136.

24 Spear, "RFK, Jr. Calls Koch Brothers 'Deadly Parasites on American Democracy.'"

25 *The Human Experiment*, directed by Don Hardy Jr. and Dana Nachman, (Santa Clara, California: KTF Films, 2013).

26 Ibid.

27 Ibid.

28 Zoe Schlanger, "A New Documentary Probes the Vast Human Experiment of Unregulated Chemicals," *Newsweek*, April 17, 2015, http://www.newsweek.com/new-documentary-probes-vast-human-experiment-unregulated-chemicals-322958.

29 *The Human Experiment*, 2013.

30 Ibid.

31 Ibid.

32 Ibid.

33 *The Human Experiment*, 2013.

34 Ibid.

35 Ibid.

36 Jesse Ventura, "WTF Monsanto?" Jesse Ventura Off the Grid, Ora.TV, March 25, 2015, https://www.youtube.com/watch?v=XJXafJXcRyk.

37 Michael Potter, President, Eden Foods, in *The Human Experiment*, 2013.

38 Perkins, *Confessions of an Economic Hit Man*, xii.

39 *The Human Experiment*, 2013.

Chapter One

1 "Quotes by Will Rogers," Will Rogers Today, retrieved November 1, 2015, http://www.willrogerstoday.com/will_rogers_quotes/quotes.cfm?qID=4.

2 Jim Schultz, *The Democracy Owner's Manual: A Practical Guide to Changing the World*, (New Brunswick, NJ: Rutgers University Press, 2002), 17.

3 Glenn Greenwald, "Top Senate Democrat: bankers 'own' the U.S. Congress," *Salon*, April 29, 2009, http://www.salon.com/2009/04/30/ownership/.

4 Greg Palast, *The Best Democracy Money Can Buy* (New York: Plume, 2004).

5 Kenneth P. Vogel, *Big Money: 2.5 Billion Dollars, One Suspicious Vehicle, And A Pimp—On the Trail Of The Ultra-Rich Hijacking American Politics* (New York: Public Affairs, 2014), viii-ix.

6 Russell Brand, *Revolution* (New York: Ballantine Books, 2014), 189.

7 Ibid.

8 Cost, *A Republic No More*, 181–182.

9 Ibid.

10 Ibid., 181.

11 Peter Schweizer, *Throw Them All Out: How Politicians and Their Friends Get Rich Off Insider Stock Tips, Land Deals, and Cronyism That Would Send the Rest of Us to Prison* (Boston: Houghton Mifflin Harcourt, 2011).

12 Ibid., 104.

13 Ibid., 110–111.

14 Ibid., 110.

15 Ibid., 75–104.

16 Ibid., 76–77.

17 Ibid., 104.

18 Ibid., 104.

19 Ibid., 85.

20 Schweizer, *Throw Them All Out*, 95–96.

21 Ibid., 96.

22 Ronnie Greene and Matthew Mosk, "Profiles in Patronage: Green bundler with the golden touch; Obama fundraiser got clean energy aid, then perch to advise Energy Secretary," The Center for Public Integrity, May 19, 2014, http://www .publicintegrity.org/2011/03/30/3845 /green-bundler-golden-touch.

23 Schweizer, *Throw Them All Out*, 96.

24 Ibid., 96.

25 Greene and Mosk, "Profiles in Patronage."

26 Ibid.

27 Schweizer, *Throw Them All Out*, 111.

28 Greenwald, "Top Senate Democrat: bankers 'own' the U.S. Congress."

29 Morton H. Halperin and Kristen Lomansey, "Playing the Add-On Game in Congress: The Increasing Importance of Constituent Interests and Budget Constraints in Determining Defense Policy," in *The Changing Dynamics of U.S.*

Defense Spending, ed. Leon V. Sigal (Santa Barbara: Praeger, 1999), 100.

30 Ibid.

31 William D. Hartung, "The Shrinking Military Pork Barrel: The Changing Distribution of Pentagon Spending, 1986–1996," in *The Changing Dynamics of U.S. Defense Spending*, ed. Leon V. Sigal (Santa Barbara: Praeger, 1999), 29.

32 Chalmers Johnson, *Dismantling the Empire: America's Last Best Hope* (New York: Metropolitan Books, 2010).

33 Schweizer, *Throw Them All Out*, 122.

34 Ibid.

35 Schweizer, *Throw Them All Out*, 123.

36 Ibid.

37 Cost, *A Republic No More: Big Government and the Rise of American Political Corruption*, 262.

38 David Sirota and Andrew Perez, "Congressional Energy Chairs Form Fundraising Committee, Rake In Oil, Gas Cash As They Push Bills For Fossil Fuel Industry," *International Business Times*, November 5, 2015, http://www .ibtimes.com/congressional-energy -chairs-form-fundraising-committee-rake -oil-gas-cash-they-push-2170149.

39 David Cay Johnston, *Perfectly Legal: The Covert Campaign to Rig Our Tax System to Benefit the Super Rich—and Cheat Everybody Else* (New York: Portfolio, 2003), 41.

40 Johnston, *Perfectly Legal*, 41–42.

41 Nicholas Confessore, "Koch Brothers' Budget of $889 Million for 2016 Is on Par with Both Parties' Spending," *New York Times*, January 26, 2015, http://www .nytimes.com/2015/01/27/us/politics /kochs-plan-to-spend-900-million-on -2016-campaign.html?_r=1.

42 Ibid.

43 Spear, "Koch Brothers: Apocalyptical Forces of Ignorance and Greed, Says RFK Jr."

44 Ibid.

45 Ibid.

46 Cost, *A Republic No More*, 228.

47 Joshua Holland, "The Fascinating History of How Corporations Became 'People,'" *AlterNet*, November 23, 2011, http://www.alternet.org/story/153201/the_fascinating_history_of_how_corporations_became_%22people%22_—_thanks_to_corrupt_courts_working_for_the_1.

48 Dan Roberts, "General Electric: Why the world's largest company still has spark," *Guardian*, January 14, 2010, http://www.theguardian.com/business/2010/jan/14/general-electric-jeff-immelt-multinational.

49 Johnston, *Perfectly Legal*, 240.

50 Holland, "The Fascinating History of How Corporations Became 'People.'"

51 Ibid.

52 Tom Stites, "How corporations became 'persons,'" May/June 2003, *UUWorld*, http://www.uuworld.org/articles/how-corporations-became-persons.

53 Steven Brill, "On Sale: Your Government. Why Lobbying Is Washington's Best Bargain," *Time Magazine*, July 1, 2010.

54 Ibid.

55 Brand, *Revolution*, 154 (emphasis in original).

56 Ibid., 42.

57 Frank Partnoy, *Infectious Greed: How Deceit and Risk Corrupted the Financial Markets* (New York: Times Books, 2003), 350.

58 Ibid., 388.

59 Ibid., 373.

60 Partnoy, *Infectious Greed*, 389–390.

61 Ibid., 390.

62 Partnoy, *Infectious Greed*, 391.

63 Ibid.

64 Ibid., 390.

65 Partnoy, *Infectious Greed*, 391.

66 Ibid.

67 Ibid.

68 Ibid., 393–394.

69 Johnston, *Perfectly Legal*, 12 (emphasis added).

70 Ibid.

71 Sue Chang, "Tech giants pay the lowest taxes among U.S. multinationals," *MarketWatch*, October 21, 2015, http://www.marketwatch.com/story/tech-giants-pay-the-lowest-taxes-among-us-multinationals-2015–10–21?siteid=yhoof2.

72 Johnston, *Perfectly Legal*, 207–210.

73 Michelle Surka, "STUDY: 72% OF FORTUNE 500 COMPANIES USED TAX HAVENS IN 2014," United States Public Interest Research Group Education Fund, October 6, 2015 (emphasis added), http://www.uspirg.org/news/usp/study-72-fortune-500-companies-used-tax-havens-2014–0.

74 Ibid.

75 Johnston, *Perfectly Legal*, 253.

76 Ibid.

77 Ibid., 266. Quoting Texas Democrat, US Representative Lloyd Doggett.

78 Johnston, *Perfectly Legal*, 7.

79 Ibid., 58.

80 Ibid.

81 Ibid., 117.

82 Ibid., 40.

83 Ibid., (emphasis added).

84 Johnston, *Perfectly Legal*.

85 Financial Samurai, "Maximum Taxable Income Amount for Social Security (FICA)," retrieved November 5, 2015, http://www.financialsamurai.com/maximum-taxable-income-amount-for-social-security-fica/.

86 Matt Taibbi, "Wall Street Isn't Winning—It's Cheating," *Rolling Stone*, October 25, 2011, http://www.rollingstone.com/politics/news/owss-beef-wall-street-isnt-winning-its-cheating-20111025.

87 Ibid.

88 Johnston, *Perfectly Legal*, 30.

89 Cost, *A Republic No More*, 266.

90 George R. Tyler, *What Went Wrong: How The 1% Hijacked the American Middle Class . . . And What Other Countries Got Right* (Dallas: BenBella Books, 2013), 279.

91 Ananya Bhattacharya, "America's 12 biggest companies now," *CNN Money*, August 3, 2015, http://money.cnn.com/gallery/investing/2015/08/03/america-biggest-companies/.

92 Tyler, *What Went Wrong*, 427.

93 Ibid.

94 Ibid., 349.

95 Tyler, *What Went Wrong*, 349–351.

96 http://www.nytimes.com/2012/01/22/business/apple-america-and-a-squeezed-middle-class.html, http://www.livemint.com/Companies/lhMmzW2muqLlDjpzm48lFM/How-US-lost-out-on-iPhone-work.html.

97 Ibid.

98 Tyler, *What Went Wrong*, 350.

99 Duhigg and Bradsher, "How US Lost Out on iPhone Work."

100 Tyler, *What Went Wrong*, 350.

101 Gretchen Morgenson, "Into the Bailout Buzzsaw," *New York Times*, July 22, 2012, http://www.realclearpolitics.com/2012/07/22/into_the_bailout_buzzsaw_285380.html.

102 Jeff Cohen, "Hillary's Candid Motto for Democratic Party: 'Represent Banks,'" *Huffington Post*, July 14, 2014, http://www.huffingtonpost.com/jeff-cohen/hillary-clinton-banks_b_5584870.html?utm_hp_ref=tw.

103 Tyler, *What Went Wrong*, 75.

104 Robert Reich, *Aftershock: The Next Economy and America's Future* (New York: Vintage Books/Random House, 2010), 110.

105 Source Watch, "Government-industry revolving door," Center for Media and Democracy (emphasis in original), retrieved September 26, 2015, http://www.sourcewatch.org/index.php/Government-industry_revolving_door.

106 Leslie Wayne, "Pentagon Brass and Military Contractors' Gold, *New York Times*," June 29, 2004, http://www.nytimes.com/2004/06/29/business/29door.html.

107 Office of the Press Secretary, "Naming of the commissioners," White House press release, January 30, 2004.

108 CBS News, "Halliburton Defends No-bid Iraq Contract," Information Clearing House, April 27, 2003, http://www.informationclearinghouse.info/article3141.htm.

109 Source Watch, "Government-industry revolving door."

110 Anna Fifield, "Contractors reap $138bn from Iraq war," *FT.com*, March 18, 2013, http://www.ft.com/intl/cms/s/0/7f435f04-8c05-11e2-b001-00144feabdc0.html#axzz3r87EV643.

111 Angelo Young, "And The Winner For The Most Iraq War Contracts Is…KBR, With 39.5 Billion In A Decade," *IB Times*, March 19, 2013, http://www.ibtimes.

com/winner-most-iraq-war-contracts-kbr-395-billion-decade-1135905.

112 CBS News, "Halliburton Defends No-bid Iraq Contract."

113 Deborah Solomon, "QUESTIONS FOR PAUL O'NEILL: Market Leader," *New York Times Magazine*, March 30, 2008, http://www.nytimes.com/2008/03/30/magazine/30wwln-Q4-t.html?_r=0.

114 The Hamilton Project, "Robert E. Rubin," retrieved October 28, 2015, http://www.hamiltonproject.org/people/robert_e._rubin/.

115 Tyler, *What Went Wrong*, 76.

116 Victoria Finkle, "The Long Shadow of Robert Rubin," *American Banker*, December 10, 2014, http://www.americanbanker.com/news/law-regulation/the-long-shadow-of-robert-rubin-1071601–1.html.

117 Clea Benson, "Summers After Government Saw Wealth Surge to $7 Million," *Bloomberg Business*, August 8, 2013, http://www.bloomberg.com/news/articles/2013–08–02/summers-after-government-saw-wealth-surge-to-17-million.

118 Ibid.

119 CBS News, "What's 'more dire' than the financial crisis?" April 14, 2015, http://www.cbsnews.com/news/treasury-secretary-henry-paulson-china-environmental-conservation/ .

120 Karen Tumulty and Massimo Calabresi, "Three Men and a Bailout: How fears of another Depression forced an unlikely trio to take charge of U.S. capitalism—and why the country will never be the same," *Time Magazine*, September 25, 2008.

121 Joe Weisenthal, "Tim Geithner Was Offered the Citi CEO Job," *Business Insider*, April 27, 2009, http://www.

businessinsider.com/tim-geithners-close-ties-with-citigroup-2009–4.

122 Jia Lynn Yang, "Jack Lew had major role at Citigroup when it nearly imploded," *Washington Post*, January 10, 2013, https://www.washingtonpost.com/business/economy/jack-lew-had-major-role-at-citigroup-when-it-nearly-imploded/2013/01/10/a913431e-5b6b-11e2–9fa9–5fbdc9530eb9_story.html.

123 Siddhartha Mahanta, "Flashback: Lew's Time at Citi And Other Disappointments," *Mother Jones*, January 9, 2012, https://web.archive.org/web/20131010032612/http://www.motherjones.com/mojo/2012/01/flashback-lews-time-citi-and-other-disappointments.

124 Daniel Halper, "Jack Lew Oversaw Up to 113 Cayman Island Investment Funds," *Weekly Standard*, February 13, 2013, http://m.weeklystandard.com/blogs/jack-lew-oversaw-113-cayman-island-investment-funds_701211.html.

125 Edward Bonnette, "The Revolving Door: Wall Street and the Secretary of the Treasury," *IVN*, February 4, 2013, http://ivn.us/2013/02/04/the-revolving-door-wall-street-and-the-secretary-of-the-treasury/.

126 Abby Martin, "Monsanto's Permanent Revolving Door in Washington," *Breaking the Set*, September 19, 2013, https://www.youtube.com/watch?v=qJXo9yRrmoM.

127 J. Woodward, "Bechtel Profits from Destruction," retrieved November 11, 2015, http://jwoodard.best.vwh.net/antiwar/bechtel/BechtelDestructFact.pdf.

128 Ibid.

129 Antonia Juhasz, "Bechtel Takes a Hit for War Profiteering," *AlterNet*, August

3, 2006, http://www.alternet.org/story /39860/bechtel_takes_a_hit_for_war_ profiteering.

130 Perkins, *Confessions of an Economic Hit Man*, 213.

131 Ibid., 214.

132 *PsychDrugs.wordpress.com*, "Eli Lilly, the Maker of Prozac, Zyprexa, Strattera and More," August 17, 2008, https:// psychdrugs.wordpress.com/2008/08/17/ eli-lilly-the-maker-of-prozac-zyprexa- strattera-evista-thiomersal-and-xigris/ citing Jeff Girth, "BUSH TRIED TO SWAY A TAX RULE CHANGE BUT THEN WITHDREW," *New York Times*, May 19, 1982, http://www.nytimes. com/1982/05/19/business/bush-tried- to-sway-a-tax-rule-change-but-then- withdrew.html?pagewanted=all.

133 *PsychDrugs.wordpress.com*, "Eli Lilly, the Maker of Prozac, Zyprexa, Strattera and More," August 17, 2008, https:// psychdrugs.wordpress.com/2008/08/17/ eli-lilly-the-maker-of-prozac-zyprexa- strattera-evista-thiomersal-and-xigris/ and John Russell, "Ex-Bush official hired at Lilly. Azar to help manage drug maker's image and direct its lobbying amid surge in lawsuits," *IndyStar.com*, May 5, 2007, http://www.indystar.com/ apps/pbcs.dll/article?AID=/20070505/ BUSINESS/705050461/-1/ZONES04.

134 *Redacted Tonight with Lee Camp*, "The Big Banks Had a Secret Agent in the Government," July 14, 2015, https:// www.youtube.com/watch?v= lNLLm0ZRAjU.

135 Ibid.

136 Matt Taibbi, "Eric Holder, Wall Street Double Agent, Comes in From the Cold: Barack Obama's former top cop cashes in after six years of letting banks run wild," *Rolling Stone*, July 8, 2015, http://www. rollingstone.com/politics/news/eric- holder-wall-street-double-agent-comes- in-from-the-cold-20150708.

137 *Redacted Tonight with Lee Camp*, "The Big Banks Had A Secret Agent In The Government."

138 Taibbi, "Eric Holder, Wall Street Double Agent, Comes in From the Cold."

139 *Redacted Tonight with Lee Camp*, "The Big Banks Had A Secret Agent In The Government."

140 David Dayen, "Why Eric Holder's new job is an insult to the American public: The former Attorney General who made 'too big to jail' a national joke now re-joins his old corporate law firm," *Salon*, July 7, 2015, http://www. salon.com/2015/07/07/why_eric_ holders_new_job_is_an_insult_to_the_ american_public/.

141 Ibid.

142 Tyler, *What Went Wrong*, 89.

143 Ibid.

144 Eric Lichtblau and Kitty Bennett, "30 Ex-Government Officials Got Lucrative Posts as Corporate Monitors," *New York Times*, May 23, 2008, http:// www.nytimes.com/2008/05/23/ washington/23justice.html?_r=0.

145 Ibid.

146 Ibid.

147 Jeanne Whalen, "Medtronic gets big cut in repatriation taxes after move to Ireland: Rates to move foreign money to U.S. drops from 35% to 5% after inversion," *MarketWatch.com*, September 28, 2015, http://www.marketwatch. com/story/medtronic-gets-big-cut-in- repatriation-taxes-after-move-to-ireland- 2015–09–28?siteid=YAHOOB.

148 Ross Douthat, "The Class War We Need," *New York Times*, July 11, 2010.

149 Egberto Willies, "Martin O'Malley announces for President and immediately hits Hillary Clinton Wall Street ties," May 30, 2015, http://www.dailykos.com/part/story/as_full?story_id=1389100.

150 Ben White, "The Goldman Sachs primary: It's Bush vs. Clinton at Wall Street's wealthiest bank," *Politico*, March 2, 2015, http://www.politico.com/story/2015/03/jeb-bush-goldman-sachs-2016-election-115672#ixzz3r7U6N3Uz.

151 Brand, *Revolution*, 239.

152 Ibid., 132.

153 Ibid., 132 (emphasis in original).

154 Brand, *Revolution*, 132.

Chapter Two

1 Stan V. Henkels, "Original minutes of the Philadelphia Committee of Citizens sent to meet with President Jackson in February, 1834," in *Andrew Jackson and the Bank of the United States* (Philadelphia: Privately Printed for Stan V. Henkels, Junior [Gollifox Press], 1928), http://kenhirsch.net/money/Andrew JacksonAndTheBankHenkels.pdf.

2 President Andrew Jackson, "Veto Message Regarding Bank of the United States," July 10, 1832.

3 Peter Schweizer, *Throw Them All Out*, 77.

4 "The Men Who Crashed the World: Part I," *Meltdown,* Directed by Terence McKenna (Ottawa, Canada: Canadian Broadcasting Corporation, 2010), DVD, https://www.youtube.com/watch?v=k5q6z_FpxIY.

5 Jesse Ventura and Dick Russell, *American Conspiracies: Lies, Lies, and More Dirty*

Lies that the Government Tells Us (New York: Skyhorse, 2010), 165.

6 Ibid.

7 Schweizer, *Throw Them All Out*, 77.

8 Charles R. Morris, *The Trillion Dollar Meltdown: Easy Money, High Rollers, and the Great Credit Crash* (New York: Public Affairs, 2008), 153.

9 Abigail Field, "Justice Denied."

10 Field, "Justice Denied." Citing former federal and state prosecutor, Mark Malone.

11 John Cassidy, "Why Didn't Eric Holder Go After the Bankers?" *New Yorker*, September 26, 2014, http://www.new yorker.com/news/john-cassidy/didnt-eric-holder-go-bankers?src=mp.

12 Cost, *A Republic No More*, 281.

13 Tyler, *What Went Wrong*, 218.

14 Ibid.

15 Ibid., 219.

16 "The Men Who Crashed the World: Part I," *Meltdown,* Directed by Terence McKenna (Ottawa, Canada: Canadian Broadcasting Corporation, 2010), DVD, https://www.youtube.com/watch?v=k5q6z_FpxIY.

17 "Adding Up the Government's Total Bailout Tab," *New York Times*—Business Day, July 24, 2011, http://www.nytimes.com/interactive/2009/02/04/business/20090205-bailout-totals-graphic.html?_r=0.

18 James Felkerson, "$29,000,000,000,000: A Detailed Look at the Fed's Bailout by Funding Facility and Recipient" (working paper no. 698, Levy Economics Institute of Bard College, Annandale-on-Hudson, NY, December 2011), http://www.levyinstitute.org/pubs/wp_698.pdf.

19 "Adding Up the Government's Total Bailout Tab," *New York Times,* 2011.

20 Thomas E. Woods Jr., *Meltdown: A Free-Market Look at Why the Stock Market Collapsed, the Economy Tanked, and Government Bailouts Will Make Things Worse* (Washington, DC: Regnery Publishing, 2009), 40.

21 Ibid., 56.

22 Brand, *Revolution*, 141. Citing David Graeber, who teaches Anthropology at the University of London and is the author of several books, including *DEBT: The First 5,000 Years* (Melville House: 2014).

23 Felkerson, "$29,000,000,000,000: A Detailed Look at the Fed's Bailout by Funding Facility and Recipient."

24 Ibid.

25 Matt Taibbi, "Obama's Big Sellout: The President Has Packed His Economic Team with Wall Street Insiders: The president has packed his economic team with Wall Street insiders intent on turning the bailout into an all-out giveaway," *Rolling Stone*, December 13, 2009, http://www.commondreams.org/news/2009/12/13/obamas-big-sellout-president-has-packed-his-economic-team-wall-street-insiders.

26 Gretchen Morgenson and Don Van Natta Jr., "Paulson's Calls to Goldman Tested Ethics," *New York Times*, August 8, 2009, http://www.nytimes.com/2009/08/09/business/09paulson.html?_r=4&ref=todayspaper&adxnnlx=1249808674-z7X0JCFkDe02pqdFpSgzFQ&pagewanted=all.

27 Matt Taibbi, "Secrets and Lies of the Bailout: The federal rescue of Wall Street didn't fix the economy—it created a permanent bailout state based on a Ponzi-like confidence scheme. And the worst may be yet to come," *Rolling Stone*, January 4, 2013, http://www.rollingstone.com/politics/news/secret-and-lies-of-the-bailout-20130104#ixzz3raJ6uDZu.

28 Robert Scheer, *The Great American Stickup: How Reagan Republicans and Clinton Democrats Enriched Wall Street While Mugging Main Street* (New York: Nation Books, 2010), 60–61.

29 Ibid., 227.

30 David Corn, "Hillary Clinton's Goldman Sachs Problem: *She talks populism, but hobnobs with Wall Street*," *Mother Jones*, June 4, 2014, http://www.motherjones.com/politics/2014/06/hillary-clintons-goldman-sachs-problem.

31 Ibid.

32 Ibid.

33 Ibid.

34 Morris, *The Trillion Dollar Meltdown*, 73.

35 Ibid.

36 Ibid., 74–75.

37 Ibid., 75.

38 Ibid., 77.

39 Ibid., 140.

40 Ibid., 153.

41 Scheer, *The Great American Stickup*, 229.

42 Morris, *The Trillion Dollar Meltdown*, 117, 152.

43 Roger Lowenstein, *Origins of the Crash: The Great Bubble and Its Undoing* (New York: Penguin Press, 2004), 189.

44 Partnoy, *Infectious Greed: How Deceit and Risk Corrupted the Financial Markets*, 296, 304.

45 Lowenstein, *Origins of the Crash: The Great Bubble and Its Undoing*, 189.

46 Ibid.

47 Ibid., 189.

48 Ibid., 190.

49 Ibid., 190.

50 Partnoy, *Infectious Greed: How Deceit and Risk Corrupted the Financial Markets*, 351.

51 Ibid.

52 Brand, *Revolution*, 140 (emphasis added).

53 Ibid., 140.

54 Taibbi, "Secrets and Lies of the Bailout," *Rolling Stone*.

55 Brand, *Revolution*, 78.

56 CoreLogic, "National Foreclosure Report," January 2014, http://www.corelogic.com/research/foreclosure-report/national-foreclosure-report-january-2014.pdf.

57 Brand, *Revolution*, 78.

58 Chris Isadore, "America's lost trillions," *CNN Money*, June 9, 2011, http://money.cnn.com/2011/06/09/news/economy/household_wealth/.

59 Colin Schultz, "The Average American Household Lost a Third of Its Net Worth During the Recession: A new study shows how much, exactly, the 2008 recession contributed to rising inequality in America," *Smithsonian*, July 29, 2014, http://www.smithsonianmag.com/smart-news/average-american-household-lost-third-their-net-worth-during-recession-180952191/?no-ist.

60 Ylan Q. Mui, "Americans have rebuilt less than half of wealth lost to the recession, study says," *Washington Post*, May 30, 2013, https://www.washingtonpost.com/business/economy/americans-have-rebuilt-less-than-half-of-wealth-lost-to-the-recession-study-says/2013/05/30/7d29a878-c930–11e2–8da7-d274bc611a47_story.html.

61 Brand, *Revolution*, 142.

62 Ventura and Russell, *American Conspiracies.*

63 Ibid.

64 Tyler, *What Went Wrong,* 463.

65 Ventura and Russell, *American Conspiracies.*

66 Ibid.

67 Jo Becker and Gretchen Morgenson, "Geithner, Member and Overseer of Finance Club," *New York Times*, April 26, 2009, http://www.nytimes.com/2009/04/27/business/27geithner.html.

68 CBS News, "When Wall St. Calls, Geithner Answers," October 8, 2009, http://www.cbsnews.com/news/when-wall-st-calls-geithner-answers/. Becker and Morgenson, "Geithner, Member and Overseer of Finance Club."

69 Glenn Greenwald, "Larry Summers, Tim Geithner and Wall Street's ownership of government: The individuals Obama chose to be his top economics officials embody exactly the corruption he repeatedly vowed to end," *Salon*, April 4, 2009, http://www.salon.com/2009/04/04/summers/.

70 Ventura and Russell, *American Conspiracies*, 176–177.

71 Matt Taibbi, "The Scam Wall Street Learned from the Mafia: How America's biggest banks took part in a nationwide bid-rigging conspiracy—until they were caught on tape," *Rolling Stone*, June 21, 2012, http://www.rollingstone.com/politics/news/the-scam-wall-street-learned-from-the-mafia-20120620#ixzz3raJzhTC9.

72 Ibid.

73 Ibid.

74 Matt Taibbi, "Obama and Geithner: Government, Enron-Style," *Rolling Stone*, December 20, 2011, http://www.rollingstone.com/politics/news/obama-and-geithner-government-enron-style-20111220#ixzz3p4t9gJVh.

75 Jeff Connaughton, "Where Are the Cops on Wall Street?" *Huffington Post*, February 4,

2011, http://www.huffingtonpost.com/jeff -connaughton/wall-street-cops- crime_b_818490.html.

76 Ibid.

77 Johnston, *Perfectly Legal*, 53.

78 Ibid.

79 Ibid., 279.

80 Ibid.

81 Ibid.

82 Associated Press, "The top 50 highest paid CEOs," http://www.salon. com/2014/05/27/top_50_highest_ paid_ceos/ and Johnston, *Perfectly Legal*, 54.

83 Lewis Krauskopf & Ankit Ajmera, "3M to cut 1,500 jobs after profit beats Street, revenue misses," October 22, 2015, *Reuters*: http://finance.yahoo.com/news /3m-cut-1–500-jobs-172438474.html

84 Jacob Davidson, "S&P to Pay Billions for Being the Watchdog That Didn't Bark: Standard & Poor's settlement is a reminder that the industry's safeguards failed in the lead-up to the financial crisis," *Time.com—Money*, February 3, 2015, http://time.com/ money/3694005/standard-and-poors- settlement-financial-crisis-rating- agency/.

85 William Michael Cunningham, "To Stop Next Crisis, Make S&P Own Up to Fraud in Settlement," *American Banker*, February 9, 2015, http://www. americanbanker.com/bankthink/to- stop-next-crisis-make-s-and-p-own- up-to-fraud-in-settlement-1072583–1. html.

86 Andrea Coombes, "Payday for lenders? Steep fees on payday loans contribute to dangerous cycle of debt: Report," *Market Watch*, November 3, 2006, http://www. marketwatch.com/story/payday-loans-

cost-consumers-billions-in-fees-every- year-report.

87 LaToya Irby, "Payday Loans and Cash Advance Businesses: Learn How to Avoid the Payday Loan Trap," retrieved November 16, 2015, http://credit.about. com/od/avoidingdebt/a/cashpaydayloan. htm.

88 Joanna Campione, "How Wall Street is taking advantage of mom and pop investors," *Yahoo! Finance*, August 10, 2015, http://finance.yahoo.com/news /the-average-investor—being- systematically-taken-advantage-of— says-new-book-130247891.html.

89 Irby, "Payday Loans and Cash Advance Businesses."

90 "How to Deal With The Credit Card Debt Of A Loved One," National Debt Relief, June 28, 2015: https://www. nationaldebtrelief.com/how-to-deal- with-the-credit-card-debt-of-a-loved- one/.

91 JP Sottile, "Our United States of Indebtedness," *Truth-out.org*, August 15, 2015, http://www.truth-out.org/news/ item/32336-our-united-states-of- indebtedness.

92 Yana Kunichoff, "Goldman Sachs' New Loan Program Enters Underregulated, Potentially Abusive Loan Marketplace," *Truth-out.org*, August 20, 2015, http:// www.truth-out.org/news/item/32433- goldman-sachs-new-loan-program- enters-underregulated-potentially- abusive-loan-marketplace.

93 Ibid.

94 Dylan Ratigan, "America for Sale: Is Goldman Sachs Buying Your City?" *Huffington Post*, June 15, 2011, http:// www.huffingtonpost.com/dylan-ratigan/ america-for-sale-is-goldm_b_877285. html.

95 Ibid.

96 Claire Bernish, "JPMorgan Hires 4-Star General Notorious for Extrajudicial Killings in Iraq," *ANTIMEDIA*, August 25, 2015, http://theantimedia.org/jpmorgan -hires-4-star-general-notorious-for-extrajudicial-killings-in-iraq/.

97 Ibid.

98 Ibid.

99 "Obama Kills Largest Corporate Attempt Yet to Flee Overseas And Dodge Taxes," *ThinkProgress*, April 6, 2016, https:// thinkprogress.org/obama-kills-largest-corporate-attempt-yet-to-flee-overseas-and-dodge-taxes-435243a357c0#. d74b20ecc.

100 Michael J. de la Merced and Leslie Picker, "Pfizer and Allergan Are Said to End Merger as Tax Rules Tighten," *New York Times*, April 5, 2016, http://www. nytimes.com/2016/04/06/business/ dealbook/tax-inversion-obama-treasury. html.

101 "Obama Kills Largest Corporate Attempt Yet to Flee Overseas and Dodge Taxes," *ThinkProgress*.

102 "Obama Speaks Out on Panama Papers, Corporate Looters, and the Politicians Who Enable Them," *ThinkProgress*, April 5, 2016, https://thinkprogress.org/ obama-speaks-out-on-panama-papers-corporate-looters-and-the-politicians-who-enable-them-95a100288377#. dl2e9ukdq.

103 Michael N. Delgass, JD, Nicole R. Hart, JD, and Eric Dostal, JD, "Why the 'Angel of Death' Tax Loophole Will Remain Alive and Well," *CPA Practice Advisor*, February 27, 2015, http://www.cpapracticeadvisor.com/ news/12049501/why-the-angel-of-death-tax-loophole-will-remain-alive-and-well.

104 Seth Hanlon, "50 Years Ago Today, JFK Called For Closing A Giant Tax Loophole…But It Still Exists," *ThinkProgress*, January 24, 2013 (emphasis added), https://thinkprogress. org/50-years-ago-today-jfk-called-for-closing-a-giant-tax-loophole-but-it-still-exists-33de0b5f01c7#.9j1coiogh.

Chapter Three

1 http://www.huffingtonpost.com/evan -f-moore/my-big-moment-in-journali _b_5645827.html

2 Editorial, "Take Back the Airwaves," *Progressive Populist*, 2002, http://www. populist.com/02.5.edit.html.

3 "The Public and Broadcasting," The Media Bureau, Federal Communications Commission, Washington, D.C., July 2008, https://www.fcc.gov/guides/public -and-broadcasting-july-2008.

4 Ibid.

5 The Sideshow Annex, "We Want the Airwaves!" retrieved November 20, 2015, http://sideshow.me.uk/annex/airwaves. htm.

6 Ibid.

7 Joe Morreale, "Concentration of Media Ownership," *Comm 264*, October 25, 2011, https://jmorreale.wordpress.com /2011/10/25/concentration-of-media-ownership/.

8 Sam Gustin, "Comcast's NBCUniversal Deal: As One Media Era Ends, Another Begins," *Time*, February 14, 2013, http://business.time.com/2013/02/14/ comcasts-nbcuniversal-deal-as-one-media-era-ends-another-begins/.

9 Institute of Media and Communications Policy, "Media Database: 1. Comcast," July 31, 2015, http://www.mediadb. eu/en/data-base/international-media-

corporations/comcastnbcuniversal-llc.html.

10 "Who Owns the Media?" *Freepress*, retrieved November 22, 2015, http://www.freepress.net/ownership/chart.

11 Morreale, "Concentration of Media Ownership."

12 "Who Owns the Media?" *Freepress*.

13 Kathy Gill, "What Is The Fourth Estate? And Why Should I Care?" *About News*, retrieved November 22, 2015, http://uspolitics.about.com/od/politicaljunkies/a/fourth_estate.htm.

14 Ibid.

15 William Astore, "The Failure of Our 'Free' Press," *Huffington Post*, January 13, 2012, http://www.huffingtonpost.com/william-astore/the-failure-of-our-free-p_b_1204288.html.

16 Ibid.

17 Ibid.

18 Ibid.

19 Glenn Greenwald, *No Place to Hide: Edward Snowden, the NSA and the U.S. Surveillance State* (New York: Metropolitan Books, 2014), 210.

20 Ibid.

21 Brand, *Revolution*, 289.

22 Ibid., 151.

23 Greenwald, "Top Senate Democrat: bankers 'own' the U.S. Congress."

24 Emily Smith, "ABC's 'secret' $105M gamble on Stephanopoulos," *Page Six*, May 18, 2015, http://pagesix.com/2015/05/18/george-stephanopoulos-future-and-105m-contract-in-danger/.

25 Spear, "Koch Brothers: Apocalyptical Forces of Ignorance and Greed, Says RFK Jr."

26 Ibid.

27 Joe Macaré and Ziggy Jeffery, "The News is the Crisis," *Truth-out.org*, November 19, 2015, https://freshpickeddeals.com/truth-out.org/the-news-is-the-crisis-735875

28 Mike Doyle, "Sign of the Times: Failure of the Fourth Estate," October 4, 2014, *Flickr*, https://www.flickr.com/photos/7931559@N08/15429701386.

29 John Horgan, "What War Propaganda Like American Sniper Reveals about Us," *Scientific American*, February 2, 2015, http://blogs.scientificamerican.com/cross-check/what-war-propaganda-like-8220-american-sniper-8221-reveals-about-us/.

30 Ibid.

31 Ibid.

32 Elizabeth Haas, Terry Christensen, and Peter J. Haas, *Projecting Politics: Political Messages in American Films* (New York: Routledge, 2015).

33 Andrew O'Hehir, "'Lone Survivor': A pro-war propaganda surprise hit," *Salon*, January 15, 2014, http://www.salon.com/2014/01/15/lone_survivor_a_pro_war_propaganda_surprise_hit/.

34 Haas, Christensen, and Haas, *Projecting Politics: Political Messages in American Films*.

35 Ibid.

36 Ibid.

37 Haas, Christensen, and Haas, *Projecting Politics: Political Messages in American Films*.

38 Calum Marsh, "*Lone Survivor*'s Takeaway: Every War Movie is a Pro-War Movie," *Atlantic*, January 10, 2014, http://www.theatlantic.com/entertainment/archive/2014/01/-em-lone-survivor-em-s-takeaway-every-war-movie-is-a-pro-war-movie/282812/.

39   Deborah Day, "'Frontline' Filmmaker Claims CIA Used 'Zero Dark Thirty' as Torture Program Propaganda," *The Wrap*, May 19, 2015, http://www.thewrap.com/shocking-new-report-claims-cia-used-zero-dark-thirty-as-torture-program-propaganda/.

40   Horgan, "What War Propaganda Like American Sniper Reveals about Us."

41   Ibid.

42   Seymour M. Hersh, "The Killing of Osama bin Laden," *London Review of Books* 37 no. 10 (May 21, 2015), http://www.lrb.co.uk/v37/n10/seymour-m-hersh/the-killing-of-osama-bin-laden.

43   Niles Williamson, "Seymour Hersh Exposes Official Lies about Bin Laden Killing," *Global Research*, May 12, 2015, http://www.globalresearch.ca/seymour-hersh-exposes-official-lies-about-bin-laden-killing/5448885.

44   Ibid.

45   Horgan, "What War Propaganda Like American Sniper Reveals about Us."

46   Dan Gillmor, "Big Media's failure to sustain fourth estate function in 2012 election," *Guardian*, November 7, 2012, http://www.theguardian.com/commentisfree/2012/nov/07/big-media-failure-fourth-estate-election.

47   Gary Kamiya, "Iraq: Why the media failed: Afraid to challenge America's leaders or conventional wisdom about the Middle East, a toothless press collapsed," *Salon*, April 10, 2007, http://www.salon.com/2007/04/10/media_failure/.

48   Charles Lewis, *935 Lies: The Future of Truth and the Decline of America's Moral Integrity* (New York: Public Affairs, 2014), xi.

49   Ibid.

50   Ibid.

51   Ibid.

52   Jonathan Schwarz, "Lie After Lie After Lie: What Colin Powell Knew Ten Years Ago Today and What He Said," *Huffington Post*, April 7, 2013, http://www.huffingtonpost.com/jonathan-schwarz/colin-powell-wmd-iraq-war_b_2624620.html.

53   Lewis, *935 Lies: The Future of Truth and the Decline of America's Moral Integrity*, xiv.

54   David Zucchino, "Army Stage-Managed Fall of Hussein Statue," *Los Angeles Times*, July 3, 2004, http://articles.latimes.com/2004/jul/03/nation/na-statue3.

55   "Reminder: Saddam Statue Was Toppled by Psy-Ops," NPR, hosted by Rachel Martin, April 9, 2008, http://www.npr.org/templates/story/story.php?storyId=89489923.

56   Max Fisher, "The Truth About Iconic 2003 Saddam Statue-Toppling," *The Wire*, January 3, 2011, http://www.thewire.com/global/2011/01/the-truth-about-iconic-2003-saddam-statue-toppling/21663/.

57   Ibid., (emphasis in original).

58   David Ray Griffin, "Building What? How State Crimes Against Democracy Can Be Hidden in Plain Sight," in *Censored: The News That Didn't Make the News—The Year's Top 25 Censored Stories—2011*, Mickey Huff, Peter Phillips, and Project Censored, eds. (New York: Seven Stories Press, 2010).

59   Ibid.

60   National Institute of Standards and Technology, "NIST Response to the World Trade Center Disaster: Federal Building and Fire Safety Investigation of the World Trade Center Disaster Part IIB – Collapse Sequence," April 5, 2005,

http://www.nist.gov/el/disasterstudies/wtc/upload/WTC_Part_IIB_CollapseSequence_Final.pdf.

61 National Institute of Standards and Technology, "NIST Response to the World Trade Center Disaster Federal Building and Fire Safety Investigation of the World Trade Center Disaster Part IIC – WTC 7 Collapse," April 5, 2005, http://www.nist.gov/el/disasterstudies/wtc/upload/WTC-Part-IIC-WTC-7-Collapse-Final.pdf.

62 Censored #18, 2007, "Physicist Challenges Official 9/11 Story," in *Censored 2008: The Top 25 Censored Stories of 2006–07*, Peter Phillips, Andrew Roth, and Project Censored, eds. (New York: Seven Stories Press: 2007).

63 ReThink911, "The Official ReThink911Video," September 2, 2013 (citing Roland Angle, PE, Civil/Structural Engineer), https://www.youtube.com/watch?v=rNR6Kbg5jJ8.

64 Ibid.

65 Censored #18, 2007, "Physicist Challenges Official 9/11 Story."

66 Ibid.

67 "ENHANCED VERSION: News Reports WTC7 Fell Before It Happens!": https://www.youtube.com/watch?v=ltP2t9nq9fI

68 Ibid.

69 Architects & Engineers for 9/11 Truth, "Science of 9/11: Who We Are," retrieved November 18, 2015, http://www.ae911truth.org/about.html.

70 911Reichstag, "9/11: DAN RATHER SAYS WTC COLLAPSES LOOK LIKE DEMOLITIONS," March 3, 2007 (CBS News, September 11, 2001), https://www.youtube.com/watch?v=Nvx904dAw0o.

71 "CNN BREAKING NEWS: America Under Attack, Bush Holds Press Briefing," *CNN.com*, September 11, 2001, http://www.cnn.com/TRANSCRIPTS/0109/11/bn.35.html.

72 Canadian Submarine Technologies, Inc., "CSTI Board of Directors," 2004, https://web.archive.org/web/20050206131007/http://canadiansub.com/Board.html.

73 Kate Johnston, "High Ranking US Major General Exposes September 11," *DiscerningKate.com*, December 10, 2012, http://discerningkate.com/2012/12/10/high-ranking-us-major-general-exposes-september-11/.

74 Ibid.

75 "The Shanksville crash," *Thingseverybodyshouldknow.wordpress.com—9/11-Look Again*, April 15, 2012, https://thingseverybodyshouldknow.wordpress.com/2012/04/15/15-the-shanksville-crash/, and Shoestring, "Shanksville, Pennsylvania, on 9/11: The Mysterious Plane Crash Without a Plane," *911 Blogger*, February 19, 2013: http://911blogger.com/news/2013–02–19/shanksville-pennsylvania-911-mysterious-plane-crash-site-without-plane.

76 Enver Masud, "9/11: United Airlines Flight 93 Shot Down?" *The Wisdom Fund*, May 7, 2007, Updated 05/02/09), http://www.twf.org/News/Y2007/0507-United93.html.

77 Ibid.

78 *Hypothesis*, directed by Brett Smith (Logic Gate Productions, 2010), DVD, https://www.youtube.com/watch?v=wkaX5n3pfZE.

79 Ibid.

80 Ibid.

81 ReThink911, "The Official ReThink911 Video," September 2, 2013, https://www

.youtube.com/watch?v=rNR6Kbg5jJ8. Citing Roland Angle, PE, Civil/ Structural Engineer.

82 Firefighters For 9/11 Truth & Unity, "Firefighters, Architects & Engineers Expose 9/11 Myths," September 2, 2015, https://www.youtube.com/watch?v=2Sft 5b2qr14&feature=youtu.be.

83 USHistory.org, "Historic Documents: The Pledge of Allegiance," retrieved November 20, 2015, http://www.ushistory .org/documents/pledge.htm.

84 Glenn Greenwald, Ewen MacAskill, and Laura Poitras, "Edward Snowden: the whistleblower behind the NSA surveillance revelations," *Guardian,* June 11, 2013, http://www.theguardian.com/ world/2013/jun/09/edward-snowden- nsa-whistleblower-surveillance.

85 Ibid.

86 http://www.huffingtonpost.com/evan -f-moore/my-big-moment-in-journali _b_5645827.html

87 Joanne Griffith, ed., *Redefining Black Power: Reflections on the State of Black America* (San Francisco: City Lights Books, 2013), 115. Citing Malcolm X speech, 1963.

88 Third World Traveler, "Noam Chomsky page," retrieved November 23, 2015, http:// www.thirdworldtraveler.com/Chomsky/ Noam_Chomsky.html.

89 James R. Hood, "AT&T showed 'extreme willingness' to help NSA spy on Americans, report alleges: More than its competitors, AT&T said to be an eager participant in government spying," *ConsumerAffairs.com*, August 16, 2015, http://www.consumeraffairs.com/news /att-showed-extreme-willingness-to-help -nsa-spy-on-americans-report- alleges-081615.html.

90 Chris Strohm, "NSA Data Have No Impact on Terrorism: Report," *BloombergBusiness.com*, January 13, 2014, http://www.bloomberg.com/ news/articles/2014–01–13/nsa-data- has-no-discernible-impact-on-terrorism- report.

91 Hood, "AT&T showed 'extreme willingness' to help NSA spy on Americans, report alleges."

92 *Terms and Conditions May Apply*, directed by Cullen Hoback (Toronto: Phase 4 Films, 2013), DVD, https://www. youtube.com/watch?v=Yn0mglH7XLk.

93 Ibid.

94 Ibid.

95 Ibid.

96 Elizabeth Flux, "Google Maps Has Been Tracking Your Every Move, And There's a Website To Prove It," *Junkee*, August 15, 2014, http://junkee.com/google-maps- has-been-tracking-your-every-move- and-theres-a-website-to-prove-it/39639.

97 Ibid.

98 "David Edwards and Muriel Kane, "Whistleblower: NSA spied on *everyone,* targeted journalists," *Rawstory.com*, January 21, 2009 (from MSNBC's *Countdown*, broadcast January 21, 2009), http://rawstory.com/news/2008/ Whistleblower_Bushs_NSA_targeted_ reporters_0121.html.

99 American Civil Liberties Union, "Q&A on the Pentagon's 'Total Information Awareness' Program," 2015: https://www .aclu.org/qa-pentagons-total-information -awareness-program.

100 John Donovan & Jackie Judd, "Balancing Privacy With 'Homeland Security'," *ABC News*, November 25, 2002: http:// abcnews.go.com/WNT/story?id =129995&page=1

101 *Terms and Conditions May Apply*, Cullen Hoback.

102 Chris Hayes, "Before PRISM there was Total Information Awareness," *MSNBC*, September 12, 2013, http://www.msnbc.com/all-in/prism-there-was-total-information-awar.

103 Ibid.

104 Timothy B. Lee, "The NSA's secrecy is bad for the NSA," *Washington Post*, June 19, 2013, https://www.washingtonpost.com/news/wonk/wp/2013/06/19/the-nsa-secrecy-is-bad-for-the-nsa/.

105 Hayes, "Before PRISM there was Total Information Awareness."

106 John Villasenor, "Recording Everything: Digital Storage as an Enabler of Authoritarian Governments," Center for Technology Innovation at Brookings, December 14, 2011, http://www.brookings.edu/~/media/research/files/papers/2011/12/14-digital-storage-villasenor/1214_digital_storage_villasenor.pdf.

107 Bruce Schneier, "My Reaction to Eric Schmidt," *Schneier on Security*, December 9, 2009, https://www.schneier.com/blog/archives/2009/12/my_reaction_to.html.

108 Ibid.

109 Cory Doctorow, "Google CEO says privacy doesn't matter. Google blacklists CNet for violating CEO's privacy," *boingboing.net*, December 9, 2009, http://boingboing.net/2009/12/09/google-ceo-says-priv.html.

110 Ibid.

111 Ibid.

112 Bruce Schneier, *Data and Goliath: The Hidden Battles to Collect Your Data and Control Your World* (New York: W.W. Norton & Company, 2015).

Chapter Four

1   Major General Smedley D. Butler, USMC (ret.), *War Is a Racket* (Port Townsend, WA: Feral House, 2003), https://archive.org/stream/WarIsARacket/WarIsARacket_djvu.txt.

2   James Joyner, "How Perpetual War Became U.S. Ideology," *Atlantic*, May 11, 2001, http://www.theatlantic.com/international/archive/2011/05/how-perpetual-war-became-us-ideology/238600/.

3   Gore Vidal, *Perpetual War for Perpetual Peace: How We Got to Be So Hated* (New York: Nation Books, 2002).

4   Norman Solomon, "Perpetual war creates endless consequences: Democrats who once spoke out against Bush's militarism have enabled Obama's," *Al Jazeera America*, July 13, 2015, http://america.aljazeera.com/opinions/2015/7/perpetual-war-creates-endless-consequences.html.

5   Hartung, "The Shrinking Military Pork Barrel: The Changing Distribution of Pentagon Spending, 1986–1996," in *The Changing Dynamics of U.S. Defense Spending*, ed. Leon V. Sigal.

6   Ibid.

7   General Dwight D. Eisenhower, "The Chance for Peace," address delivered before the American Society of Newspaper Editors, April 16, 1953: https://www.eisenhower.archives.gov/all_about_ike/speeches/chance_for_peace.pdf

8   Lauren Lyster, "Want to Cut Government Waste? Find the 8.5 Trillion the Pentagon Can't Account For," *Yahoo Finance: Daily Ticker*, November 25, 2013, http://finance.yahoo.com/blogs/daily-ticker/want-cut-government-waste-8-5-trillion-pentagon-142321339.html.

9 Global Research News, "Report Reveals $8.5 Trillion Missing from Pentagon Budget," *Global Research*, June 5, 2015 (emphasis in original), http://www.globalresearch.ca/report-reveals-8–5-trillion-missing-from-pentagon-budget-2/5453618.

10 Scot J. Paltrow, "Behind the Pentagon's doctored ledgers, a running tally of epic waste," *Reuters.com*, November 18, 2013, http://www.reuters.com/investigates/pentagon/#article/part2.

11 Ibid.

12 Paul Blumenthal, "Congress Had No Time to Read the USA PATRIOT Act," *Sunlight Foundation*, March 2, 2009, https://sunlightfoundation.com/blog/2009/03/02/congress-had-no-time-to-read-the-usa-patriot-act/.

13 Zbigniew Brzezinski, "How to Make New Enemies," October 25, 2004, The *New York Times*: http://query.nytimes.com/fullpage.html?res=9C0CE1D8163DF936A15753C1A9629C8B63

14 Vidal, *Perpetual War for Perpetual Peace.*

15 Ibid.

16 Johnson, *Dismantling the Empire: America's Last Best Hope*, 170.

17 Ibid., 170–171.

18 Ibid., 171.

19 Ibid., 170.

20 Johnson, *Dismantling the Empire: America's Last Best Hope*, 162.

21 Ibid.

22 Ibid., 141.

23 Zalin Grant, "WHO MURDERED THE CIA CHIEF? William E. Colby: A Highly Suspicious Death," *Zalin Grant's War Tales,* (Pythia Press, 2011), http://www.pythiapress.com/wartales/colby.htm; Christina Wilkie,

"Former CIA Director's Death Raises Questions, Divides Family," *Huffington Post*, December 5, 2011, http://www.huffingtonpost.com/2011/12/05/former-cia-directors-death-raises-questions-divides-family_n_1130176.html; Art Bell, "Why Was Former CIA Director William Colby Assassinated?," *Archive.org*, August 8, 2004, http://archive.org/details/WhyWasFormerCiaDirectorWilliamColbyAssassinated; Christopher Ruddy, "Theories on Colby's Death Abound," *Newsmax*, May 7, 1996, http://archive.newsmax.com/articles/?a=1996/5/07/153650.

24 Chalmers Johnson, *Dismantling the Empire: America's Last Best Hope* (New York: Metropolitan Books, 2010).

25 John Vibes, "U.S. Military Agents Deployed To 147 Different Countries In 2015, 75% Of the Planet," *Activist Post*, November 13, 2015, http://www.activistpost.com/2015/11/u-s-military-agents-deployed-to-147-different-countries-in-2015–75-of-the-planet.html.

26 Johnson, *Dismantling the Empire: America's Last Best Hope*, 183.

27 Ibid.

28 National Priorities Project, "Fighting for a U.S. federal budget that makes sense for all Americans: Military Spending in the United States," retrieved December 10, 2015, https://www.nationalpriorities.org/campaigns/military-spending-united-states/.

29 Johnson, *Dismantling the Empire: America's Last Best Hope*, 159.

30 Elisabeth Bumiller, "Costly Aircraft Suggests Cuts Won't Be Easy," *New York Times*, November 19, 2011, http://www.nytimes.com/2011/11/20/us/costly-osprey-symbol-of-fight-to-cut-pentagon.html.

31 Jack McCain, "Your Periodic Reminder
That the V-22 is a Piece of Junk," *War Is
Boring*, July 16, 2014, https://medium.
com/war-is-boring/your-periodic-
reminder-that-the-v-22-is-a-piece-of-
junk-db72a8a23ccf#.xhh18mjri.

32 US Air Force, "CV-22 Osprey,"
February 6, 2015, http://www.af.mil/
AboutUs/FactSheets/Display/tabid/224/
Article/104531/cv-22-osprey.aspx.

33 Bumiller, "Costly Aircraft Suggests Cuts
Won't Be Easy."

34 McCain, "Your Periodic Reminder That
the V-22 is a Piece of Junk."

35 US Air Force, "CV-22 Osprey."

36 Ibid.

37 Ibid.

38 Bumiller, "Costly Aircraft Suggests Cuts
Won't Be Easy."

39 Ibid.

40 November 25, 2015: http://www.business
insider.com/us-new-13-billion-
warship-2015-6

41 Ibid.

42 Jeremy Bender, "A former Navy captain
just identified the biggest flaw in the
US aircraft-carrier strategy," *Business
Insider*, April 24, 2015, http://www.
businessinsider.com/navy-captain-us-
should-rethink-aircraft-carriers-2015-4.

43 Ibid.

44 Ibid.

45 Lee Ferran, Megan Chuchmach, and
Mark Schone, "Final F-22 Fighter
Delivered, McCain Says $79B Jets Still
Have No Mission," *ABC News*, May 3,
2012, http://abcnews.go.com/Blotter/
final-22-fighter-delivered-sen-john-
mccain-79b/story?id=16270127.

46 Ibid.

47 Tony Capaccio, "The F-22's Belated
Combat Debut Against Islamic State
Earns Praise," *BloombergBusiness.
com*, February 18, 2015, http://www.
bloomberg.com/news/articles/2015–
02–18/f-22-s-belated-debut-against-
islamic-state-praised-by-commander.

48 Bob Cox, "F-22 Safety Concerns Linger,"
Fort Worth Star-Telegram, August 26,
2012, http://www.military.com/daily-
news/2012/08/26/f22-safety-concerns-
linger.html.

49 Ferran, Chuchmach, and Schone, "Final
F-22 Fighter Delivered, McCain Says
$79B Jets Still Have No Mission."

50 Ibid.

51 James Fallows and Jackie Lay, "The
Pentagon's $1.5 Trillion Mistake,"
Atlantic, December 29, 2014, http://www
.theatlantic.com/video/index/384088/
the-pentagons-15-trillion-mistake/.

52 AJ Vicens, "The F-35 is still FUBAR,"
Mother Jones, March 17, 2015, http://
www.motherjones.com/politics/2015
/03/f35-jet-fighter-safety-problems.

53 Ibid.

54 Fallows and Lay, "The Pentagon's $1.5
Trillion Mistake."

55 Gillian Rich, "Can The F-35 Beat The
A-10 In Close-Air Support?" *Investor's
Business Daily*, August 21, 2015, http://
news.investors.com/business/082115–
767623-can-the-f35-beat-the-a10-in-
close-air-support.htm#ixzz3u2bxTLko.

56 David Francis, "How DOD's $1.5
Trillion F-35 Broke the Air Force,"
CNBC, July 31, 2014, http://www.cnbc.
com/2014/07/31/how-dods-15-trillion-
f-35-broke-the-air-force.html.

57 Brendan Fischer, "A Banana Republic
Once Again?" *The Center for Media
and Democracy's PR Watch*, December
27, 2010, http://www.prwatch.org/news

/2010/12/9834/banana-republic-once-again.

58   Ibid.

59   "Letter from Francis Gary Powers, September 26, 1961," in Francis Gary Powers, Jr. and Douglas E. Campbell, *Letters From A Soviet Prison: The Personal Journal and Correspondence of CIA U-2 Pilot Francis Gary Powers* (manuscript).

60   Ibid.

61   Jeremy Scahill, Sverre Tysl, and Noel Byrne, PhD, "Behind Blackwater Inc.," January 26, 2007, in *Project Censored: The News That Didn't Make the News —The Year's Top 25 Censored Stories-2007*, Peter Phillips, Andrew Roth and Project Censored, eds. (New York: Seven Stories Press, 2007), http://www.projectcensored.org/7-behind-blackwater-inc/.

62   Jeremy Scahill, *Blackwater: The Rise of the World's Most Powerful Mercenary Army* (New York, Nation Books, 2007).

63   Nathan Hodge, "Company Once Known as Blackwater Ditches Xe for Yet Another New Name," *Wall Street Journal*, December 12, 2011, http://www.wsj.com/articles/SB10001424052970204319004577089021757803802.

64   Scahill, *Blackwater: The Rise of the World's Most Powerful Mercenary Army.*

65   Ibid.

66   Ibid.

67   Andrew Hobbs, Brittney Gates, and Kelsey Arnold, "Blackwater (Xe): The Secret US War in Pakistan," October 2, 2010, in *Censored: The News That Didn't Make the News—The Year's Top 25 Censored Stories- 2011*, Mickey Huff, Peter Phillips, and Project Censored, eds. (New York: Seven Stories Press, 2010), http://www.voltairenet.org/article175040.html.

68   Ibid.

69   Ibid.

70   Ibid.

71   Jeremy Scahill, "The Secret US War in Pakistan: Inside sources reveal that the firm works with the US military in Karachi to plan targeted assassinations and drone bombings, among other sensitive counterterrorism operations," *Nation*, November 23, 2009, http://www.thenation.com/article/secret-us-war-pakistan/.

72   Mark Mazzetti and Matt Apuzzo, "Deep Support in Washington for CIA's Drone Missions," *New York Times*, April 25, 2015, http://www.nytimes.com/2015/04/26/us/politics/deep-support-in-washington-for-cias-drone-missions.html; James Risen and Mark Mazzetti, "Blackwater Guards Tied to Secret C.I.A. Raids," *New York Times*, December 10, 2009, http://www.nytimes.com/2009/12/11/us/politics/11blackwater.html.

73   Antonia Juhasz, Special to CNN, "Why the War in Iraq was fought for Big Oil," *CNN.com*, April 15, 2013, http://www.cnn.com/2013/03/19/opinion/iraq-war-oil-juhasz/.

74   Young, "And the Winner For The Most Iraq War Contracts Is…KBR, With 39.5 Billion In A Decade."

75   James Risen, "U.S. Identifies Vast Mineral Riches in Afghanistan," *New York Times*, June 13, 2010, http://www.nytimes.com/2010/06/14/world/asia/14minerals.html?pagewanted=all&_r=1; *Charleston Gazette*, "Why we are in Afghanistan," *Global Exchange*, retrieved December 12, 2015, http://www.globalexchange.org/news/why-we-are-afghanistan.

76 Professor Michel Chossudovsky, "The Spoils of War: Afghanistan's Multibillion Dollar Heroin Trade - Washington's Hidden Agenda: Restore the Drug Trade," *Global Research*, May 25, 2015, http://www.globalresearch.ca/the-spoils-of-war-afghanistan-s-multibillion-dollar-heroin-trade/91; Abby Martin, "How Opium is Keeping US in Afghanistan: CIA's Shady History of Drug Trafficking," *MediaRoots.org*, January 3, 2014, http://mediaroots.org/opium-what-afghanistan-is-really-about/; Bob Flanagan, "Retired CIA Agent: 'We Run The Afghan Opium Trade,'" *World News Daily Report*, September 9, 2015, http://worldnewsdailyreport.com/retired-cia-agent-we-run-the-afghan-opium-trade/.

77 President Dwight D. Eisenhower, "Farewell Address," PBS, January 17, 1961, http://www.pbs.org/wgbh/americanexperience/features/primary-resources/eisenhower-farewell/.

Chapter Five

1 James Baldwin, *The Fire Next Time* (New York: Vintage, 1962).

2 David Kaiser and Lovisa Stannow, "Prison Rape and the Government," *New York Review of Books*, March 24, 2011, http://www.nybooks.com/articles/archives/2011/mar/24/prison-rape-and-government/.

3 Ibid.

4 Ibid.

5 John Dodge, "U.S. Leads World in Prison Population By Wide Margin; Failed Drug Policies Blamed," *CBS Chicago*, May 6, 2014, http://chicago.cbslocal.com/2014/05/06/u-s-leads-world-in-prison-population-by-wide-margin-failed-drug-policies-blamed/.

6 Ibid.

7 Beth Buczynski, "Shocking Facts About America's For-Profit Prison Industry," *Truth-out.org*, February 6, 2014, http://www.truth-out.org/news/item/21694-shocking-facts-about-americas-for-profit-prison-industry.

8 Glenn Greenwald, *Drug Decriminalization in Portugal: Lessons for Creating Fair and Successful Drug Policies* (Washington, DC: Cato Institute, 2009), www.cato.org/pubs/wtpapers/greenwald_whitepaper.pdf; Barry Hatton and Martha Mendoza, "Portugal's Drug Policy Pays Off; US Eyes Lessons," Associated Press, December 26, 2010, http://www.washingtontimes.com/news/2010/dec/26/portugals-drug-policy-pays-off-us-eyes-lessons/?page=all.

9 Buczynski, "Shocking Facts About America's For-Profit Prison Industry."

10 Dodge, "U.S. Leads World in Prison Population by Wide Margin; Failed Drug Policies Blamed."

11 Scott Kaufman, "Noam Chomsky: Reagan was an 'extreme racist' who re-enslaved African-Americans," *Raw Story*, December 11, 2014, http://www.rawstory.com/2014/12/noam-chomsky-reagan-was-an-extreme-racist-who-re-enslaved-african-americans/.

12 Ibid.

13 Ibid.

14 Aaron Miguel Cantú, "Ring of Snitches: How Detroit Police Slapped False Murder Convictions on Young Black Men," *Truth-out.org*, March 31, 2015, http://truth-out.org/news/item/29950-ring-of-snitches-how-detroit-police-slapped-false-murder-convictions-on-young-black-men.

15 Erik Eckholm, "In a Safer Age, U.S. Rethinks its 'Tough on Crime' System," *New York Times*, January 13, 2015, http://www.nytimes.com/2015/01/14/us/with-crime-down-us-faces-legacy-of-a-violent-age-.html?_r=0.

16 Christopher Ingraham, "The U.S. has more jails than colleges. Here's a map of where those prisoners live," *Washington Post*, January 6, 2015, http://www.washingtonpost.com/blogs/wonkblog/wp/2015/01/06/the-u-s-has-more-jails-than-colleges-heres-a-map-of-where-those-prisoners-live/.

17 Ram Subramanian, Ruth Delaney, Stephen Roberts, et al, "Incarceration's Front Door: The Misuse of Jails in America," *The Vera Institute of Justice, Center on Sentencing and Corrections*, July 29, 2015, http://www.vera.org/sites/default/files/resources/downloads/incarcerations-front-door-report_02.pdf.

18 Tara Herivel and Paul Wright, eds, *Prison Profiteers: Who Makes Money from Mass Incarceration* (New York: The New Press, 2007).

19 *Yahoo! Finance*, "The GEO Group, Inc. (GEO)" and "Corrections Corporation of America (CXW)," retrieved February 3, 2015. Note: Like many corporations, Corrections Corporation of America has changed its name to one that is more euphemistic in an attempt to disassociate itself from ethically questionable issues like profiting from prison sentences. They are currently known as CoreCivic, Inc.

20 Ray Downs, "Who's Getting Rich off the Prison-Industrial Complex?" *Vice*, May 7, 2013, http://www.vice.com/read/whos-getting-rich-off-the-prison-industrial-complex.

21 Herivel and Wright, *Prison Profiteers: Who Makes Money from Mass Incarceration*.

22 Ibid.

23 Ibid., xi.

24 Ibid., 261.

25 Buczynski, "Shocking Facts About America's For-Profit Prison Industry."

26 Herivel and Wright, *Prison Profiteers: Who Makes Money from Mass Incarceration*, xi (emphasis in original).

27 Buczynski, "Shocking Facts About America's For-Profit Prison Industry."

28 Ibid.

29 Jennifer Gonnerman, "Million-Dollar Blocks: The Neighborhood Costs of America's Prison Boom," November 16. 2004, in Herivel and Wright, *Prison Profiteers: Who Makes Money from Mass Incarceration*, 27–35.

30 Herivel and Wright, *Prison Profiteers: Who Makes Money from Mass Incarceration*, xii.

31 Ibid., 81.

32 German Lopez, "Slavery or rehabilitation? The debate about cheap prison labor, explained," *Vox*.com, September 7, 2015, *Vox*, http://www.vox.com/2015/9/7/9262649/prison-labor-wages.

33 Herivel and Wright, *Prison Profiteers: Who Makes Money from Mass Incarceration*, xvi-xvii.

34 Ibid.

35 Ibid., 165.

36 Ibid.

37 Herivel and Wright, *Prison Profiteers: Who Makes Money from Mass Incarceration*, 95.

38 Regina Willis, "How Prisoners Are Organizing a Nationwide Strike from Behind Bars," *Truth-out.org*, September 8, 2016, http://www.truth-out.org/news/item/37537-how-prisoners-are-organizing-a-nationwide-strike-from-behind-bars.

39 Victoria Law, "Two Years After Pelican Bay Hunger Strike, What's Changed for People Inside the Prison?" *Truth-out.org*, July 8, 2015, http://www.truth-out.org/news/item/31778-two-years-

after-pelican-bay-hunger-strike-what-s-changed-for-people-inside-the-prison.

40 Ibid.

41 Ibid., 33.

42 Herivel and Wright, *Prison Profiteers: Who Makes Money from Mass Incarceration*, 34.

43 Ibid., 119.

44 Ibid., 3.

45 Ibid.

46 Ibid., 8–9.

47 Carrie Johnson, "Justice Department Will Phase Out Its Use of Private Prisons," National Public Radio, *All Things Considered*, August 18, 2016, http://www.npr.org/sections/thetwo-way/2016/08/18/490498158/justice-department-will-phase-out-its-use-of-private-prisons.

48 Sam Knight, "Justice Department Announces Initiative to End Use of For-Profit Prisons," *Truth-out.org*, August 18, 2016, http://www.truth-out.org/news/item/37292-justice-department-announces-initiative-to-end-use-of-for-profit-prisons.

49 Matt Zapotosky and Chico Harlan, "Justice Department says it will end use of private prisons," *Washington Post*, August 18, 2016, https://www.washingtonpost.com/news/post-nation/wp/2016/08/18/justice-department-says-it-will-end-use-of-private-prisons/?utm_term=.01e48c762f8b.

50 Ibid.

51 Lindsay Koshgarian, "Prisons or Jobs," *National Priorities Project*, August 20, 2016. Citing Cristina Constantini and Jorge Rivas, "Shadow Prisons," *Fusion*, February 4, 2015 and "U.S. Deaths in Immigration Detention," *Human Rights Watch*, July 7, 2015.

52 Ibid.

53 "Johnny Cash - San Quentin (Live from Prison)," YouTube video, 3:06, from a performance on February 24, 1969, posted by "ultrarobin," March 4, 2006, https://www.youtube.com/watch?v=1zgja26eNeY.

Chapter Six

1 Joseph Mercola, DO, "The 6 Types of Pills Big Pharma Wants You Hooked on for Life," *Mercola.com*, May 14, 2012, http://articles.mercola.com/sites/articles/archive/2012/05/14/mercks-adhd-drugs-unsafe.aspx.

2 Kelly Patricia O'Meara, "Contrary to News Headlines, Robin Williams Was on Drugs at the Time of His Death—Antidepressant Drugs," *CCHR International (Citizens Commission on Human Rights)—The Mental Health Watchdog*, November 10, 2014, http://www.cchrint.org/2014/11/10/robin-williams-was-on-drugs-at-the-time-of-his-death-antidepressant-drugs/; Caroline Graham, "I blame the drugs Robin Williams took to fight Parkinson's claims friend: Actor Rob Schneider says he is convinced medication caused star's suicide," *Daily Mail*, August 16, 2014, http://www.dailymail.co.uk/tvshowbiz/article-2726920/Actor-Rob-Schneider-says-convinced-Parkinson-s-medication-caused-star-s-suicide.html.

3 Mark Wachtler, "Rob Schneider says Big Pharma killed Robin Williams," *Whiteout Press*, August 20, 2014, http://www.whiteoutpress.com/articles/2014/q3/rob-schneider-says-big-pharma-killed-robin williams/.

4 Michelle Surka, "STUDY: 72% OF FORTUNE 500 COMPANIES USED TAX HAVENS IN 2014," *United States Public Interest Research Group Education Fund*, October 6, 2015, http://www.uspirg.org/news/usp/study-

72-fortune-500-companies-used-tax-havens-2014–0.

5   Jacky Law, *Big Pharma: Exposing the Global Healthcare Agenda* (New York: Carroll & Graf, 2006).

6   Statista, "Revenue of the worldwide pharmaceutical market from 2001 to 2014 (in billion U.S. dollars)," retrieved December 30, 2015, http://www.statista.com/statistics/263102/pharmaceutical-market-worldwide-revenue-since-2001/.

7   Mark Wachtler, "Statistic of the Week" (from *Natural News) Whiteout Press*, January 2, 2016, http://www.whiteoutpress.com/.

8   Mike Ludwig, "How Much of Big Pharma's Massive Profits Are Used to Influence Politicians?" *Truth-out.org*, September 30, 2015, http://www.truth-out.org/news/item/33010-how-much-of-big-pharma-s-massive-profits-are-used-to-influence-politicians.

9   Martha Rosenberg, "Disgraced FDA Official Goes Back to Big Pharma: Former FDA number two is doing what he did best on the FDA—push for the sale of unsafe drugs on the market," *AlterNet*, January 8, 2008, http://www.alternet.org/story/72513/disgraced_fda_official_goes_back_to_big_pharma.

10 Jack Campbell, Ashley Allen, and Douglas A. McIntyre, "The Ten Worst Drug Recalls in The History Of The FDA," *24/7 Wall St.*, December 10, 2010, http://247wallst.com/investing/2010/12/10/the-ten-worst-drug-recalls-in-the-history-of-the-fda/2/.

11 Mercola, DO, "The 6 Types of Pills Big Pharma Wants You Hooked on for Life."

12 Mike Ferrara, "Vioxx Killed Half a Million? The Facts Are Grim," *Legal Examiner*, May 1, 2012, http://cherryhill.legalexaminer.com/fda-prescription-drugs/vioxx-killed-half-a-million-the-facts-are-grim/.

13 Campbell, Allen, and McIntyre, "The Ten Worst Drug Recalls in The History Of The FDA."

14 Dani Veracity, "Leaked documents show Merck knew of Vioxx dangers, yet hid them for years," *Natural News*, August 6, 2005, http://www.naturalnews.com/010613.html.

15 Campbell, Allen, and McIntyre, "The Ten Worst Drug Recalls in The History Of The FDA."

16 Tim Jake, "What You Need to Know About the Celebrex Recall," *SooperArticles.com*, November 4, 2009, http://www.sooperarticles.com/health-fitness-articles/drugs-articles/what-you-need-know-about-celebrex-recall-22022.html.

17 SeegerWeiss LLP, "Drug Warning: Celebrex," retrieved January 5, 2016, http://www.seegerweiss.com/drug-injury/celebrex/.

18 Jeffrey Dach, MD, "Protect Your Family from Bad Drugs," 2016, http://www.drdach.com/Bad_Drugs.html.

19 Ibid.

20 Kathryn Doyle, "New analysis says 2001 study of Paxil for teens misrepresented results," *Reuters*, September 28, 2015, http://www.reuters.com/article/2015/09/28/us-health-paxil-teen-depression-idUSKCN0RS1V120150928.

21 "Paxil for Teen Depression Prescribed on Misrepresented Results: New Analysis," *Yahoo! Health*, September 28, 2015, citing Kathryn Doyle, *Reuters*, https://www.yahoo.com/health/paxil-for-teen-depression-prescribed-on-153018240.html.

22 Doyle, "New analysis says 2001 study of Paxil for teens misrepresented results."

23 Ed Silverman, "Johnson & Johnson Loses Trial Over Risperdal And Male Breasts," *Wall Street Journal*, February 24, 2015, http://blogs.wsj.com/pharmalot/2015/02/24/johnson-johnson-loses-trial-over-risperdal-and-male-breasts/.

24 Ibid.

25 Emily Willingham, "Janssen Pharmaceuticals Accused of Hiding Risperdal's Breast Effects In Boys," *Forbes*, August 29, 2015, http://www.forbes.com/sites/emilywillingham/2015/08/29/janssen-pharmaceutical-accused-of-hiding-risperdals-breast-effects-in-boys/.

26 Ed Silverman, "Johnson & Johnson Loses Trial Over Risperdal And Male Breasts."

27 Ibid.

28 TMZ Staff, "Robin Williams—Suicide Triggered by Depression, Parkinson's, Paranoia," *TMZ.com*, November 7, 2014, http://www.tmz.com/2014/11/07/robin-williams-autopsy-results-drugs-depression-suicide-parkinsons/.

29 Ibid.

30 Ibid.

31 O'Meara, "Contrary to News Headlines, Robin Williams Was on Drugs at the Time of His Death—Antidepressant Drugs."

32 Christie D'Zurilla, "Robin Williams' life was punctuated by struggles with alcohol, cocaine," *Los Angeles Times*, August 12, 2014, http://www.latimes.com/entertainment/gossip/la-et-mg-robin-williams-dead-death-rehab-alcohol-cocaine-20140811-story.html.

33 Natasha Singh and Ariane Nalty, "EXCLUSIVE: Robin Williams' Widow Forgave Him, Doesn't Blame Him 'One Bit' for Taking His Own Life," *Yahoo.com*, November 3, 2015, https://gma.yahoo.com/exclusive-robin-williams-widow-forgave-him-doesn-t-124422315—abc-news-celebrities.html.

34 D'Zurilla, "Robin Williams' life was punctuated by struggles with alcohol, cocaine."

35 Ibid.

36 Ibid.

37 Cavan Sieczkowski, "Robin Williams Checks into Rehab for Continued Sobriety," *Huffington Post*, July 1, 2014, http://www.huffingtonpost.com/2014/07/01/robin-williams-rehab_n_5548396.html.

38 Singh and Nalty, "EXCLUSIVE: Robin Williams' Widow Forgave Him, Doesn't Blame Him 'One Bit' for Taking His Own Life."

39 D'Zurilla, "Robin Williams' life was punctuated by struggles with alcohol, cocaine."

40 Sarah Larimer, "Robin Williams coroner's report: Paranoia, depression and Parkinson's, but no alcohol or illegal drugs," *Washington Post*, November 7, 2014, https://www.washingtonpost.com/news/style-blog/wp/2014/11/07/robin-williams-autopsy-no-alcohol-or-illegal-drugs-in-his-system/.

41 Ibid.

42 O'Meara, "Contrary to News Headlines, Robin Williams Was on Drugs at the Time of His Death—Antidepressant Drugs."

43 Wachtler, "Rob Schneider says Big Pharma killed Robin Williams."

44 Singh and Nalty, "EXCLUSIVE: Robin Williams' Widow Forgave Him, Doesn't Blame Him 'One Bit' for Taking His Own Life."

45 Holly Fame, "New Info on Robin Williams Death—Suicide Triggered By Dementia?" November 12, 2014, http://www.hollyfame.com/new-info-on-

robin-williams-death-suicide-triggered-by-dementia/.

46 Wachtler, "Rob Schneider says Big Pharma killed Robin Williams," (emphasis in original).

47 Ibid.

48 Ibid.

49 Ibid.

50 Ibid.

51 Ibid.

52 Wachtler, "Rob Schneider says Big Pharma killed Robin Williams," (emphasis in original).

53 Ibid.

54 O'Meara, "Contrary to News Headlines, Robin Williams Was on Drugs at the Time of His Death—Antidepressant Drugs."

55 *Food Matters: Prevent Illness, Reverse Disease & Maintain Optimal Health… Naturally*, directed by James Colquhoun and Laurentine Ten Bosch (Australia: Permacology Productions, 2008), DVD.

56 O'Meara, "Contrary to News Headlines, Robin Williams Was on Drugs at the Time of His Death—Antidepressant Drugs."

57 Citizens Commission on Human Rights International, "Remeron Side Effects," 2015, (emphasis in original), http://www.cchrint.org/psychiatric-drugs/antidepressantsideeffects/remeronsideeffects/.

58 *Drugwatch*, "Risperdal Black-Box Warning," October 21, 2015, http://www.drugwatch.com/risperdal/black-box-warning/.

59 DrugDETOX.org, "REMERON," 2014, http://www.drugdetox.org/druginfo/remeron.php.

60 Mental Health Daily, "Robin Williams Suicide Causes: Dementia or Antidepressants to Blame?" 2015, http://mentalhealthdaily.com/2014/12/24/robin-williams-suicide-causes-dementia-or-antidepressants-to-blame/.

61 Mental Health Daily, "Seroquel (Quetiapine) Withdrawal Symptoms: How Long Do They Last?" 2014 (emphasis in original), http://mentalhealthdaily.com/2014/05/20/seroquel-quetiapine-withdrawal-symptoms-how-long-do-they-last/.

62 Associated Press, "Experts raise concerns over Seroquel to treat depression," *USA Today*, October 2, 2009, http://usatoday30.usatoday.com/news/health/2009–04–08-fda-seroquel_N.htm.

63 Ibid.

64 Samantha Chang, "Robin Williams suicide caused by Parkinson's related dementia, hallucinations," *Examiner.com*, November 10, 2014, http://www.examiner.com/article/robin-williams-took-depression-drugs-before-suicide-suffered-from-paranoia.

65 Larimer, "Robin Williams coroner's report: Paranoia, depression and Parkinson's, but no alcohol or illegal drugs."

66 Ibid.

67 "Robin Williams Cleaned Up His Own Blood After Cutting Wrists, New Documentary Claims," *In Touch Weekly*, April 22, 2015, http://www.intouchweekly.com/posts/robin-williams-cleaned-up-his-own-blood-after-cutting-his-wrists-new-documentary-claims-56743.

68 Mental Health Daily, "Seroquel (Quetiapine) Withdrawal Symptoms: How Long Do They Last?"

69   "Robin Williams Cleaned Up His Own Blood After Cutting Wrists, New Documentary Claims," *In Touch Weekly*.

70   Anna Almendrala, "Robin Williams' Widow Writes a Devastating Account Of His Final Year," *Huffington Post*, September 30, 2016, http://www.huffingtonpost.com/entry/inside-robin-williams-devastating-final-year-of-life_us_57eee8ace4b024a52d2f25be?ncid=engmodushpmg00000006.

71   Ibid.

72   Ibid.

73   Susan Schneider Williams, BFA, "The terrorist inside my husband's brain," *Neurology* 87 no. 13 (September 27, 2016) 1308–1311, http://www.neurology.org/content/87/13/1308.full.

74   Ibid.

75   John P. Cunha, DO, FACOEP, "Sinemet Side Effects Center," *Rx List*, August 31, 2016, http://www.rxlist.com/sinemet side-effects-drug-center.htm.

76   Ibid.

77   Liz Neporent, "Doctors Blast Rob Schneider's Parkinson's Drug Twitter Rant," *ABC News*, August 19, 2014, http://abcnews.go.com/Health/experts-blast-rob-schneiders-parkinsons-drug-twitter-rant/story?id=25041317.

78   RxList, "SINEMET CONSUMER (CONTINUED)," September 1, 2016, http://www.rxlist.com/sinemet-drug/consumer-side-effects-precautions.htm.

79   O'Meara, "Contrary to News Headlines, Robin Williams Was on Drugs at the Time of His Death—Antidepressant Drugs."

80   Mental Health Daily, "Seroquel (Quetiapine) Withdrawal Symptoms: How Long Do They Last?"

81   Cunha, DO, FACOEP, "Sinemet Side Effects Center."

82   Brenda Goodman, MA and Laura J. Martin, MD, MPH, "Compulsions in Parkinson's Tied to Treatment," *WebMD Health News*, January 8, 2013, http://www.rxlist.com/script/main/art.asp?articlekey=166791.

83   "Mirapex," *Drugs.com,* July, 2016, https://www.drugs.com/pro/mirapex.html.

84   Schneider Williams, BFA, "The terrorist inside my husband's brain."

85   RxList, "Mirapex Patient Information," retrieved October 21, 2016, http://www.rxlist.com/mirapex-drug/medication-guide.htm.

86   Schneider Williams, BFA, "The terrorist inside my husband's brain."

87   Cunha, DO, FACOEP, "Sinemet Side Effects Center."

88   *Food Matters,* directed by James Colquhoun and Laurentine Ten Bosch.

89   Ibid.

90   Ibid.

91   Ibid.

92   Mike Adams, "Yet another psych drug shooter: Oregon gunman Christopher Mercer was taking five types of medication, likely vaccine-damaged with autism spectrum disorder," *Natural News*, October 6, 2015, http://www.naturalnews.com/051453_Christopher_Mercer_psychiatric_medications_autism_spectrum_disorder.html.

93   "Another Mass Shooting, Another Psychiatric Drug? Federal Investigation Long Overdue," *CCHR International (Citizens Commission on Human Rights)*, The Mental Health Watchdog, 2012, http://www.cchrint.org/2012/07/20/the-aurora-colorado-tragedy-another-

senseless-shooting-another-psychotropic-drug/.

94 Kelly Patricia O'Meara, "Are Psychiatric Drugs, Documented to Cause Violence, Fueling the Increase in Murders That is Puzzling Criminal Experts?" CCHR International-The Mental Health Industry Watchdog, September 30, 2016, https://www.cchrint.org/2016/09/30/are-psychiatric-drugs-fueling-increase-in-murders/.

95 "Psychiatric Drugs & Violence—The Facts," *CCHR International (Citizens Commission on Human Rights)*— The Mental Health Watchdog, 2013 (emphasis in original), http://www.cchrint.org/psychiatric-drugs/drug_warnings_on_violence/.

96 "Another Mass Shooting, Another Psychiatric Drug? Federal Investigation Long Overdue," The Mental Health Watchdog.

97 Ibid.

98 Ibid.

99 *Food Matters: Prevent Illness, Reverse Disease & Maintain Optimal Health . . . Naturally*, Directed by James Colquhoun & Laurentine ten Bosch (Permacology Productions: 2008), DVD.

100 *Making a Killing: The Untold Story of Psychotropic Drugging*, directed by Toby Burwell and Randall Stith (Los Angeles: Citizens Commission on Human Rights, 2008), DVD, https://www.youtube.com/watch?v=qHlLRge45sg.

101 "Another Mass Shooting, Another Psychiatric Drug? Federal Investigation Long Overdue," The Mental Health Watchdog.

102 O'Meara, "Are Psychiatric Drugs, Documented to Cause Violence, Fueling the Increase in Murders That is Puzzling Criminal Experts?"

103 Mercola, DO, "The 6 Types of Pills Big Pharma Wants You Hooked on for Life."

104 Martha Rosenberg, "Are Veterans Being Given Deadly Cocktails to Treat PTSD? A potentially deadly drug manufactured by pharmaceutical giant AstraZeneca has been linked to the deaths of soldiers returning from war. Yet the FDA continues to approve it," March 5, 2010, *AlterNet*, http://www.alternet.org/story/145892/are_veterans_being_given_deadly_cocktails_to_treat_ptsd.

105 Ibid.

106 *Trace Amounts: Autism, Mercury and the Hidden Truth*, directed by Eric Gladen and Shiloh Levine (Gathr Films, 2015), DVD.

107 Stephanie Seneff, PhD, "Roundup and GMO and the Rise of Modern Disease," April 28, 2014, https://people.csail.mit.edu/seneff/Oahu2015.pdf.

108 Anne Dachel, *The Big Autism Cover-Up: How and Why the Media Is Lying to the American Public* (New York: Skyhorse Publishing, 2014).

109 Tara Haelle, "CDC: Child Autism Rate Now 1 in 45 After Survey Method Changes," *U.S. News & World Report*, November 13, 2015, http://health.usnews.com/health-news/articles/2015/11/13/cdc-child-autism-rate-now-1-in-45-after-survey-method-changes.

110 Dachel, *The Big Autism Cover-Up*.

111 *Trace Amounts: Autism, Mercury and the Hidden Truth*, directed by Eric Gladen and Shiloh Levine.

112 Ibid.

113 Ibid.

114 *Trace Amounts: Autism, Mercury and the Hidden Truth*, directed by Eric Gladen and Shiloh Levine.

115 Ibid.

116 Robert F. Kennedy, Jr., *Thimerosal: Let the Science Speak: The Evidence Supporting the Immediate Removal of Mercury—a Known Neurotoxin—from Vaccines* (New York: Skyhorse Publishing, 2015).

117 *Trace Amounts: Autism, Mercury and the Hidden Truth*, directed by Eric Gladen and Shiloh Levine.

118 Ibid.

119 Bruce Carlson, "Kalorama: Vaccines a 25.5 Billion Dollar Business in 2014," *PR Newswire*, February 13, 2015, http://www.prnewswire.com/news-releases/kalorama-vaccines-a-255-billion-dollar-business-in-2014–300035312.html.

120 *Trace Amounts: Autism, Mercury and the Hidden Truth*, directed by Eric Gladen and Shiloh Levine.

121 Ibid.

122 Centers for Disease Control and Prevention, "Thimerosal in Flu Vaccine: Questions & Answers," October 16, 2015, http://www.cdc.gov/flu/protect/vaccine/thimerosal.htm.

123 *Trace Amounts: Autism, Mercury and the Hidden Truth*, directed by Eric Gladen and Shiloh Levine.

124 Dr. Joseph Mercola, "Mercury In Vaccines Was Replaced With Something Even MORE Toxic," *Mercola.com*, January 27, 2009, http://articles.mercola.com/sites/articles/archive/2009/01/27/mercury-in-vaccines-was-replaced-with-something-even-more-toxic.aspx.

125 Kevin Barry, *Vaccine Whistleblower: Exposing Autism Research Fraud at the CDC* (New York: Skyhorse Publishing, 2015).

126 Megan Pond, "The Flu Vaccine–What Your Doctor Won't Tell You (Or Probably Doesn't Even Know)," *VaxTruth.org*, September14, 2011, http://vaxtruth.org/2011/09/the-flu-vaccine-what-your-doctor-wont-tell-you-or-probably-doesnt-even-know/.

127 *Trace Amounts: Autism, Mercury and the Hidden Truth*, directed by Eric Gladen and Shiloh Levine.

128 Minnesota Department of Health, "Thimerosal and Childhood Vaccines: What You Should Know," retrieved January 1, 2016, http://www.health.state.mn.us/divs/idepc/immunize/hcp/thimerosalfs.html.

129 Julie Obradovic, "The Only Thimerosal Free Vaccination Schedule," *Age of Autism: The Daily Web Newspaper of the Autism Epidemic*, November 19, 2008, http://www.ageofautism.com/2008/11/the-only-thimer.html; Minnesota Department of Health, "Thimerosal and Childhood Vaccines: What You Should Know."

130 Centers for Disease Control and Prevention, "Thimerosal in Flu Vaccine: Questions & Answers;" Minnesota Department of Health, "Thimerosal and Childhood Vaccines: What You Should Know."

131 Nolan Higdon, Michael Smith, and Mickey Huff, "The H1N1 Swine Flu Pandemic: Manipulating Data to Enrich Drug Companies," *Project Censored: The News That Didn't Make the News*, October 2, 2010, http://www.projectcensored.org/the-h1n1-swine-flu-pandemic-11-manipulating-data-to-enrich-drug-companies/.

132 Lily Dane, "The US Government Has Paid Out $3 Billion To Vaccine-Injured Americans Since 1989," *Activist Post*, February 5, 2005, http://www.activistpost.com/2015/02/the-us-government-has-paid-out-3.html.

133 Ray Moynihan and Alan Cassels, *Selling Sickness: How the World's Biggest Pharmaceutical Companies Are Turning Us All Into Patients* (New York: Nation Books, 2006).

134 Ibid.

135 *Orgasm Inc.*, directed by Liz Canner (First Run Features: 2011), DVD.

136 Kevin McCoy, "Valeant buys maker of 'female Viagra' for $1 billion," *USA Today*, August 20, 2015, http://www.usatoday.com/story/money/2015/08/20/valeant-buying-sprout-pharma-1b-deal/32039235/.

137 *Orgasm Inc.*, directed by Liz Canner.

138 Ray Moynihan, "The making of a disease: female sexual dysfunction - *Is a new disorder being identified to meet unmet needs or to build markets for new medications?*" British Medical Journal 326 no. 45 (January 4, 2003): 45–47, http://www.ncbi.nlm.nih.gov/pmc/articles/PMC1124933/.

139 Ibid.

140 *Orgasm Inc.*, directed by Liz Canner.

141 Ibid.

142 *Orgasm Inc.*, directed by Liz Canner.

143 Ibid.

144 Ibid.

145 Ibid.

146 Ibid.

147 Ibid.

148 *Big Bucks, Big Pharma: Marketing Disease and Pushing Drugs*, produced by Ronit Ridberg (Media Education Foundation: 2007), DVD, https://www.youtube.com/watch?v=c7ke4RT9aAY.

149 *Big Bucks, Big Pharma: Marketing Disease and Pushing Drugs*, produced by Ronit Ridberg.

150 Ibid.

151 Ibid.

152 Alicia Rebensdorf, "Sarafem: The Pimping of Prozac for PMS: Sarafem, a new FDA-approved treatment from Eli Lilly, promises to make you 'more like the woman you are,'" *AlterNet*, June 11, 2001, http://www.alternet.org/story/11004/sarafem%3A_the_pimping_of_prozac_for_pms.

153 Harvard University, "Biographical Sketch of Marcia Angell, M. D., F.A.C.P.," 2001, http://web.med.harvard.edu/health caucus/ac_angell.html.

154 *Big Bucks, Big Pharma: Marketing Disease and Pushing Drugs*, produced by Ronit Ridberg.

155 *Big Bucks, Big Pharma: Marketing Disease and Pushing Drugs*, Produced by Ronit Ridberg

156 Ibid.

157 Ibid.

158 Law, *Big Pharma: Exposing the Global Healthcare Agenda.*

159 *Food Matters*, directed by James Colquhoun and Laurentine Ten Bosch.

160 Mercola, DO, "The 6 Types of Pills Big Pharma Wants You Hooked on for Life," (emphasis in original).

161 *Food Matters*, directed by James Colquhoun and Laurentine Ten Bosch.

162 Ibid.

Chapter Seven

1 Palast, *The Best Democracy Money Can Buy.*

2 Tom Philpott, "Move Over, Monsanto: The Pesticide and GMO Seed Industry Just Spawned a New Behemoth," *Mother Jones*, December 14, 2015, http://www.motherjones.com/

tom-philpott/2015/12/dupont-dow-merger-spwans-new-pesticidegmo-seed-behemoth.

3   Sandra Steingraber, *Living Downstream: An Ecologist's Personal Investigation of Cancer and the Environment*, Boston: Addison-Wesley, 1997.

4   Jonathan Stoumen, Adrienne Magee, Julie Bickel, et al, "Drinking Water Contaminated by Military and Corporations," *Project Censored: The News That Didn't Make the News*, April 28, 2010, http://www.projectcensored.org/17-drinking-water-contaminated-by-military-and-corporations/.

5   Philpott, "Move Over, Monsanto: The Pesticide and GMO Seed Industry Just Spawned a New Behemoth."

6   Hanzai E, "The Complete History of Monsanto, The World's Most Evil Corporation," *Waking Times*, June 20, 2014, http://www.wakingtimes.com/2014/06/20/complete-history-monsanto-worlds-evil-corporation/.

7   "Monsanto's Dirty Dozen," GMO Awareness, May 12, 2011, http://gmo-awareness.com/2011/05/12/monsanto-dirty-dozen/.

8   Hanzai E, "The Complete History of Monsanto, The World's Most Evil Corporation."

9   "Monsanto's Dirty Dozen," GMO Awareness.

10 Hanzai E, "The Complete History of Monsanto, The World's Most Evil Corporation."

11 "Monsanto's Dirty Dozen," GMO Awareness.

12 Ibid.

13 Ibid.

14 Hanzai E, "The Complete History of Monsanto, The World's Most Evil Corporation."

15 "Monsanto's Dirty Dozen," GMO Awareness.

16 Hanzai E, "The Complete History of Monsanto, The World's Most Evil Corporation."

17 Ibid.

18 "Monsanto's Dirty Dozen," GMO Awareness.

19 Ibid.

20 Hanzai E, "The Complete History of Monsanto, The World's Most Evil Corporation."

21 Ibid.

22 "Monsanto's Dirty Dozen," GMO Awareness.

23 Ibid.

24 Daniel Cressey, "Widely used herbicide linked to cancer: As the World Health Organization's research arm declares glyphosate a probable carcinogen, *Nature* looks at the evidence," *Nature*, March 24, 2015, http://www.nature.com/news/widely-used-herbicide-linked-to-cancer-1.17181.

25 Ibid.

26 "Monsanto's Dirty Dozen," GMO Awareness.

27 Ibid.

28 Ibid.

29 Zen Honeycutt, "Glyphosate Found in Childhood Vaccines," September 10, 2016, *EcoWatch* (citing MIT scientist Dr. Stephanie Seneff), http://www.ecowatch.com/glyphosate-vaccines-1999343362.html.

30 Ibid.

31 James Spounias, "The Seed of Corporate Greed," *AFP (American Free Press)*, August 18, 2015, http://americanfreepress.net/the-seed-of-corporate-greed/.

32 Ibid.

33 *Food, Inc.*, directed by Robert Kenner (New York: Magnolia Home Entertainment, 2009), DVD.

34   Philpott, "Move Over, Monsanto: The Pesticide and GMO Seed Industry Just Spawned a New Behemoth."

35   Center for Food Safety, "Dow: Destroying Our World," 2016, http://www.centerforfoodsafety.org/video/2519/cfs-videos/dow-destroying-our-world/3005/dow-destroying-our-world.

36   Ibid.

37   Rhea Suh, President, Natural Resources Defense Council, "WHERE HAVE ALL THE MONARCHS GONE??" 2015 Action Letter, (emphasis in original).

38   Hawai'i SEED, *Facing Hawai'i's Future: Essential Information About GMOs* (Koloa, Hawaii: Hawai'i SEED, 2013): http://www.hawaiiseed.org/resources/articles/facing-hawaiis-future-book/.

39   "Peer Review of GMO Safety Studies Finds Significant Flaws," GMO Awareness.

40   A Sheep No More, "The Revolving Door Between Monsanto, the FDA, and the EPA: Your Safety in Peril," *Sheep Media*, January 15, 2014, http://asheepnomore.net/2014/01/15/revolving-door-monsanto-fda-epa-safety-peril/#arvlbdata.

41   TLB Staff, "The Monsanto Pandora's Box Nightmare of GMO Global Genocide: Unleashed and Irreversible," *Liberty Beacon*, March 10, 2013, http://www.thelibertybeacon.com/2013/03/10/the-monsanto-pandoras-box-nightmare-of-gmo-global-genocide-unleashed-and-irreversible/.

42   Joseph Mercola, DO, "New Study Shows Bee Research Tainted by Corporate Funding," *Mercola.com*, August 12, 2014, http://articles.mercola.com/sites/articles/archive/2014/08/12/neonicotinoids-bee-deaths.aspx.

43   Ibid.

44   Natural Resources Defense Council, "SAVE OUR BEES," retrieved January 12, 2016, http://www.nrdc.org/wildlife/animals/bees.asp.

45   Mercola, DO, "New Study Shows Bee Research Tainted by Corporate Funding."

46   *Vanishing of the Bees*, directed by George Langworthy an Maryam Henein (London: Dogwoof Pictures, 2009), DVD.

47   Ibid.

48   Joseph Mercola, DO "Taxpayer Money Helps Pay for Monsanto Devastation," *Mercola.com*, February 24, 2015 (emphasis in original), http://articles.mercola.com/sites/articles/archive/2015/02/24/monarch-butterfly-glyphosate.aspx.

49   Ibid.

50   John Pleasants, "Monarch Butterflies and Agriculture" in Karen S. Oberhauser, Kelly R. Nail, and Sonia Altizer, eds., *Monarchs in a Changing World: Biology and Conservation of an Iconic Butterfly* (Sacramento: Comstock Publishing, 2015), http://www.centerforfoodsafety.org/issues/311/ge-foods/fact-sheets/3096/infographic-monsanto-vs-monarchs.

51   GREENPEACE, "Briefing: Environmental and health impacts of GM crops - the science," September 2011, http://www.greenpeace.org/australia/PageFiles/434214/GM_Fact%20Sheet_Health_%20and_Env_Impacts.pdf.

52   Sandra Steingraber, *Living Downstream: An Ecologist's Personal Investigation of Cancer and the Environment*, Boston: Addison-Wesley, 1997.

53   *Vanishing of the Bees*, directed by George Langworthy and Maryam Henein.

54   Sandra Steingraber, *Living Downstream: An Ecologist's Personal Investigation of Cancer and the Environment*, Boston: Addison-Wesley, 1997.

55 *Food, Inc.*, Directed by Robert Kenner.

56 Ibid.

57 "How Has the Childhood Obesity Rate Changed in the Last 30 Years?" *SPARK*, retrieved January 12, 2016, http://www.sparkpe.org/blog/how-has-the-childhood-obesity-rate-changed/.

58 *Super Size Me*, directed by Morgan Spurlock (New York: Virgil Films, 2010), DVD.

59 *Food, Inc.*, directed by Robert Kenner.

60 Jeffrey Smith, "Health Risks," *IRT (Institute for Responsible Technology)*, http://responsibletechnology.org/gmo-education/health-risks/.

61 Ibid.

62 Toxics Action Center, "THE PROBLEM WITH PESTICIDES," 2015, http://www.toxicsaction.org/problems-and-solutions/pesticides.

63 Ibid.

64 Stephanie Seneff, PhD, "Roundup and GMO and the Rise of Modern Disease," April 28, 2014, https://people.csail.mit.edu/seneff/Oahu2015.pdf.

65 Toxics Action Center, "THE PROBLEM WITH PESTICIDES."

66 Zen Honeycutt, "Glyphosate Found in Childhood Vaccines," *EcoWatch*, September 10, 2016 (citing MIT scientist Dr. Stephanie Seneff), http://www.ecowatch.com/glyphosate-vaccines-1999343362.html.

67 Beth Kowitt, "THE WAR ON BIG FOOD," *Fortune*, June 1, 2015, 70.

68 Kevin Zeese and Margaret Flowers, "The Growing Global Challenge to Monsanto's Monopolistic Greed," *Truth-out.org*, May 22, 2013, http://www.truth-out.org/opinion/item/16516-the-growing-global-challenge-to-monsantos-monopolistic-greed.

69 GMO Séralini, "Séralini retraction is black mark on scientific publishing—Georgetown professors," January 13, 2014 (citing Adriane Fugh-Berman, MD and Thomas G. Sherman, PhD), http://www.gmoseralini.org/scralini-retraction-is-black-mark-on-scientific-publishing-georgetown-professors/.

70 Jonathan Benson, "Monsanto buys leading bee research firm after being implicated in bee colony collapse," *NaturalNews*, April 26, 2012, http://www.naturalnews.com/035688_Monsanto_honey_bees_colony_collapse.html.

71 Hanzai E, "The Complete History of Monsanto, The World's Most Evil Corporation."

72 Katelyn Parks and Kenn Burrows "Agribusiness Giants Attempt to Silence and Discredit Scientists Whose Research Reveals Herbicides' Health Threats," *Project Censored: The News That Didn't Make the News*, October 1, 2014, http://www.projectcensored.org/19-agribusiness-giants-attempt-silence-discredit-scientists-whose-research-reveals-herbicides-health-threats/.

73 Ibid.

74 Camila Domonoske, "50 Years Ago, Sugar Industry Quietly Paid Scientists to Point Blame At Fat," National Public Radio, September 13, 2016, http://www.npr.org/sections/thetwo-way/2016/09/13/493739074/50-years-ago-sugar-industry-quietly-paid-scientists-to-point-blame-at-fat.

75 Markham Heid, "We're All Guinea Pigs in a Decades-Long Failed Diet Experiment," *Vice US*, September 18, 2016, http://www.vice.com/en_uk/read/were-all-guinea-pigs-in-a-failed-decades-long-diet-experiment.

76 Gary Taubes and Cristin Kearns Couzens, "Big Sugar's Sweet Little Lies - How the industry kept scientists from asking: Does sugar kill?," *Mother Jones*, November/December 2012, http://www.motherjones.com/environment/2012/10/sugar-industry-lies-campaign.

77 Heid, "We're All Guinea Pigs in a Decades-Long Failed Diet Experiment."

78 Ibid.

79 Ibid.

80 Ibid.

81 Domonoske, "50 Years Ago, Sugar Industry Quietly Paid Scientists to Point Blame at Fat."

82 Ibid.

83 Ibid.

84 Ibid.

85 Ibid.

86 Honor Whiteman, "Coca-Cola, PepsiCo funded almost 100 health organizations over 5 years," *MNT (Medical News Today)*, October 10, 2016, http://www.medicalnewstoday.com/articles/313363.php.

87 Amy Capetta, "Soda Companies Funded Nearly 100 Health Organizations Despite Conflict of Interest, According to Investigation," *Yahoo!*, October 10, 2016, https://www.yahoo.com/beauty/soda-companies-funded-nearly-100-health-231231055.html.

88 Ibid.

89 Whiteman, "Coca-Cola, PepsiCo funded almost 100 health organizations over 5 years."

90 Jason Silverstein, "Coca-Cola Company and PepsiCo funded nearly 100 national health organizations, study says," *New York Daily News*, October 10, 2016, http://www.nydailynews.com/news/national/coca-cola-pepsico-funded-100-health-groups-study-article-1.2825544.

91 Ibid.

92 The Kohala Center, "Local Foods in Hawai'i's Schools: A report on the challenges to local food procurement in Hawai'i and the opportunities to advance beyond them," September 2015, http://kohalacenter.org/docs/reports/2015_LocalFoodHawaiiSchools.pdf.

93 Rachael Rettner, "Most Americans Still Don't Eat Their Fruits & Veggies," *Live Science*, July 09, 2015, http://www.livescience.com/51500-fruit-vegetable-consumption-united-states.html.

94 D.S. Kittinger, S.T. Mayet, S. Niess, et al, "Examining the predictive value of the Theory of Planned Behavior and stages of change on fruit and vegetable intake," *Hawaii Journal of Public Health* 1 (2008) 45–51, https://fsu.digital.flvc.org/islandora/object/fsu:204633/datastream/PDF/view.

Chapter Eight

1 Marjorie Cohn, JD, "Human Rights and Global Wrongs," *Truth-out.org*, January 2016, http://www.truth-out.org/news/item/24035-human-rights-and-global-wrongs.

2 Antonia Juhasz, "Why the war in Iraq was fought for Big Oil," *CNN.com*, http://www.cnn.com/2013/03/19/opinion/iraq-war-oil-juhasz/.

3 Ibid.

4 Ibid.

5 Ibid.

6 *The Charleston Gazette*, "Why we are in Afghanistan," *Global Exchange*, retrieved January 14, 2016, http://www.globalexchange.org/news/why-we-are-afghanistan.

7   Naomi Oreskes, "Exxon's Climate Concealment," *New York Times*, October 9, 2015, http://www.nytimes.com/2015/10/10/opinion/exxons-climate-concealment.html.

8   The Daily Take Team, The Thom Hartmann Program, "Exxon's Climate Cover-Up," *Truth-out.org*, October 20, 2015, http://www.truth-out.org/opinion/item/33311-exxon-s-climate-cover-up.

9   Thom Hartmann, "Citibank warns about the cost of climate inaction," *Thom Hartmann Program*, September 10, 2015, http://www.thomhartmann.com/blog/2015/09/citibank-warns-about-cost-climate-inaction.

10   Simon Thomsen, "'I don't give a f— if we agree': Arnold Schwarzenegger just gave a climate-change speech that will give you chills," *Business Insider Australia*, December 8, 2015, http://www.businessinsider.com/arnold-schwarzeneggers-went-on-an-epic-rant-about-climate-change-2015-12.

11   Senator Bernie Sanders (@BernieSanders), Twitter, January 20, 2016.

12   Cohn, J.D., "Human Rights and Global Wrongs"

13   Nick Cunningham, "The 10 Worst Energy-Related Disasters of Modern Times," *Oilprice.com*, October 5, 2014, http://oilprice.com/Energy/Energy-General/The-10-Worst-Energy-Related-Disasters-In-History.html.

14   Palast, *The Best Democracy Money Can Buy*.

15   Kelley Zaino, Stephanie Dyer, and Sascha von Meier, "The True Cost of Chevron," *Project Censored: The News That Didn't Make the News*, October 2, 2010, http://www.projectcensored.org/the-true-cost-of-chevron/.

16   Ibid.

17   Cunningham, "The 10 Worst Energy-Related Disasters of Modern Times."

18   "Duke Energy," *PolluterWatch*, retrieved January 22, 2016, http://polluterwatch.com/duke-energy.

19   Kristen Lombardi, Center for Public Integrity, "'Upsets': Chemical releases disrupt lives but rarely result in punishment," *NBC News*, May 21, 2013, http://investigations.nbcnews.com/_news/2013/05/21/18401250-upsets-chemical-releases-disrupt-lives-but-rarely-result-in-punishment.

20   Ibid.

21   Associated Press, "California oil spill gushed like hose 'without a nozzle,' investigators say," *Fox News*, June 26, 2015, http://www.foxnews.com/us/2015/06/26/california-oil-spill-gushed-like-hose-without-nozzle-investigators-say.html.

22   "California Oil Spill," *CBS News*, retrieved January 22, 2016, http://www.cbsnews.com/pictures/california-coastline-oil-spill/.

23   Erik Ortiz, "California Oil Spill: Biologists Eyeing Extent of Damage to Waters, Wildlife," *NBC News*, May 21, 2015, http://www.nbcnews.com/news/us-news/california-oil-spill-biologists-eyeing-extent-damage-waters-wildlife-n362756.

24   Suzanne Goldenberg, "A single gas well leak is California's biggest contributor to climate change," *Guardian*, January 5, 2016, http://www.theguardian.com/environment/2016/jan/05/aliso-canyon-leak-california-climate-change

25   CREDO Action, "Tell President Obama and the EPA: Stop the worst methane

leak in history," retrieved January 22, 2016: http://act.credoaction.com/sign/porter_ranch?.

26 SoCalGas, "Aliso Canyon Storage Facility Project," January 2015, http://www2.socalgas.com/safety/aliso-canyon/.

27 SoCalGas, "Pipeline Safety is Our Priority," retrieved January 21, 2016, https://www.socalgas.com/stay-safe/pipeline-and-storage-safety/pipeline-safety-is-our-priority.

28 Zeese and Flowers, "The Growing Global Challenge to Monsanto's Monopolistic Greed."

29 *Gasland*, directed by Josh Fox (Docurama, 2010), DVD.

30 Edwin Dobb, "The New Oil Landscape: The fracking frenzy in North Dakota has boosted the U.S. fuel supply- but at what cost," *National Geographic*, March 2013, 28–59.

31 Ibid.

32 Carolanne Wright, "The Fracking Industry's Answer to Toxic Wastewater: Spray It on Public Roadways," *Wake Up World*, January 16, 2016, http://wakeup-world.com/2016/01/16/the-fracking-industrys-answer-to-toxic-wastewater-spray-it-on-public-roadways/.

33 *Gasland*, directed by Josh Fox.

34 Dobb, "The New Oil Landscape: The fracking frenzy in North Dakota has boosted the U.S. fuel supply—but at what cost."

35 *Gasland*, directed by Josh Fox.

36 Ibid.

37 Dobb, "The New Oil Landscape: The fracking frenzy in North Dakota has boosted the U.S. fuel supply- but at what cost."

38 *Gasland*, directed by Josh Fox.

39 Ibid.

40 Ibid.

41 Ibid.

42 *Gasland*, directed by Josh Fox.

43 Ibid.

44 Ibid.

45 Collin Eaton, "Halliburton execs point to U.S. shale as profits leap 70 percent," *Fuel Fix*, October 20, 2014, http://fuelfix.com/blog/2014/10/20/halliburton-profits-leap-70-percent/.

46 *Gasland*, directed by Josh Fox.

47 Ibid.

48 Ibid.

49 Ibid.

50 *Gasland*, directed by Josh Fox.

51 Ibid.

52 Danielle Waugh, "Filmmaker Blasts Energy Alternative," *ABC News*, June 25, 2010, http://abcnews.go.com/Entertainment/Technology/filmmaker-blasts-energy-alternative/story?id=10993095.

53 *Gasland*, directed by Josh Fox.

54 Ibid.

55 Ibid.

56 *Pump: The Movie*, directed by Joshua Tickell and Rebecca Harrell Tickell (Submarine Deluxe, 2014), DVD.

57 Ibid.

58 Ibid., citing Edwin Black, *Internal Combustion: How Corporations and Governments Addicted the World to Oil and Derailed the Alternatives* (Washington, DC: Dialog Press, 2008).

59 *Pump: The Movie*, directed by Joshua Tickell and Rebecca Harrell Tickell.

60 Ibid.

61 Coral Davenport, "U.S. Will Allow Drilling for Oil in Arctic Ocean," *New York Times*, May 11, 2015, http://www.

nytimes.com/2015/05/12/us/white-house-gives-conditional-approval-for-shell-to-drill-in-arctic.html?_r=0.

62   International Monetary Fund, "Counting the Cost of Energy Subsidies," July 17, 2015, http://www.imf.org/external/pubs/ft/survey/so/2015/new070215a.htm.

63   Stefanie Spear, "RFK, Jr. Calls Koch Brothers 'Deadly Parasites on American Democracy,'" The Ring of Fire Network, September 13, 2015, http://ringoffireradio.com/2015/09/13/rfk-jr-calls-koch-brothers-deadly-parasites-on-american-democracy/.

64   Ibid.

65   International Monetary Fund, "Counting the Cost of Energy Subsidies."

66   Ibid.

67   Nick Surgey, "Fossil Fuel Industry Paid for Meetings with GOP Attorneys General to Plan Attack on Clean Power Plan," Truth-out.org, September 8, 2016, http://www.truth-out.org/news/item/37534-fossil-fuel-industry-paid-for-meetings-with-gop-attorneys-general-to-plan-attack-on-clean-power-plan.

68   Spear, "RFK, Jr. Calls Koch Brothers 'Deadly Parasites on American Democracy.'"

69   Blair Koch, "Communities Push for Legal Rights to Regain Power Over Fracking Companies," Truth-out.org, October 24, 2015, http://www.truth-out.org/news/item/33322-communities-push-for-legal-rights-to-regain-power-over-fracking-companies.

70   Matilda Lee, "Sandra Steingraber: There's a taboo about telling industry and agriculture that practices must change to prevent cancer," The Ecologist, November 30, 2010, http://www.theecologist.org/Interviews/687501/sandra_steingraber_theres_a_taboo_about_telling_industry_and_agriculture_that_practices_must_change_to_prevent_cancer.html.

71   Robert Shetterly, "Sandra Steingraber," Americans Who Tell the Truth: Models of Courageous Citizenship, 2015, http://www.americanswhotellthetruth.org/portraits/sandra-steingraber.

72   Nancy C. Lutkehaus, Margaret Mead: The Making of an American Icon (Princeton, NJ: Princeton University Press: 2008), 261.

73   William Rivers Pitt, "Greed Dies Hard in a Poisoned Land," Truth-out.org, August 18, 2015, http://www.truth-out.org/opinion/item/32389-greed-dies-hard-in-a-poisoned-land.

74   Energy Justice Network, "Coal Firing Facilities: National Map," retrieved January 29, 2016, http://www.energyjustice.net/map/coaloperating.

75   Source Watch, "Existing U.S. Coal Plants," retrieved January 29, 2016, http://www.sourcewatch.org/index.php/Existing_U.S._Coal_Plants.

76   Senator Jeff Merkley, "TELL CONGRESS: KEEP FOSSIL FUELS IN THE GROUND!" CREDO Mobilize, December 6, 2015, http://www.jeffmerkley.com/petition/keep-it-in-the-ground.

INDEX